Standing by the Ruins

Standing by the Ruins

ELEGIAC HUMANISM IN WARTIME
AND POSTWAR LEBANON

Ken Seigneurie

FORDHAM UNIVERSITY PRESS   *New York*   2011

THIS BOOK IS MADE POSSIBLE BY A COLLABORATIVE GRANT
FROM THE ANDREW W. MELLON FOUNDATION.

Fordham University Press has no responsibility for the
persistence or accuracy of URLs for external or third-
party Internet websites referred to in this publication
and does not guarantee that any content on such
websites is, or will remain, accurate or appropriate.

Fordham University Press also publishes its books
in a variety of electronic formats. Some content that
appears in print may not be available in electronic
books.

Library of Congress Cataloging-in-Publication Data

Seigneurie, Ken.
   Standing by the ruins : elegiac humanism in wartime
and postwar Lebanon / Ken Seigneurie.—1st ed.
      p.   cm.
   Includes bibliographical references and index.
   ISBN 978-0-8232-3482-0 (cloth : alk. paper)
   ISBN 978-0-8232-3483-7 (pbk. : alk. paper)
   1. Arabic literature—Lebanon—History and
criticism.   2. Literature and society—Lebanon.
3. Popular culture—Lebanon.   4. Lebanon—
Intellectual life—20th century.   I. Title.
PJ8078.S45   2011
892.7'0995692—dc22

                                        2011016161

Printed in the United States of America

13 12 11   5 4 3 2 1

First edition

In memory of George Robert Seigneurie (1988–2010)

CONTENTS

FIGURES

PLATES

ACKNOWLEDGMENTS

This book is the product of talk as much as it is of reading, watching, and writing. I am grateful to my many mentors and friends whose generosity and wisdom in conversation has made the research and writing of this book so enjoyable. Some have played a preponderant role over an extended period. Susan Stanford Friedman has supported my research for a decade now, and it was she who suggested in fall 2006, right after a war, "Why not write a book about Lebanon?" Angelika Neuwirth has consistently encouraged me to write about modern Arabic literature since the early years of this century when it became clear to some that Lebanese literature was on a roll. Marianne Marroum has been a frank and helpful reader of almost everything I have written in the past decade. Rashid al-Daif consistently encouraged me to resume my study of Arabic after a long hiatus and has provided a consistently supportive voice. Jonathan Hall's companionable conversation throughout the penultimate year of composition brought many loose ends together.

Others have played more punctual roles. I am especially grateful to two eminent senior scholars who read and offered judicious comments on the manuscript: David Damrosch, the brilliant comparatist, and Roger Allen, the great Arabist. Their advice and encouragement have been pivotal in bringing this book to fruition. I have also benefitted from sound advice at key moments from Djelal Kadir, Azade Seyhan, John J. Donohue, S.J., Ziad Majed, Stuart McDougal, Heather Dawkins and Gayatri Chakravorty Spivak. Their work has also set the bar for me in all aspects of academic work, and I count on their indulgence as I inevitably slip under it. Other scholars made up the Beirut intellectual environment in which I was so happy to swim for so long: Wafa' Abd al-Nour, Lina Abyad, Samira Aghacy, Tarif Bazzi, Vahid Behmardi, Sobhi Boustany, Hassan Daoud, Rebecca Dyer, Abir Hamdar, Maher Jarrar, Assaad Khairallah, Andrew Long, Patrick McGreevy, Robert Myers, Samar Mujaes, Levon Nordiguian, Andreas Pflitsch, Nada Saab, Cheryl Toman, Christophe Varin, Elizabeth Vauthier, Edgard Weber and David Wrisley. My student assistants over the years have made me look more efficient than I am. Hala Daouk deserves special mention, especially for undertaking the job of obtaining copyright permissions. Zoha Abdulsater, Rebecca Ammar, Sarah Ghamlouche, and Faten Yaacoub have all given generously of their time in the production process. In fact, it would be unfair not to mention all my undergraduate and graduate students at Lebanese American University in Beirut. In the often mysterious cross-fertilization between teaching and research, I sometimes had the impression this book was part of our ongoing classroom dialogue. The same teaching-research dynamism has animated the final year of writing and research on this project at Simon Fraser University in Surrey, British Columbia, and thanks go to Miriam Klait for her assistance there.

Institutions are an important part of this book. I acknowledge that a year-long sabbatical at half-salary and a generous conference travel budget awarded by the University Research Council of Lebanese American University–Beirut, were key conditions in the production of this book. Special thanks go to the dedicated library staff of the Riyad al-Nassar Library at LAU. Under the leadership of Aida Namaan and now Cendrella Habre, theirs is among the most efficient libraries in which I have had the pleasure of working. Houeida Charara, Sawsan Habre, Aida Hajjar, Bughdana Hajjar, and Kamal Jaroudy have ensured that it was always a pleasure to do library research.

In Canada, where I spent the 2009–10 academic year working on this book, I am grateful to Dean Lesley Cormack and her successor, John Craig, of the Faculty of Arts and Social Sciences at Simon Fraser University for their support in the final stages of composition of this manuscript. I am also grateful for the SFU President's Research Start-up Grant. which funded a key trip to Beirut in summer 2010 where I completed manuscript revisions. Thanks also go to Gloria Ingram, Lindsay Parker, and Erin Westwood of the Program in World Literature at SFU—Surrey for helping me in the crucial business of securing travel funding and in document preparation. I also thank Holly Hendrigan of the SFU–Surrey Library for her energy and effort in supporting this research and securing key sources.

At Fordham University Press, I thank Helen Tartar for her confidence in and support of this project. Thomas Lay, Tim Roberts, and Susan Murray deserve thanks for their knowledge, advice, and hard work in bringing this book to press. At the German Orient Institute in Beirut, I thank Stephen Leder and Thomas Scheffler for inviting me to lecture and granting me the status of Affiliated Researcher in the summer of 2010.

Other influences have been more indirect. This book is an attempt to capture something of the intellectual and artistic atmosphere of Beirut, which exceeds by far the objects of study I have chosen. Though I know some of the people mentioned here only by their work, they have been an inspiration in my quest to identify what I call elegiac humanism in Lebanese culture. Given even more time than the four years I have already spent on this project, I would linger over the work of the poet-journalist Abbas Beydoun and try to convey his joie de vivre as he used to recite poems to rip-roaring applause on Friday nights in the Jadal Byzanty nightclub. I would study the work of another poet-journalist, Sabah al-Zwayn, for her irrepressible good faith and social conscience. I would tarry over the work of journalist-novelist Mohammad Abi-Samra for his principled but never strident political consciousness. And I would consider the work of the journalist-scholar Hazim Saghie for his trenchant analyses of the complex relationship between culture and politics in Lebanon and the Arab world. My limitations as a scholar have kept me from knowing in adequate depth the work of many others who make up the wry and wonderful atmosphere of Beirut that has fascinated me for some fourteen years now.

Finally, I must apologize to my daughter, Pascale, for not using the title she suggested for this book, "Kaboom! Why Lebanon Keeps Making That Noise." Great title, wrong book. Most of all, I express my gratitude to May Semaan Seigneurie for her faith and patience in my work and in our life together.

NOTE ON TRANSLITERATIONS

The Arabic transliterations in this text follow the rules established by the *International Journal of Middle East Studies* (http://web.gc.cuny.edu/ijmes/pages/transliteration.html) except that titles in Lebanese dialect are transliterated for the sake of clarity.

And I say goodbye to these stones
that have begun to ramble
and have blackened all at once

—Abbas Beydoun

Introduction

Shoring These Ruins against My Fragments

For what I am calling humanism can be provisional, historically contingent, antiessentialist (in other words, postmodern), and still be demanding.

—KWAME ANTHONY APPIAH, *In My Father's House*

Ruins are everywhere twenty years after the civil war of 1975–90. Some are preserved as monuments with commemorative plaques. People eke out livings in others among the cracks and shell-pocks. Some are covered in giant colorful advertisements four stories high in weather-resistant plastics that can last for months. Others stand abandoned, stripped of wood, porcelain, and moveable steel. Ruins do not generally disturb the everyday lives of people, yet they matter. This book will explore how the representation of ruins in Lebanese culture has formed an aesthetic of resistance against a dominant war ethos.

Standing by the Ruins concentrates on a small current of Lebanon's cultural output over the past three decades. I argue not that it is representative of Arab or Lebanese society as a whole but rather that it is one of numerous currents, each flowing variously according to its wont in response to constantly changing historical and political conditions. I privilege the novels, films, and popular culture studied here because I find them aesthetically satisfying and partaking of a fascinating family resemblance. Part of my interest may be traced to what I see as a strong and principled artistic response to conditions that are becoming increasingly common the world over: ongoing war, sectarian extremism, economic exploitation, and despair. In these products of a people's history and ingenuity I find an alternative to cultural practices that are complicit with the ideologies of coercion and zero-sum conflict. I want this book to convey the sense I have acquired in Beirut that the cultural realm, while evoking delight, can also preserve the cultural values of courage, generosity, and conviviality in societies undergoing long-term civil conflict. This book therefore seeks to identify and explore an aesthetic practice and its associated ethos within Arab culture. Prior to examining the formation and development of this aesthetic in the chapters of this study, it is necessary to argue for the plausibility of five contextual claims that will lay the groundwork for the analyses that follow.

A PIONEER OF THE PRESENT

Lebanon is probably not the best example of a nation bowed under long-term political violence and intimidation, but it will do. In some ways, this tiny nation, circa 1975, was even a pioneer of the global present. On the eve of its 1975–90 civil war, it lay, like numerous other nations from Finland to the Persian Gulf, athwart a fault line between the Soviet and American tectonic plates. Yet unlike most of these nations—Eastern Europe on the one hand, Turkey and Israel on the other—it was less firmly anchored to one side or the other. Its weak government floated westward while its Leftist movement boasted intellectual credentials and tended eastward. This ideological ambivalence in the early 1970s allowed the Lebanese to relativize cold war certitudes fifteen years before history would allow the rest of the world to do so. Lebanon also straddled the gulf between Islam and Christianity with a population divided between them and sharing a border with the Jewish state of Israel. Thus long before "fundamentalism" became a household word, Lebanon's confessional system of government and close proximity to the Jewish state of Israel and Alawite-dominated Syria put it at the epicenter of late-twentieth-century monotheistic sectarianisms. In the wake of Jordan's 1970 "Black September," Lebanon also became the battleground of choice in the Israeli-Palestinian conflict, providing the theater for the increasingly sectarian profile of that conflict a quarter century before 9/11. Last and perhaps most fundamental, the gross disparity between rich and poor in Lebanon contributed to a serious class conflict in which workers contended with a laissez-faire economy and a virtually limitless supply of emigrant labor long before neoliberalism established similar conditions worldwide. In these ways, the early 1970s Lebanese crisis concentrated in one small land many of the political, ideological, sectarian, and class vulnerabilities that define our era.[1]

Lebanon's economic policies and political structure also prefigured the present. A weak, decentralized government provided for a liberal economy that functioned openly at the behest of the global marketplace and foreign players. A confessionalist constitution encouraged weak national allegiance and allowed religion-based communities to establish their own laws regarding marriage, divorce, and inheritance. In the absence of limits, some communities achieved a high degree of control over public spaces and services while others created institutions parallel to those of the state in health care, public transport, utilities, education, defense, and public safety. If in the world today, privatization and cultural identitarianism are the norm, a nation that blazed this trail decades ago merits attention.

With all these preconditions in place, what lay only on the horizon of possibility in 1975 for other multicultural nations actually occurred in Lebanon. First, a cold war proxy struggle broke out not unlike numerous others from Korea to Mozambique.[2] It was part of the battle between great utopic visions unfolding against another local backdrop, pitting local nationalist Christian interests against a coalition of Leftist parties that took up Palestinian and Muslim causes.[3] Then something unusual happened. Within two years, the sectarian cart began pulling the secular horse. The reversal marked the bankruptcy of the struggle between "actually existing socialism" and liberal capitalism more than a decade before 1989: "The Lebanese civil war created its own order . . . : the autonomy of the sects mutated into armed control and 'sectarian cleansing,' while the wild laissez-faire economy transformed into mafia predation. This new order was a new form of war: the war waged by the militias against the state and its citizens."[4] Third, the rise of sectarianism was not simply atavistic. The proliferating sectarian groupings that supplanted secular ideologies were themselves infused with modern utopianism based on fascistic or communist models.[5] Theodor Hanf writes unironically of "Jacobinism" and a rejection of coexistence, noting that "the Lebanese parties to the conflict after the outbreak of war were essentially the same as those before. But their leaders were now harder, as ready to take but less ready to give."[6] Wittingly or not, some sought to transpose the "successful" Zionist model of utopian sectarian war to Lebanon. The war devastated hitherto neutral Lebanon from 1975–90. That war then ripped through Iran in 1979, Afghanistan since the 1980s, Algeria in the early 1990s, Yugoslavia and Chechnya in the late 1990s, Sudan and Iraq since the early years of this century, and perhaps Pakistan today. Thus 1970s Lebanon arguably played a key mediating role in post–cold war sectarian movements.[7]

A noteworthy characteristic of this war was the flattening of age-old complexities into monovalent identities: "Militia power not only practiced ethnic, sectarian and political 'cleansing' of territories but also committed what Juan Goytisolo has aptly called 'memoricide,' the eradication of all memories of coexistence and common interests between Lebanese. Instead, they imposed their discourse of 'protection' on their own 'people': the 'other' wants to kill you, but we are here to save your lives."[8] It is among this book's contextual claims that the late-twentieth century Lebanese sectarian war may be regarded as a cautionary tale for a globalized, multicultural twenty-first century. The history of Lebanon since 1975 illustrates the danger of supplanting managed animosities with utopian solutions.

If, as some Lebanese say only half in jest, sectarianism is a national pathology, it is no less the case that a countervailing open-

ness to difference is equally distinctive. The competition between these visions may be seen as part of a century-long struggle
throughout the eastern Mediterranean. In the wake of the fall
of the Ottoman Empire, the cosmopolitan identities of many
great Levantine cities—Istanbul, Izmir, Aleppo, Haifa, and Al-
exandria—were gradually leached through national and sectarian identities. Beirut, on the other hand, by the 1970s was even
more heterogeneous than a century earlier. For many this was a
source of pride, for others a threat: "Neighboring rulers regarded
Lebanon as a provocative nest of capitalism. . . . Lebanon's tolera-
tion of a free press and free expression was a thorn in their flesh.
Whoever lost in an Arab power struggle found political asylum
in Lebanon."[9] In this struggle between cosmopolitan and sectarian visions of identity, the latter has generally prevailed, but there
remains a minor key cultural discourse of coexistence. If it has
been hitherto untheorized, this is perhaps because despite its psy-
chosocial value, it carries little economic or political ballast. This
book traces its development from the war into what few would
mistake for peacetime as this multicultural experiment in the Levant muddles on.

CULTURAL KNOCK-ON

Following World War II, neoromantic, existentialist, and social
realist aesthetic forms dominated literary production in the Arab
world.[10] Over the course of the second half of the twentieth century, writers increasingly adopted stances of political commitment.[11]
As commitment literature (al-adab al-multazim) goes, it was ca-
pacious, often carrying along with it a range of humanist ideals.[12]
After the 1967 defeat of secular Arab nations, commitment literature honed an increasingly polemical edge: "Up to the 1970s
the meaning of the slogan iltizām [commitment] was the subject
of heated debates in the Arab literary scene. The meaning of the
term had been changing continuously during these years. Under
the influence of growing hostilities before and during the Arab-
Israeli confrontation of 1967 the term became increasingly mili-

tant and anti-Israeli in tone."[13] Not altogether surprisingly, part of the debate included a fateful tendency to imitate immensely successful Israeli aesthetic practices. Ghassan Kanafani's *Fi al-Adab al-Sihyuni* (On Zionist Literature) urged Arab writers to be equal to the challenge of ultracommitted Zionist literature.[14] Ahmad Mohammad A'tiya in 1974 compared the alleged frivolousness of Arabic literature to the efficacy of Hebrew literature and implied that Arab writers had much to learn from their Hebrew-language counterparts.[15] Claiming that Arabs had to "fight then write," he called for the linkage of literature and society to an all-out war effort: "The Arab writer is separated from the Arab fighter. In fact [social] reality is separated from the battle. And we find no trace of unity between literature and the battle except in rare instances. The behavior of the Arab revolutionary writer is completely separate from real revolutionary acts and stops at the penning of ideologies."[16] It was a doomed effort. A'tiya's stridency suggests a negative feedback loop in which the intellectuals' injunction to "feel commitment" is indistinguishable from the alienating coercion of authoritarianism. Faced with increasingly alienated laypeople, the committed intellectual can do little more than shout louder and condemn the disjunction between behavior and "real revolutionary acts." Thus whereas early in the war, "all parties were in the 'resistance' against something,"[17] by the late 1970s secularism was a spent force as commitment became increasingly indistinguishable from compulsion (*ilzām*). Social realist modes trailed off over the course of the decades that followed, but the notion of total commitment passed smoothly into the sectarian ideologies by tapping into the well of revanchist identitarianism. The recoding of commitment from secular to sectarian priorities took place swiftly and almost silently since it was not in the interest of sectarian forces to draw attention to their debt to secularism and it was not in the interest of residual secular forces to highlight the reappropriation of their methods for other ends. Thus a will to imitate a committed Zionist aesthetic was fulfilled in the committed sectarianism that flourishes in Lebanon to this day.

For many writers and artists, the sudden discredit visited upon secular utopian ideals left a vacuum where social realism had been. "Commitment," Klemm writes, "floated (and still floats) as a hollow word through literary circles."[18] Other aesthetic practices fared no better. Modernist experimentation was coded as "art for art's sake" and tarred as an abdication of responsibility. Neoromantic idealizations of the rural ethos that had appealed to generations of emigrants from village to city appeared increasingly divorced from reality. These prewar aesthetic practices had been predicated on a centered consciousness pitted against variously defined hegemonies. The social realist prophet, the modernist gadfly, and the neoromantic alienated soul provided strong alternative subject positions to the various deindividualized collectivities associated with the state, conformism, or modernity. In the mid-1970s context of violent factionalism, the sovereign subject found its caricatural apotheosis in the warlords who strove to recreate the world from their own vantage. Writers and artists intuited that the nation needed more than gadflies, but already had too many prophets. Consequently, Barbara Harlow notes the rise of an aesthetic of alienation (*ightirāb*), and Badawi notes that with respect to Arabic prose fiction as a whole, there occurred a "withdrawal into the author's inner universe."[19] Excellent novels were written in this mode, in particular Tawfiq ʿAwwad's 1972 *Tawahin Bayrut* (translated as *Death in Beirut*) and Ghada Samman's *Bayrut '75*, both of which anticipated the disillusionment of the first years of the war.[20] Yet the clarity of these artistic visions was directed toward diagnosing the decay into war, not offering an alternative sustaining vision.

It is a commonplace that culture mediates the grasp of reality, but not just any cultural mediation will do. The principal prewar novelistic genres in Lebanon were derived largely from Western aesthetic paradigms and predicated on an assumed need for libidinal release within repressive, centralized society. Such an aesthetic made a certain amount of sense in a prewar patriarchal society, but during a war in which some twenty armed factions fought over a prostrate central government, the preservation of civil society was a more important priority.[21] The breakdown of the state into factions—what the rest of the world would subsequently call "Lebanization"—forced a rethinking of subject-centered discourses and thereby to some extent freed the Lebanese novel and film from Western models.

The war conditioned at least two aesthetic responses. Both were hybrids drawn from Western and Arab sources and displaying, unsurprisingly, a longing for order and peace. Both were also steeped in an ethical reading of history, and both remain operative to this day. They differ, however, in their characteristic epistemological frames and in the reading practices each encourages. This book analyzes both but focuses on that which is lesser known.

MYTHIC UTOPIAN FUTURES

While some found that the multiple and shifting justifications for war undermined any subject-centered discourse and exposed political commitment as a mug's game, others found it easy to replace one utopic vision by another. These new sectarians avoided the problem of fragmentary subjectivity by subordinating individual conscience to communal imperatives. Culture mediated the readjustment of consciousness toward sectarian commitment by drawing on the codes and symbols of both social realism and a much older mythic aesthetic.[22] Angelika Neuwirth has argued that even commitment literature in its secular heyday carried a strongly mythic valence:

> The mythic dimensions of the close relation between death and
> *Eros*, between violent loss of individual life and its redemp-
> tive power experienced by the collective, are still preoccupying
> modern-day Arabic poetics. Subtexts whose elements evoke the
> mythic *hieros gamos* are traceable in texts from early Islamic
> literature as well as from classical and modern poetry. This find-
> ing makes the acceptance of the heroic fighter as a redemptive
> figure, as a "bridegroom of the earth," which can be observed in
> contemporary politically committed literature, somewhat easier
> to understand. The modern concept draws on imagery that does

not stem from contemporary liberation movements as one might expect, but rather goes back in history as far as early Islamic times.[23]

In Lebanon, the dominant wartime and postwar aesthetic continues to stress commitment as in social realism but makes explicit the link to sacred myth. It combines the single-minded will to change the world with an ethos of redemptive self-sacrifice such as found in mythic or religious figures such as Tammuz, Hussein, or Jesus. In this modern aesthetic, the shedding of blood, which in myth or religion remains symbolic, is literalized in the commitment to transform the world according to a putatively religious model. Its deep appeal lies in its capacity to kindle nostalgic and utopian sentiments all at once by recoding an image of the past as simultaneously a utopic image of the desired future.

To get a sense of the ubiquity and rhetorical power of mythic utopianism, it is necessary to examine a mass art form such as popular music or the art of the poster. Little work has been done in this area, but Zeina Maasri's April 2008 poster exhibit in Beirut and her book *Off the Wall*, published in 2009, provide a virtual iconography of the mythic aesthetic.[24] In some ways, these war posters were like those of any war as they sought to attract supporters and steel the will of fighters. Yet the number of armed factions and the contested sense of Lebanese identity meant that perhaps this civil war demanded more marketing than most. Militias hawked themselves in a rhetoric of easily grasped mythemes: "the inevitable victory of the oppressed" or "holding the line against barbarians." In each case, a utopic future shimmered in the offing beyond heroic sacrifice. Proleptically responding to the objection that such talk is cheap, parties stressed the gold standard of commitment—blood: "Political parties competed in declaring their share of zealous fighting by proclaiming the amount of martyrs they had 'offered' up to the common cause of the front. The number of fallen heroes becomes an indicator of a party's share of participation on a front and a proof of its commitment and sacrifice in the defense of an existential cause."[25] The term "amount of martyrs" is appropriate. In the mythic utopian aesthetic, flesh and blood are value-quantities in an imaginary moral economy or cosmic election. Since presumably nobody chooses a vain death, the more flesh and blood offered up, the more just the cause and the greater the likelihood one's party will be chosen to usher in the utopic future. Blood replaces discursive thought and the ballot box such that it can almost be said that the value of martyrdom is proportional to the impoverishment of language and the moral corruption of society. The implicit logic is that nothing short of righteous violence and self-sacrifice can redeem a fallen world.

All parties to the war were adept at recoding redemptive self-sacrifice from secular into sectarian registers. Maasri cites one example: "Hezbollah's posters in the beginning were based on a compounding of previous experiences in political posters: Socialist realism, the Palestinian resistance and the Iranian Revolution posters. . . . The Iranian poster model was most useful since it imbued the anti-imperialist struggle with a politico-religious discourse that is pertinent to Hezbollah and familiar to its Shiite community."[26] Thus Hezbollah, "The Party of God," succeeded in welding highly emotive religious discourse to secular utopianism.

If the Christian and Islamic militias were able to reinhabit the secular revolutionary aesthetic so easily, it was because "utopia" is a signifier by definition severed from sociopolitical reality and exceptionally open to slippage.[27] A vision of "Lebanon" in 1974 as socialist utopia morphs easily into "Christian homeland" or "Islamic republic" in 1986. Indeed, to this day, the lack of consensus over the nation's identity means that to a greater extent than most, Lebanon as a nation is an empty signifier. Maasri describes the discursive displacement effected on the memory of the Druze leader Kamal Jumblatt (see Plate 1): "During the 1980s in Lebanon, as inter-confessional battle multiplied over territorial rule and sectarian consciousness tightened, Kamal Jumblatt 'the symbol of progressive and secular Arab Lebanon' gave way to a traditional Druze za'im in the representations of the PSP [Progressive Socialist Party]. . . . A change of image and reconstitution of the past into a present reality seemed necessary."[28] Under the imperatives of war, the objects of memory shift valences, but the narratives are remarkably similar. Thus the mythic aesthetic proved resilient and effective at mobilizing masses over long periods of time and across widely varying ideological environments.

Crucial to the logic of mythic utopianism is the establishment of a fallen world in need of redemption. In order to demonstrate the threat of "barbarous masses" or "oppressive reactionaries," posters and memorials often invoke war ruins (see Plates 2–4). Destroyed edifices and scenes of martyrdom are a key link in an implicit narrative that typically unfolds as: (1) atrocity in the past; (2) ruin in the present; (3) imminent threat of repetition; (4) necessity for preventive action; and (5) future utopia. Ruins in the present provide the tangible link to a traumatic past and a potentially utopic future. It is a compelling, tight narrative that leaves nothing to chance or ambiguity. Yet as popular as mythic utopianism can be—its revanchist narrative easily becomes a self-fulfilling prophecy—many Lebanese rejected it. This book seeks to shed light on why and how they forged an alternative.

ELEGIAC PASTS

The fact that mythic utopianism was dominant in wartime society but did not figure prominently in the Lebanese war novel, film, or some popular culture is worth pondering. To be sure, many writers and filmmakers were doubtless circumspect about throwing in with another cause after secular utopianism had waned, but this begs the question of why others apparently felt no such compunction. One might follow Neuwirth to a certain point that the literary objectification of sacred myth tends to block reader cathexis of self-sacrifice:

> The myth of *Tammūz* offers a particularly significant example
> since the pattern of interaction underlying it, the shedding of the
> blood of a sacred victim deemed necessary for the revitalization
> of world order, certainly belongs to the key concepts of religious
> symbolic language. Still, once this myth is reflected in profane
> literary works of our century, it does not serve to affirm the bind-

ing form of a religious demand for sacrifice, but . . . rather to
question the act of offering sacrifice which may be imposed for
completely profane, even morally doubtful, political reasons.[29]

Yet such a structural argument cannot explain how literature can,
at other times, be pressed into the service of justifying redemptive self-sacrifice. One contextual element of the twentieth-century Lebanese novel is its development in dialogic relation with the
twentieth-century Western literary tradition, which, at least since
World War I, has often been critical of redemptive self-sacrifice.
Yet while the Lebanese war and postwar novels may well derive
from Western models, their paths have bifurcated in an important way.

The new aesthetic that informs the novels, films, and popular
cultural productions studied here is distinguished by its treatment
of memory.[30] Like mythic utopianism, it is centered on a nostalgic vision evoked by war ruins, but there the similarity ends. The
war posters Maasri studies code ruins according to group identities and imply clear political responses. In stark contrast, wartime
novels linger over ruins in set pieces and recursively described
scenes. Feature films devote slow, silent panning shots to ruins as
if to hover over a mystery. These novels and films invite us to tarry
over ruins as open-ended signifiers. A character's contemplation
of a bullet-riddled statue or a narrator's musing before a dusty balcony strewn with dead house plants leaves open the question of
causality and briefly halts the forward-driving narrative. Ruins
here are metonyms of a complex, dubious past—the statue was
once revered, the plants alive—pointing to loss without presum-
ing to explain it. Ruins here do not concretize a *casus belli* according to a moralized syllogism, but unfurl time's tight progress and
suspend cause-effect reasoning to evoke the ambiguity and pathos
of that which is forever lost. So the new aesthetic may fairly be described as "elegiac."

From the standpoint of mythic utopianism, which provides a
readily understandable narrative that moves from past atrocity to
present action and future utopian redemption, the elegiac aesthet-

ic seems curiously backward-looking and truncated. It seems to contrast a sorrow-ridden present with an implicitly idealized past but stops short of providing a hopeful vision of the future. Thus, it apparently offers little more than a longing for what has been irrecoverably lost. Between the two aesthetic visions of the past, one offers group identity and purpose, the other alienated suffering for losses that cannot be recouped anyway.

The new aesthetic seems even more counterintuitive given that if one wishes to reject mythic utopianism, fruitful alternatives do exist. Numerous recent studies have shown how nostalgia, elegy, and ruins can function in a variety of ways beyond licensing essentialized group history or apparently sterile longing. Most of these studies consider the potential efficacy of nostalgia broadly as "a form of idealization that seeks to motivate a personal emotional reaction in the reader or viewer."[31] Nostalgia and its elegiac literary vehicle, therefore, can be a key means of constructing forward-looking "usable pasts." In the Western tradition: "Elegies cannot just describe loss: they have to refigure it as a species of transformation and provide an early glimpse of an afterlife for their subject."[32] This "afterlife" does not have to be utopic but can be practical. Contemporary Anglophone authors, for example, "exploit nostalgia's tendency to interweave imagination, longing, and memory . . . to envision resolutions to the social dilemmas of fragmentation and displacement."[33] Ruins, too, can serve multiple purposes. Throughout Western literary history, ruins have served variously as reminders of mortal pride, projections of psychological anxiety, remnants of a corrupt social order, preludes to Christian resurrection, and apocalyptic cautionary tales.[34] Within the context of such an efficacious use of ruins and nostalgia, the Lebanese writers' and filmmakers' focus on irrecoverable loss and longing seems downright quietist. One wonders how this aesthetic can be satisfying as it provides neither a sense of closure nor the dominant aesthetic's satisfying balance between past injustice and future utopia.

Yet it is perhaps the very success of mythic utopianism in its sectarian form that makes an alternative necessary. Violence cannot be ambiguous in mythic utopianism, but must be either atrocity crying out for retribution or righteous punishment for past wrongs. Death cannot be senseless, but must be either a martyrdom that inches the group ever-closer to the utopic future or a scorned enemy's just desserts. The neatness of this economy of blood, longing, and fulfillment betrays an iron will to ignore the irrecoverable. In wartime Lebanon, however, this leftover inexplicability grew as the war, doing what all wars do best, dragged on. The elegiac aesthetic, in implicit response to rationalized bloodshed, thematized the sheer loss inflicted by war. Relevant here is Francesco Orlando's notion of the antifunctional in literature: "Just as literature welcomes an immoral return of the repressed, by which a moral repression is contradicted, and an irrational return of the repressed, by which a rational repression is contradicted, so we may suppose that it welcomes . . . a return of the *antifunctional* repressed, by which a functional repression is contradicted."[35] Without getting too structuralist about it, we can note that if mythic utopianism commodifies blood in a moralized economy of atrocity and retribution, the new aesthetic takes ruins and the irrecoverable loss they index as anticommodities whose misuse value is to expose the dominant aesthetic economy.[36] A paradoxical effect is that the attention to the uncircumscribable leftover creates a value in itself: the pathos of irrecuperability.

The remarkable family resemblance among the works studied here suggests that writers and filmmakers are drawing on a common tradition. Since their use of ruins and nostalgia is distinct from that of much Western literature, it is reasonable to direct attention to the forms and genres of memory literature in Arabic. In all of Arabic culture, nothing is more redolent of memory and longing than "stopping by the ruins" (*wuqūf ʿala al-aṭlāl*), which may also be rendered as "standing by the ruins." This topos was already well established in pre-Islamic Arabic poetry.[37] It is the principal element of the *nasīb* or amatory prologue of the ancient Arabic *qaṣīda* or ode. Typically, the *nasīb* recounts the Bedouin speaker-poet's discovery of a deserted campsite where he once shared happy times with his beloved. He contemplates, often in the company of a couple of companions, the ruin-traces (*aṭlāl*) of the camp: weed-grown paths, old tent pegs, fag ends from a campfire. From these reminders of bygone joys, he delivers himself to unbridled longing as he weeps and complains before the fate that separated him from his beloved.

> In the first section of the *qaṣīda* the poet halts, stands, and remembers. It is his remembrance, however, that introduces all the ultimately important things in their "occurrence in succession," or rather in their presence in his mind in that order. The poet's first, supposedly visually concretized but in a true sense still mental, image is that of the ruinous remains of habitation, which, as *ṭalla*, a word of implicitly archaizing overtones, presents a frame of time of the utmost remoteness, where there is only an evanescence of objects. As such it is coupled with the psychological frame of some great personal loss. There follows an image, still more the creation of the remembering mind than of direct visual apprehension, of the emerging reality of desolation and emptiness, in which the airy figment of the *ṭalal* becomes the personal lost "circle" of perfection, the abode as *dār*. Also, the *dār* as the circle of erstwhile habitation changes into, or is placed within, the seasonally more specific lyrical quadrature of the lost springtimes of *rabīʿ*, the pasture ground that once was green; and then lost loves appear in the realm that hesitates between dream and reverie only to disappear again there where those other memories, or wishes, of the past lie buried. These are the things that happen at various levels of remembrance as the *qaṣīda* opens.[38]

Eventually, the poet pulls himself together and resumes his travels, the wounds of loss endured, not expunged. The topos conveyed in the words of one critic, "a whole people's historical reservoir of sorrow, loss, yearning—above all, yearning."[39] I shall claim here that this topos is the articulation of a "structure of feeling" widely distributed throughout the Arab world and its dialogically inflected sister cultures such as the Persian, Jewish, and Eastern Christian. I hope to show that the yearning reflected in the ruins topos is of a particular kind and corresponds to a structure of feeling: an affective element of consciousness "with specific internal relations, at once interlocking and in tension," which is always in process and often "taken to be private."[40]

The representation of loss, yearning, and coping arguably epitomizes the conflicting imperatives of self and society: "The poet of the *nasīb* . . . 'extends his mind' towards the past. . . . The initial situation of the *nasīb* is always sad and unsatisfactory, because love and happiness are gone. The poet either recalls the past in order to redeem his diminished self-esteem, or he is visited by memories of the beloved and repeats in his imagination the experience of former happiness. He then lives through an emotional crisis, he weeps violently and finally recovers and has done with it. In compliance with the demands of tribal society he 'cuts his bond.'"[41] Thus through art, the disordered soul is both indulged and chastened in catharsis and denial as the demands of social stability prevail. Yet to argue for the social utility of the ruins topos is to consider it under a functional light and deemphasize its aesthetic appeal, which is the pleasure of longing as such:[42] "The reason for starting poems with the *nasīb*, and more specifically stopping by the ruins, is that it is the key to unlocking the poem and winning over the reader. . . . The longevity of this kind of poetry may be attributed to its beauty and the aesthetic feeling of nostalgia it evokes."[43] Thus the aesthetic kindling of nostalgia is an end in itself that need serve no ulterior purpose. Indeed, one scholar seeks to elide mimesis in order to identify the poetic image with the value of longing as such: "We do not notice in these poets any distance in feeling, an overindulgence in artifice, or a deliberate strangeness in imagery. We do not feel that we are confronted with scenes that the poets had imagined or situations they had envisioned or events they had pictured. Instead, we understand that the poet is writing about things he has seen and heard, about experiences he lived through and loved ones he has been separated from. We feel, in fact, that we are standing in front of these ruins."[44] In sum, "to long is to live"; and to long well is to live fully. It is an embrace of suffering humanity over triumphant humanity and to this extent betokens the courage to see the irrecuperability of pain that utopic triumphalism must airbrush away.

Clearly, the image of longing over ruins in the Arabic tradition holds a different place than corresponding topoi such as the *ubi sunt* tradition in European culture.[45] To this day, no educated Arab from Iraq to Morocco is ignorant of the canonical odes, which are as fundamental to Arab culture as the epic is to the West, reflecting and constantly reestablishing aesthetic and social structures of feeling that transcend social class, religious affiliation, and gender categories. It is part of a constellation of cultural values that permeate social relations of all kinds. Not altogether surprisingly, it has also been a lightning rod from medieval times to the present, criticized for its formalism and backward-looking ethos.[46] In a compelling monograph tracing the evolution of the *nasīb*, Jaroslav Stetkevych shows how the basic pattern of standing before ruins and yearning for what is irretrievably lost has served love poets and poets of home and heritage for centuries, stable enough for conservatives during times of disorder and flexible enough for innovators seeking to escape conventional strictures. Today, it remains a staple of popular poems and songs including those of the divas Umm Kalthoum and Fayrouz, whose voices can transport listeners to ecstasies of longing.[47]

The nostalgia evoked by the ruins topos is distinct from a literary enchantment characteristic of war literatures.[48] The speaker-poet of Imruʾ al-Qays's pre-Islamic *muʿallaqa* addresses his comrades: "Halt, let us weep, you and I, as we remember beloved and campsite / At the winding dune's crest, between al-Dakhul and Hawmal."[49] The speaker-poet evokes suffering that can be aesthetically contemplated but not eliminated. Indeed, the ache of absence is intensified in a heroic effort to embrace the full range of human experience. Another critic notes that the ruins topos establishes "a space and mood of unparalleled melancholy in its invocation that all is lost" and suggests that it encrypts an unconscious desire to escape teleology.[50] This insight might well apply to the Lebanese war novelists' and filmmakers' deployment of the ruins topos. Through the evocation of open-ended longing for the past, these artists, in effect, strive to transcend the utopian telos of sectarian war.

Among the more striking developments in the twentieth century is the still poorly documented migration of the ruins topos to the Arabic novel. In an important article published in 2000, Hilary Kilpatrick first revealed how mid-twentieth-century Arab novelists began reappropriating standing by the ruins in archaeological sites, modern cities, or "ruined" societies. She posited that this topos is "connected with the role of memory in literature today as a device for structuring experience."[51] As metonyms of the past, ruins can be memory's—and art's—point of contact with historical experience. Specifically, if as Kilpatrick affirms, the role of memory in literature today is to structure experience, then without putting too fine a point on it, the Lebanese experience that has begged structuring for the past half century is that of violence.

The difference among violences makes a difference and conditions the way wartime novels and films reappropriate the ruins topos. Lebanon was something of a particle accelerator for mid-1970s revolutionary violence that elsewhere was quelled. In North America and western Europe, the state kept revolutionary violence in check. Likewise in the Arab world, Egypt, Jordan, and Syria quelled, often violently, potential threats to sovereignty. Only in Lebanon did a weak government condone revolutionary elements and armed domestic militias, all of which felt emboldened to realize their dreams in the frictionless atmosphere until clashing against each other in 1975–76.[52] The parties to war soon shattered into their sectarian constituents, and these, in turn, accelerated throughout the years that followed thanks to a slingshot effect of domestic, regional, and international forces until they too broke into intrasectarian wars such as that which afflicted the Shiite Muslim and Christian communities. Thus while the domestic profile of the Lebanese civil war may well have begun as a problem of excluded margins, it degenerated into a war of margins over an absent center that was epitomized in novels and films by the ruined city center. Numerous imagined communities—"Christian homeland," "Islamic republic," "secular nation-state," "province of Greater Syria," and "Israeli buffer zone"—realized themselves to greater or lesser extents over given patches of land. And into each, the mythic aesthetic of redemptive self-sacrifice funneled bodies according to an impeccable moral justification that hardly differed from one community to the next. Observing this, Lebanese artists and intellectuals, such as several of the writers and filmmakers studied here, could see what suppressed and would-be revolutionaries elsewhere around the world at the time could only intuit: the ferocity of high moral intentions.

Through their use of the standing-by-the-ruins topos, Lebanese writers and filmmakers translate the tradition of longing for that which is irrecoverably lost to a wartime environment. When the protagonist of Burhan 'Alawiyya's feature film *Beirut: The Meeting* gazes upon the ruin of the Holiday Inn, we do not know whether he does so as a victim or as a former fighter. The distinction is as irrelevant as whether Imru' al-Qays's speaker-poet left his beloved or vice-versa. The character's growing consciousness of both victimization and responsibility unfolds simultaneously in his open-ended longing. Through the reappropriated ruins topos, memory and nostalgia are sharpened in order to deepen consciousness of the past but without licensing identitarianism. Standing by the ruins thus avoids the notorious danger of nostalgia: "Nostalgia is paradoxical in the sense that longing can make us more empathetic toward fellow humans, yet the moment we try to repair longing with belonging, the apprehension of loss with a rediscovery of identity, we often part ways and put an end to mutual understanding."[53] By positing longing as an aesthetic value independent of its object, the ruins topos conditions empathy rather than identity. By refusing the self-other binary of the mythic utopian "package," it also bears the potential to convey moral complexity.

It is not necessary to claim that the reappropriation of the ruins topos is specifically willed, but rather to note that it is a tool always at hand to artists working in the Arabic tradition. It would, in fact, probably take an effort to depict memory and longing in Arabic without some intersection with the classical topos. By the early 1980s, writers and filmmakers were drawing implicitly from a cultural treasure to respond to what would become a major problem of the twenty-first century: how to maintain a vision of human dignity in the face of irresponsible government, civil anarchy, and sectarian violence. Their reappropriation of the ruins topos conjures images of a projected past to counter the "memoricide" and dehumanization of sectarian war. This elegiac visioning is akin to mourning, which bears an ethical valence: "Might not the mourner's wishful revisioning of the past, through which she unrealistically sustains relationship, also signify profoundly as an ethical openness to the other? Or more specifically, to put this idea in mourning's own terms, how does a vulnerability to the other, an imaginative proximity to her suffering and death, also define what it means to be ethical?"[54] Inasmuch as the characters' contemplation of ruins in these novels and films is always independent of identities, they tend toward "an imaginative proximity" to the suffering of others. This book casts into relief the importance of such a move in building a sense of the human solidarity necessary for establishing civil society.

ELEGIAC HUMANISM

The "humanist" profile of the ruins-centered aesthetic will be lost on no one by now. An aesthetic that denies the comfort of identitarianism in the name of human dignity is a kind of humanism, although one might wish to avoid the term altogether. It remains hotly contested, a bone we cannot quite bury or venerate deeply enough. Controversy stalks its definition as history and disciplinary need have chased it through numerous fields—history, literature, philosophy, anthropology, and theology to name only a few. It is so semantically overdetermined that it often seems to mean something and its opposite simultaneously.[55] Yet what other concept could provide an alternative to the mythic-utopian conviction that human life is a quantum of matter-energy in the service of greater forces? Since several excellent books have been published with the aim of clarifying the overlapping and contradictory meanings associated with humanism, I shall concentrate on situating the term as it is used here in the context of current and historical debates.[56]

Many critiques of humanism establish genealogies of the concept that feature a point "where it all went wrong": for Michael Hardt and Antonio Negri, it is the Renaissance; for Stephan Toulmin, Descartes is the turning point; for Max Horkheimer and Theodor Adorno, it is the Enlightenment; for Frantz Fanon, it is the colonial moment; and for David E. Cooper, it is nineteenth-century Prometheanism.[57] Most of these critics admit of at least a theoretical redemption of the term. Other thinkers associated with poststructuralism point to features that indelibly sully humanist thought: Martin Heidegger objects to the metaphysical nature of the humanist subject; Michel Foucault exposes humanism as a naturalization of the Western episteme; Louis Althusser exposes its ideological obfuscation; and Gayatri Chakravorty Spivak identifies humanism as a cultural catachresis.[58] To this day, the argument, articulated from various angles, remains strong that humanism is an internalization of coercion through knowledge production.[59] It is increasingly common, however, to read of salvage operations on humanism that rebut overly schematic antihumanist claims.[60]

With no pretension of adding to or rebutting any of these individually complex arguments, it is nevertheless necessary here to open a discursive space that suspends the wholesale damning of humanism. The first batch of critiques—the wrong-turn thesis—seeks to redirect rather than erase humanism. The present study, inasmuch as it argues for the primacy of one historical tendency over others, has something in common with this group. The second includes the categorical rejectionists of humanism, but these are not necessarily the most tenacious of arguments since to eliminate humanism out of hand may be refreshing, but it begs the question of what a less coercive ethos would look like. All knowledge production is fraught. The most challenging opponents of humanism take issue with the eighteenth-century category of "man," which has until recently dominated the notion of a human-centered universe. Paul Sheehan takes it as axiomatic that humanism is the "discourse of the modern subject derived from the Cartesian tradition of reason, logic, cognition, reflexivity; and its Kantian moral affiliates of responsibility, duty, respect, self-sovereignty, agency. In this tradition a reasoning being is also a moral being."[61] This is the kind of Eurocentric vision objected to in much poststructuralist antihumanism. Its vision of human exceptionalism privileges a culturally specific notion of autonomous, rational subjectivity over variously defined others who are then normatively marginalized. The poststructuralist critique of this Enlightenment-era subject has been salutary in numerous ways, not least in exposing otherwise invisible hegemonic discourses.

Yet as necessary and compelling as these critiques are, the humanism with which they take issue is arguably not humanism at all. To a significant extent, the differences between Renaissance humanism and that of the Enlightenment are great enough to be hardly amenable to the same term.[62] Cooper traces European humanism to late-medieval nominalism that denies any necessary relationship between concepts and the world and affirms that "*habit* alone accounts for the way we apply concepts."[63] This medieval exposure of the gulf between words and things led to a disorienting contingency of the natural world but also a liberating sense of the boundlessness of human potential—a proto-humanism "centered on an esteem for creative agency."[64] Thus the Renaissance view of human identity is increasingly open-ended: "We . . . encounter in Renaissance thought hints of a very different conception of the self: doubts of the value and power of reason and a blurring of the boundaries between the several supposedly distinguishable faculties arranged in order below it, language implying a view of the self as a mysterious and undifferentiated unity, its quality a reflection of another faculty previously little recognized, 'the heart.'"[65] The case has been made that the intellectual roots of the poststructuralist emphasis on language lie in the same late-medieval nominalism that "created at least the negative conditions that allowed the humanist cult of the word to develop and flourish."[66] By this light, contemporary antihumanism and Renaissance humanism are therefore not so much distinct from each other as versions of the general conviction that humans are uncircumscribable beings possessed of mystery and therefore endowed with "dignity." I understand this to be the only strictly humanist proposition. Accordingly, most poststructuralist critiques of the Enlightenment avatar of humanism may be seen as a reform movement within the larger history of humanism.

The relative freeing of the word from theocentric meaning during the fourteenth and fifteenth centuries introduced an ongoing dialectic about the extent of human capacities. By disabling the human capacity to grasp noncontingent truth, nominalism gave rise, paradoxically, to an enabling ontology described by Pico della Mirandola and celebrated by Renaissance thinkers such as Erasmus. This exalted view of human potential in turn conditioned a range of modest, "realist" convictions: in philosophy, that the only universe we can know is a human universe; in linguistics, that language is equivocal and relative; in historiography, that history is human rather than divinely ordained; in literary scholarship, that texts are human creations and not congealed truths; in pedagogy, that doubt and curiosity are necessary means to learning; and in political science, that messy expediency trumps moral certitude.[67] This tendency toward circumspection in its turn licenses a host of beliefs some of which are neither circumspect nor recognizably humanist. Thus, from the humanist conviction that the only world we can know is a human world, the means to this limited knowledge—reason—can find itself exalted as an essential human quality. In this way, "humanism" gets entangled in a properly antihumanist conviction such as the Enlightenment-era definition of humans as rational beings, which in turn leads to the kind of modern Prometheanism described by Cooper and Toussaint. Inasmuch as both modern Prometheanism and the mythic utopianism that fueled the Lebanese sectarian war are predicated on a will to transform an imperfect world according to ideological certainties, they are of a piece.

If wartime and postwar cultural productions studied here have a distinctly humanist ring, it is partly because the Arabic literary

tradition with which they keep faith does too. This is only sometimes controversial such as in the spring of 2008, when the "Aristotle Affair" burst into the French popular press.[68] A renowned
medievalist, Sylvain Gouguenheim, had just published a book
denying an Arab role in the transmission of the ancient Greek
heritage to the European Renaissance. Le Monde printed a favor-
able review on 3 April; Le Figaro followed suit; and within days
the book's print run of four thousand was exhausted. The lash
soon snapped back as numerous academics panned Aristote au
Mont Saint-Michel: Les racines grecques de l'Europe chrétienne
and eventually published a 200-signature petition on 28 April.[69]
The Aristotle Affair is only the most recent skirmish in a centu-
ries-old debate over the origins of humanistic heritage. After relatively broad-minded Dante and Boccaccio, fourteenth-century
Petrarch was in some respects not only the first European Renaissance humanist but also the first to deny an Arab role in contributing to European knowledge.[70] Within the past forty years, the
weight of scholarly opinion has shifted in favor of some still not
fully specified contribution of Arab culture to the European humanist tradition.[71]

Among the medieval Arab antecedents of European humanist
thought, three stand out. First, humanism as a project to recover
and assimilate the ancient Greek heritage is characteristic of not
only fifteenth-century Italian scholarship but also of tenth-century Baghdadi scholarship: "The humanism that flourished in the
Renaissance of Islam was an offspring of the humanism ideal that
germinated in the period of Hellenism and Graeco-Roman antiquity. Its primary features are: (1) adoption of the ancient phil-
osophic classics as an educational and cultural ideal in the formation of mind and character; (2) a conception of the common
kinship and unity of mankind; and (3) humaneness, or love of
mankind."[72] Second, humanism as an educational program associated with the studia humanitatis of the Italian Renaissance
corresponds closely to the adab tradition in classical Islam.[73] In
this connection, George Makdisi has made the most sustained argument for a relation of influence between the adab educational

program and the late-medieval *ars dictaminis* in Europe, summarizing much of his work in the statement: "This is how I see the development of humanism in Italy: the impetus for humanism was given by the Arabs who also supplied the model. The substance was sought in classical antiquity . . . from Cicero."[74] Third, humanism as a conviction of the "dignity of man" is congruent with the work of Buyid Dynasty scholars of the Abbaside Empire.[75] Kraemer quotes a passage from the influential tenth-century writer Ibn ʿAdi: "It also behooves the one who loves perfection to train his soul to harbor friendship (*maḥabba*) toward all men, and to have affection and compassion for them. For men are one tribe (*qabīl*), related to one another, joined together by humanity (*insāniyya*). And the adornment of the divine power is in all and in each and every one of them, it being the rational soul. It is by means of this soul that man becomes human. And it is the noblest of the two parts of man, which are the soul and the body."[76] Finally, while numerous scholars have posited plausible avenues of influence between the medieval Arabic literary world and contemporaneous Europe, María Rosa Menocal has gathered perhaps the most compelling evidence for a medieval Mediterranean symbiosis of cultures.[77] Combined with the scholarship of Makdisi, Kraemer, Arkoun, de Libéra, and others, Menocal's book shifts the burden of proof to those who claim that it was possible to avoid significant intercultural contact among vast Mediterranean civilizations such as the Arabo-Persian, the Byzantine, and the west European along with their flourishing minorities such as the Jews and Syriac Christians.

To argue for historical connections between Arab and Western humanisms is not to affirm a naïve one-to-one semantic equivalence between key medieval Arabic terms and European equivalents, or to claim that the nineteenth-century coinage "humanism" unproblematically applies to both European and Arab cultures. A quarter century ago, Mohammed Arkoun cautioned against treating ideas as stable, transhistorical entities.[78] To be sure, ideas evolve with history, and the histories of different peoples sharing similar ideas evolve differently. Nevertheless, without denying the

effects of history and equivocation, it is not rash to suppose that
beliefs and structures of feeling can persist over time and pass
between cultures, especially when they are anchored to resilient
forms and topoi such as the hybrid Andalusian *muwashshaḥa*
song-form Menocal describes or the standing-by-the-ruins topos,
as I claim. In this way, ideas along with their associated structures
of feeling can plausibly communicate across cultures and time according to the linguistic model of signifier-signified transmission
whereby, for example, the ruins topos functions as signifier and
open-ended longing as signified. Even Arkoun, whose attention to
cultural specificity is scrupulous, writes of his intention to discern
in the writings of the tenth-century Arab humanist, Miskawayh:

> une fonction psycho-social, une part dans l'élaboration, la diffusion
> ou la conservation d'un *humanisme* caractéristique de toute une ci-
> vilisation. . . . ils [les écrits de Miskawayh] se présentait comme l'ani-
> mateur—parmi d'autres—d'un réseau de significations qui, dans la
> cité bûyide, offraient à toute une humanité des principes de vie, des
> critères de jugement, des valeurs communes de référence.[79]

> [a psychosocial function, a share in the elaboration, diffusion or
> conservation of a *humanism* that is characteristic of an entire
> civilization. . . . (The writings of Miskawayh) present themselves
> as a generating force among others of a network of significations
> that, in the Buyid city, offered principles of life, criteria of judge-
> ment and common referential values to an entire people.]

In sum, the point is not to argue that medieval Arab humanism
is the same as that of the fifteenth-century Italian *humanisti* or as
that of late-twentieth-century Lebanese humanist novelists and
filmmakers. Rather, just as the mythic aesthetic is a reappropriation of a discourse of redemptive self-sacrifice drawn from ancient
myth and monotheistic religion, so the contemporary elegiac aesthetic is a reappropriation of humanist thought from its numerous sources east and west. Indeed, "humanism" must henceforth
be understood as shorthand for a broader Mediterranean (at least)
cultural product including not only Muslim Arab but also Eastern Christian, Jewish, Persian, Berber, and Egyptian constitu-

ents.[80] This book suggests that the contemporary reappropriation of this discourse in Lebanese "elegiac humanism" is just one of many potential new humanisms predicated on the conviction that human identity is relational, open-ended, and, by virtue of this uncircumscribability, possessed of dignity.

A CULTURE IN RUINS

If I have successfully argued my claims, the reader will find it plausible that: (1) key elements of the social and political contexts of 1975–76 Lebanon have become generalized in the post–cold war globalized world; (2) Lebanon's social and political turmoil in the early 1970s demanded a rapid cultural paradigm shift; (3) the dominant wartime aesthetic was a mythic utopianism that drew from secular and religious discourses of redemptive self-sacrifice; (4) some wartime writers and filmmakers adapted an ancient Arabic literary topos to develop an alternative elegiac aesthetic discourse; and (5) this elegiac aesthetic presupposed and endorsed a hybrid humanist discourse. It remains to make good on the claim that all this bears relevance to the world beyond Lebanese culture.

The elegiac humanist aesthetic stands in contrast to mythic utopianism, whose great appeal, and not only in Lebanon, lies in its hitching of a daring Prometheanism to a comfortable identity-based ideology. Mythic utopianism in its sectarian Christian, Muslim, or Jewish forms has often been considered opposed to modernity and not an integral part of it. Yet in its secular priorities, ideological certitudes, and goal-driven strategies, sectarian utopianism is modern.[81] It is susceptible to the same criticism that is commonly leveled at Enlightenment-era "humanism," which I will henceforth call "anthropologism" since it attempts to define what humans are and is distinguished from the open-ended ontology of Renaissance humanism.

I have tried to show how Middle Eastern sectarian ideologies regard human beings as things to be used in the service of various utopian projects. This corresponds to Martin Heidegger's indictment of Western anthropologism's preestablished "interpretation of beings":

> The *humanitas* of *homo humanus* is determined with regard to
> an already established interpretation of nature, history, world,
> and the ground of the world, that is, of beings as a whole.
>   Every humanism is either grounded in a metaphysics or is
> itself made to be the ground of one. Every determination of the
> essence of man that already presupposes an interpretation of be-
> ings without asking about the truth of Being, whether knowingly
> or not, is metaphysical. . . . The first humanism, Roman human-
> ism, and every kind that has emerged from that time to the pres-
> ent, has presupposed the most universal "essence" of man to be
> obvious.[82]

From the certainty of "established interpretations" grows the
boldness to realize utopia via *technē*, and to regard the earth and
everything in it as quantities standing at the ready for rational
employment.[83] Contemporary Middle Eastern utopian ideologies,
among them Jewish Zionism, Arab Ba'athism, Syrian Social Na-
tionalism, Lebanese Christian Phalangism, and Islamism are no
strangers to such modern monovalent interpretations, yet the old
orientalist saw that the problem of the modern episteme is a Western problem dies hard.

The couching of modern utopianism in mythic discourses
makes it no less totalizing than universalist ideologies. Both establish a network of we-they binaries such as are deployed in
various imperialisms, and both are characterized by marginal-
ization and assimilation. Jacques Derrida, seeing residual anthropologism in Heidegger's thought, writes: "The *we* is the unity of absolute knowledge and anthropology, of god and man, of
onto-theo-teleology and humanism. 'Being' and language—the
group of languages—that the *we* governs or opens: such is the
name of that which assures the transition between metaphysics
and humanism via the *we*."[84] Derrida associates this imperious
we with Enlightenment humanism, but again, the *we* of sectarian anthropologism is no less imperious. To pretend otherwise—
that, for example, religious fundamentalism offers an alternative
to modern anomie—is to suspend for no good reason the critical
acumen that is brought to bear on Western anthopologism. To

accept the problem as a solution also, crucially, prevents envisioning alternatives to sectarian anthropologism such as elegiac humanism may offer.

Since Heidegger and Derrida are both skeptical about any easy exit from anthropologism, they are cagey about an alternative. They do sketch a few characteristics of what a post-anthropologistic discourse might look like. For Heidegger, it is crucial for thinking to be "in its element." He stresses that Being is the element of thinking, "the 'quiet power' of the favoring-enabling that is of the possible. . . . When I speak of the 'quiet power of the possible' I do not mean the *possibile* of a merely represented *possibilitas*, nor *potentia* as the *essentia* of an *actus* of *existentia*; rather, I mean Being itself, which in its favoring presides over thinking and hence over the essence of humanity, and that means over its relation to Being. To enable something here means to preserve it in its essence, to maintain it in its element."[85] The "quiet power of the possible" comes across here as a will to forestall epistemological closure. To preserve something "in its essence" is to preserve otherness, to let Being "preside over" thinking. Indeed, since Being cannot be circumscribed, any pretension to positive definitions is a sure sign that thinking has slipped out of its element: "When thinking comes to an end by slipping out of its element it replaces this loss by procuring a validity for itself as *technē*, as an instrument of education and therefore as a classroom matter and later a cultural concern."[86] By defining what man is—the rational animal, the image of God, the chosen people, the community of believers—anthropologism in its various guises closes off Being from reflection and compensates for the loss via ever more desperate articulations of *technē*. Given that Being is inaccessible, what is needed, according to Heidegger, is to seek "the nearness of Being." Accordingly, Heidegger notes the importance of silence, of learning "to exist in the nameless."[87] The resistance to closure is one means by which it is possible to foster openness to Being. In this book's analyses of numerous novels, films, and rituals, images recur of persons standing silently by the ruins of an uncircumscribable past, trying but never succeeding in achieving closure because loss in this aesthetic is irrecuperable.

Derrida is, of course, even more reticent about the capacity of language to represent Being.[88] He sees residual anthropologism in Heidegger's work: "We can see then that Dasein, though *not* man, is nevertheless *nothing other* than man. It is, as we shall see, a repetition of the essence of man permitting a return to what is before the metaphysical concepts of *humanitas*."[89] Once the "man" here is recognized as a historically conditioned signifier, this fact exposes the universalist denotation of "man" as wishful thinking—a dogma in the service of the power that employs it. Thus the mediation of language compromises any attempt at realizing in language a noncontingent human dignity. Derrida refuses to deny or soft-peddle these facts of language but is nevertheless not a relativist. In the thankless task of trying to find a language for human dignity, he has recourse to metaphor. He writes of a "trembling" that indexes the "co-belonging and co-propriety of the name of man and the name of Being."[90]

In his later work, Derrida points to, without ever pretending to express, what one might be forgiven for considering an enlightened humanist ideal. Discussing Blanchot's "Marx's Three Voices," Derrida recuperates the problematic "we":

> We are asked by them [the three voices], in the first place, to think the "holding together" of the *disparate* itself. Not to maintain together the disparate, but to put ourselves there where the disparate itself *holds together*, without wounding the dis-jointure, the dispersion, or the difference, without effacing the heterogeneity of the other. We are asked (enjoined, perhaps) to turn *ourselves* over to the future, to join ourselves in this *we*, there where the disparate is turned over to this singular *joining*, without concept or certainty of determination, without knowledge, without or before the synthetic junction of the conjunction and the disjunction. The alliance of a *rejoining* without conjoined mate, without organization, without party, without nation, without State, without prop-

erty (the "communism" that we will later nickname the new International).[91]

While he refuses to shore the fragments of human diversity under the Eurocentric category of "man," Derrida nevertheless seeks a "holding together" of humanity. He does not seek a common language, a common law—in short, commensurability—since he argues this always implies coercion. Instead, he calls for a willingness to turn "*ourselves* over to the future," which I read as a will to expand the horizons of discourse beyond the logics of the present. There is here a humble respect for the mystery of human identity as it unfolds in time that is akin to the Renaissance notion of open-ended human identity and to the elegiac humanism characteristic of a minority current in Lebanese wartime and postwar culture.

In this book, I try to show how this minority current has implicitly adopted an aesthetic of silence, open-ended ontology, and tentativeness about language that is congruent with the notion of human dignity toward which Derrida points.[92] The novels and films studied here do not presume an impossible stance outside hegemonic power, but rather seek to imaginatively point beyond it. In their open-ended evocation of loss and longing, they refuse the consolation of future justice. What has been lost is gone forever, and life is the less for it. As characters behold ruins and long for their long-absent human referents, the work of nostalgia and mourning opens up a mental space that provides an alternative to the mythic utopian recuperation of memory. From the standpoint of bereaved reflection, utopic or programmatic action appears increasingly implausible. In their place, these texts evoke an always absent vision of noncontingent human dignity that contrasts with the naturalized coercions of ongoing war.

Chapter 1, "Absence at the Heart of Yearning: Civil War and Postwar Novels," concentrates on five wartime and postwar writers. Tracing the emergence and development of the elegiac humanist aesthetic, this chapter argues that each writer employs the standing-by-the-ruins topos to open a window onto memory and imagination, contrasting "then and now," "here and there." Thus Hassan Daoud's character-narrator in his 1983 *Binayat Mathilde* (*The House of Mathilde*) stands in the ruins of an apartment building, letting them infuse him with its once-bustling everyday life; Hoda Barakat's protagonist's development in her 1990 *Hajar al-Dahik* (*The Stone of Laughter*) is reflected in a series of standing-by-the-ruins scenes in one apartment; Rashid al-Daif's protagonist-narrator in his 1995 ʿ*Azizi al-Sayyid Kawabata* (*Dear Mr Kawabata*) initially rejects the nostalgia of ruins before recovering a sense of their role in anchoring memory; Najwa Barakat's 1999 *Ya Salam* (Good Heavens) willfully represses the representation of ruins only to thematize their return as psychopathology; and Rabiʿ Jaber's character-narrator in his 2005 *Berytus: Madina taht al-Ard* (Berytus: City Underground) falls into a war ruin as the first step in a literalized journey through war memory. From these elegiac moments, the novels studied here denaturalize the ideological certitudes of war by sanctioning an open-ended vision of human identity.

Chapter 2, "'Speak Ruins!': The Work of Nostalgia in Feature Film," begins with a brief discussion of the role of nostalgia in a few popular Lebanese movies of the 1960s. These often delightful films tend to reinforce a fantasy vision of Lebanese society. During the first years of the war, a new generation of foreign-educated Lebanese filmmakers emerged to overturn this view of the past. This chapter studies their reappropriation of the ruins topos in five feature films. I argue here that ruins "speak" of repressed trauma to characters who learn to read them symptomatically. Thus Burhan ʿAlawiyya's protagonist in his 1981 *Bayrut, al-Liqaʾ* (*Beirut: The Meeting*) stands before the iconic ruin of the Holiday Inn, "hearing" its challenge and embarking on a mission to literally and symbolically cross the Christian-Muslim divide; Maroun Baghdadi's protagonist in his 1991 *Hors la vie* (*Beyond Life*) is imprisoned in ruins whose spaces force him to see other perspectives on the war; Johanna Hadjithomas and Khalil Joreige's characters in their 1999 *al-Bayt al-Zahr* (*The Pink House*) live in a ruin that concretizes war memories they would prefer to ignore;

Jean Chamoun's protagonist in his 2000 *Tayf al-Madina* (*In the Shadows of the City*) is surrounded by ruins but begins to fathom the war only when he understands them as metonyms for lost human referents; and Assad Fouladkar's 2004 *Lamma Ḥikyit Maryam* (*When Maryam Spoke*) uses the topos of the ruin-corpse to "speak" to the protagonist of his lost love. In each of these films, ruins communicate muselike to characters who otherwise exist in confusion or denial of traumatic history.

Chapter 3, "Elegiac Humanism and Popular Politics: The Independence Uprising of 2005," proleptically responds to the objection that this aesthetic is a marginal avant-garde phenomenon with little real-world relevance.[93] Its object of study is the cultural component of the broad, nationwide social movement that swept over Lebanon in spring 2005. A range of popular cultural forms associated with the movement clearly departed from the typical style of demonstrations in the Arab world. This chapter claims that the efficacy of the Independence Uprising was due to its reappropriation of the social structures of mourning in a manner remarkably akin to the reappropriation of the standing-by-the-ruins topos by wartime and postwar novelists and filmmakers. I argue that these cultural productions are a popular rhetoric of elegiac humanism. By examining graffiti, songs, banners, and chants, this chapter reveals a broader, culturewide means of responding to mythic utopianism. In the effort to cast into relief the particularities of this rhetoric, the chapter contrasts it with the popular rhetorics of the Syrian regime and its Hezbollah allies. While this lends the chapter and the book as a whole a polemical edge, my intent is to show the real-world deployment of what might otherwise be dismissed as a quietist aesthetic.

The conclusion of this study explores the current state of the elegiac humanist aesthetic that flourished in the postwar and peaked during the ten-week Independence Uprising of the spring of 2005. Since then, fears have been rife and amply justified that resurgent sectarianism will rip the nation apart for a second time within a generation. Without undue pessimism, in the conclusion I show how the 2006 "July War" between Hezbollah and the Israeli Defense Forces conditioned a resurgence of mythic utopianism along with a newly invigorated commercial aesthetic. Nevertheless, I suggest that the presence of an elegiac humanist aesthetic across several media over the course of a quarter century is not coincidental and that its waning is not definitive. Elegiac humanism is a manifestation of a resilient, long-standing element of eastern Mediterranean culture. Indeed, it shares a conditioning cultural logic with sectarianism. Just as sectarian attitudes are a part of the fabric of Lebanese culture, so is the humanism that transcends the nation's religious divisions. Yet since elegiac humanism almost by definition does not manifest itself in political parties, it remains a uniquely cultural phenomenon and a poor sister of sectarianism. Thus, if this book begins by tracing today's upsurge in sectarianism to mid-1970s "Lebanization," it also argues that Lebanese culture bears within itself a new humanist alternative.

Ultimately, the conclusion reinforces what I hope will be a gathering conviction on the part of the reader that human beings living under exiguous political circumstances are not destined to either repeat the coercions of their oppressors or submit to the abuses inflicted upon them. Rather, the conclusion reinforces the thesis that novels, films, and popular culture can teach us to read the ruin-traces of violence in a way that breaks the logic of righteous retribution and emphasizes the dignity of human life and death. If this empowering vision has faded and often fails to counter sectarianism, its example still nourishes hope during the long reign of modern ongoing war.

CHAPTER ONE

Absence at the Heart of Yearning

Civil War and Postwar Novels

In the introduction, I historicized the rise of the Lebanese war novel as a response to the failure of realist commitment literature. I traced this aesthetic transition to a shift in the narrativization of civil war from cold-war to ethnic-sectarian paradigms. I argued that events in Lebanon delegitimated the notion of a global East-West struggle behind ethnic-sectarian brush wars. By 1977, the war in Lebanon was recognized as an ethnic-sectarian struggle spinning beyond the orbit of a bipolar world. This political paradigm shift put paid to the Lebanese realist novel. Both realism and the cold war relied on a single horizon of meaning.[1] Each side in the Cold War, like each realist novel, claimed for itself close correspondence to neutral reality. The new multipolar ethnic-sectarian conflict carried with it new teleologies that pointedly ignored this cold war–realist paradigm. A proliferation of local narratives, each one proclaiming Truth, escorted Lebanon further into chaos. It was the worst thing in modern Lebanese history but the best thing for its literature. After a half-century monopoly, realism—like the cold-war narrative—became an overnight anachronism, and from its grip emerged the Lebanese war novel.[2]

It was a grueling birth. The rapid shift from a war between re-actionaries and revolutionaries to an atavistic feud among dispa-rate bands of Christians, Druze, and Muslims swept away ideo-logical certitudes. Activists who had been prepared to lay down their lives for secular convictions were suddenly told that this was all wrong and that it was really better to die for religious-sectarian reasons. Some, whether out of conviction or economic necessity, made the shift, but in either case it required no little abridgement of memory. Others, who had imagined that martyrdom should ideally be reserved for the same cause from one day to the next, found themselves alienated by their memory of commitment to a now-discredited ideology. So those who continued to participate in wartime politics had to either forget or admit that life was a quantum of matter-energy that could be exchanged for a mouth-ful of words. The others found themselves on the margins, fruit-lessly brooding over loss and defiled dignity.

As opportunistic, nasty, and short as the life of active commit-ment often was, it was ostensibly vibrant and forward-looking. Moreover, an exciting new postmodern aesthetic that stressed ahistoricity and depthless semiosis apparently endorsed the for-getful movers and shakers of war over the memory-laden mar-ginals. So from the standpoint of expediency, it is something of a surprise that Lebanese war novelists by and large refused to take the wide path of Promethean forgetfulness. Instead, they began thematizing ways to marshal memory beyond the revanchism that fueled wartime martyrdom. The easy explanation is that the ideological codes of the novelistic genre as inherited from west-ern Europe often, or at least sometimes, dictate a moral posture against violence. Besides being overly simplistic, this view of non-Western artistic production as always derivative of foreign models fails to account for the formal specificities of the novels under study. This chapter argues that Lebanese novelists' most significant borrowing is from Arabic memory literature and that this gives their novels their distinctive character within contem-porary world literature. Lebanese novelists implicitly reappro-priated classical Arabic literary techniques along with their associated values in order to formulate an aesthetic response to a traumatic present.[3]

Arguments for grouping disparate texts into a subgenre usually rely on a wide, representative selection from a range of works.[4] This chapter studies only five Lebanese Arabic novels of the past thirty-five years for a couple of reasons.[5] First, no claim is made for the universality of the thesis. Numerous fine novels present tantalizing but arguably insufficient affinities with the subgenre I sketch out.[6] The novels under study here all deal with not only memory but a particular way of exploring memory. Second, other novels could have been included among the objects of study here: Emily Nasrallah's *Flight against Time*, Iman Humaydan Younes's *B as in Beirut*, Hoda Barakat's *Tiller of the Waters*, and Elias Khoury's *Voyage of Little Gandhi*, to name just four.[7] The critical method employed here, however, demands space in order to identify the ways formal features intersect with plot. Thus I have chosen novels that span a wartime and postwar publishing history and that illustrate the variety of "memory narratives" amenable to the critical approach. I also believe that each has much to offer as world literature, so early in the analysis of each novel I suggest a thematic grouping including well-known novels from other cultures. Perhaps most of all, these novels as a group—Hassan Daoud's 1983 *Binayat Mathilde* (*The House of Mathilde*), Hoda Barakat's 1990 *Hajar al-Dahik* (*The Stone of Laughter*), Rashid al-Daif's 1995 *ʿAzizi al-Sayyid Kawabata* (*Dear Mr Kawabata*), Najwa Barakat's 1999 *Ya Salam* (Good Heavens), and Rabiʿ Jaber's 2005 *Berytus: Madina taht al-Ard* (Berytus: City Underground)—present a trenchant literary response to Lebanon's traumatic past. Each is thematically distinct beyond the common interest in memory and the actualization of a literary topos. It is hoped that exploring the formal unity of such a diverse group will offer a compelling argument for the relevance of this chapter's thesis to other contemporary Lebanese Arabic novels and perhaps beyond.

The literary heritage is arguably tributary to the way many Arabs experience memory. Within that heritage, the literary topos of "stopping by the ruins" (*wuqūf ʿala al-aṭlāl*) is an important current. I shall try to show how the structure of feeling conditioned by this topos infuses the thematization of memory in the contemporary Lebanese novel. In the introduction, I limned the general features of "stopping by the ruins" and affirmed that numerous novels and films along with popular culture quietly incorporate it in their depiction of ravaged buildings, objects, and people. The point, however, is not to simply state that the abandoned campsite of the ancient ode (*qaṣīda*) has now become the burned-out home and that the ex-lover has become one's absent family member, neighbor, or associate. Rather, substitutions couple the elegiac mood of the ancient topos to a contemporary political and moral problem. Typically, whereas the ancient poet stands by the ruins of the abandoned campsite and yearns for his lover reft from him by fate, the protagonist in the modern novel stands by war ruins and yearns for a past prior to war. The memory of the prewar past stands in contrast to the debased wartime present and the implausible utopic future. In this way, contemporary writers counter the dominant wartime aesthetic by exposing the violence of revanchist memory and the futility of redemptive self-sacrifice.

It is not unfair to say that the Lebanese war novel is part of a broader struggle in Lebanon to maintain a civil society of the mind when it is absent from the street. While it grew as an alternative to social realism, this literature is not unmindful of the social relevance of literature. The difference between the new elegiac humanist aesthetic and the social realism it has gradually displaced, at least in literature, lies in its recognition that any impulse toward change must be built on a firm reading of history, not just a vision of the future. Thus this chapter explores how the ruins topos is variously used to construct a history upon which the foundations of a civil society may be built.

The aesthetic practice that I identify among these writers is partly attributable to common conditions experienced by many who lived in wartime Lebanon and were exposed to its unique blend of freewheeling cosmopolitanism and ideological pressure. Most Lebanese novelists, for example, are of working- or middle-class origins. Another remarkable common feature of their

backgrounds is their educational roots. Most attended the public, virtually free, Lebanese University. Today, when the Faculty
of Letters of the Lebanese University has fallen on hard times—
even harder, it must be said, than those that afflict the humanities
worldwide—it is nothing short of astounding that so much talent could have been developed by this institution throughout the
1960s, 1970s, and 1980s. It was a great national vision that has not
received its due recognition: public money devoted to educating
the nation's youth regardless of their social, religious, or sectarian
identities produced generations of writers and artists who have
returned the investment many-fold. Sooner or later, this work will
find its way into schools as part of the national curriculum and
take its rightful place in the ongoing dialogue that makes up any
nation's identity.

Politically, the older generation of writers studied here, Rashid
al-Daif, Hassan Daoud, and Hoda Barakat, jettisoned program-
atic Leftism by the late 1970s. They retain, however, along with
the younger generation of Najwa Barakat and Rabi' Jaber, abid-
ing convictions in favor of personal freedoms, social justice, and
progress. These sociopolitical convictions do not superimpose
easily on Western political categories of Left, Right, and Center,
which makes their work all the more interesting for Western readers. Notwithstanding their disillusionment with politics in the
wake of the civil war, most of these writers played an active role in
support of the 2005 Independence Uprising, and have shared in
the bitterness of seeing the ruling class squander the movement's
historic opportunity.

Finally, very few Lebanese Arab novelists can support themselves, even at the end of a long career, on the sales of their books
alone. The rise of religious extremism since the 1980s means that
entire swaths of the country that once boasted bookshops featuring a wide range of poetry and prose now feature narrow gam-
uts of religious and sectarian literature. The restricted readership
is not limited to Lebanon. In the general decay of Arab societies
over the course of recent decades, the twentieth-century centers
of Arab culture—Cairo, Beirut, and Baghdad—no longer hold the

places they once did, and new centers such as Dubai have yet to assume an important role. Hassan Daoud notes a resulting parochialization: "Lebanese literature stays in Lebanon; Moroccan literature stays in Morocco." Another result of the rise of sectarianism and the decay of cultural cross-fertilization is that publishing contracts for Lebanese writers have gone from a norm of 3,000 copies in the 1980s to fewer than 1,500 today despite the rise in population.[8] Most writers must hold full-time jobs in journalism or the university. Anecdotes of young writers waking up at 4:30 a.m. to work on a poem or novel before putting in a full day's work are common the world over; most Arab writers still do such schedule-wrenching in middle age. Yet despite conditions that force literature to be an amateur pursuit, the work of these writers, I argue here, has attained professional standards and carved out a unique place for itself in the history of Lebanese and Arabic literature.

RUINS AND ELEGY IN *THE HOUSE OF MATHILDE* (*BINAYAT MATHILDE*)

Like numerous Lebanese novelists, Hassan Daoud (born Hasan Zabib in 1950) lives in Beirut and is of working-class origins. He comes from a Shiite Muslim family from the south of the country and graduated from the Lebanese University with a master's in Arabic literature in 1973. During the first years of the war, he was a member of the Lebanese Communist Party. He left the party in 1978 along with numerous other writers and artists when they were reproached for, among other things, remarking that the party was "behaving like a Muslim party." He has worked for three Arabic-language newspapers, *al-Safir*, *al-Hayat*, and *al-Mustaqbal* for about a decade each since 1979 and is currently the editor of *al-Nawafid*, the cultural supplement of the Beirut-based daily *al-Mustaqbal*. He began exploring prose fiction in the early 1980s and enjoys recounting how his friend, the poet-journalist Abbas Beydoun, responded to his first attempts at writing in the orotund mode of classical rhetoric: "Well, my friend, this is all very clever but it makes my belly hurt." His first novel, *Binayat Mathilde* (*The House of Mathilde*), marked a clean break from commitment literature and classical rhetoric and, as a result, it confused many readers. He recalls a friend asking, "What do a bunch of ladies shuffling around in an old building have to do with anything?" Since then he has become among the most successful of Lebanese novelists and his understated narrative voice is an important influence on the younger generation. Daoud, like many Lebanese artists, is not effusive in expressing his political convictions, but he actively participated in the 2005 Independence Uprising and was equally disappointed by the failure of the political class to heed its lessons. About the apartment building at the center of *The House of Mathilde*, he notes that it is based on the building his family lived in near the Sanaya Garden when they moved to Beirut.[9]

Consider what happens in societies that have no agreed-upon way of managing change. Typically, social conservatism and the imperatives of change become deadlocked, and society lurches from stagnation to chaos and back again. Hassan Daoud's 1983 novel, *Binayat Mathilde*, deftly translated by Peter Theroux as *The House of Mathilde*, traces such a struggle. What is atypical about this short three-part novel is its focus on the history of one Beirut apartment building in the years prior to and during the 1975–90 Lebanese civil war. In shunning the depiction of politicians, warlords, and militia members to focus on the lives of dozens of the building's inhabitants, this novel makes the controversial case that civil war and the habits of everyday life in private homes were of a piece. This is not to ignore national, regional, and international factors but to depict their points of articulation in private lives. The war, according to this view, was neither simply an in-house choice nor an outside affliction, but the outcome of historical conditions and social predilections.

The House of Mathilde is told from the standpoint of a man looking back onto the lives led in and around an apartment building since before his family's arrival when he was a child up to the narrative present when the ruined building houses only his aunt. Its skillful use of the building-as-microcosm trope bears comparison with that of other well-known texts in world literature: *The Yacoubian Building* by Alaa al-Aswany; *Miramar* by Naguib Mahfouz; *Life: A User's Manual,* by Georges Perec; and *The Death of Vishnu* by Manil Suri. The account of dozens of people who move in and out of the building in *The House of Mathilde* maps the displacement of a predominantly European and Lebanese Christian population by Lebanese Muslims and refugees who flee the impoverished and war-riven south of the country. The narrative also traces the inevitable shift in social-class demographics as the refugees take work as bakers and mechanics and gradually displace the jewelers and petite bourgeoisie. Yet another axis of change follows the decline of male authority within a patriarchal system as men during the war are forced to spend more time at home where women hold sway. While the characters are hardly conscious of these big social changes, their personal actions reflect and contribute to them as the nation and their homes slant into chaos.

The first part of the novel describes the apartment building and its inhabitants from a time shortly after it was built. This section is roughly organized around the arrival of the narrator's family as the unwitting agent of change. The second section, taking place during the run-up to war, chronicles an increase in the demographic flux of the building and includes the departure of the narrator's family. In both these sections, the layered social conflicts that contribute to the outbreak of war remain implicit. Only in the third section of the novel do these tensions rise in tandem with those of the war, reaching climax in the startling and near simultaneous murder of a building inhabitant, Mathilde, and an explosion that nearly destroys the building itself. Thus it is only in retrospect that the reader can discern in the first two-thirds of the novel the subjacent tensions that lead to war.[10] The text, in other words, is constructed so as to correspond to personalized memory.

The account of this character-narrator is very much an interpreted history featuring a strong perceptual filter. Characters often remain unnamed and are referred to only as "my aunt," "the Russian lady," or "the other Russian lady." Other characters are known by their first name, "Mathilde" or "Madame Laure," and still others are cited fully, "Ibrahim al-Kilani." This way of naming corresponds to the idiosyncratic way children know their elders and stresses that the adult narrator's knowledge of events is recalled from his childhood. As he stands in the ruin of the apartment building at the beginning of the novel, his memory of its inhabitants is imbued with the way they appeared to his young eyes.

The absence of direct discourse in this novel shifts even more weight to the narrator's focalization. All represented thoughts and dialogue pass through his consciousness, and because he seems rational and fair-minded, he enjoys a good deal of readerly good faith. Yet by identifying with this narrator's unusually limited focalization, the reader is smoothly and almost imperceptibly eased out of a realist frame of reference into the private world of the narrator. While the narrator seems more or less reliable, he often has access to other characters' intimate thoughts and is in place to make observations to which he never could have been privy. At other times, he confesses he does not know what others are thinking. Thus as the narrator muses on the past, he makes it; he does not transcribe it.

The narrator's personal, constructed history is one of the ways in which this novel dovetails with the epistemological context established by the ancient Arab poets. Like the *jāhilīya* poet, and unlike the chronicler or realist novelist, the narrator sees the past through its traces in the present and infuses personal meaning into both. Of all the novels of the Lebanese civil war that employ standing by the ruins, none inhabits the topos more fully than *The House of Mathilde*. It opens with the narrator's three-page prose vision of a dilapidated Beirut apartment building:

> My aunt was alone in the building. No one stood at the large
> windows that lighted the stairs and separated the floors. No
> one opened their door. It seemed to me that the doors had been
> locked for a long time. They were imposing and silent, and the
> big iron padlocks that dangled from them suggested that the old

furniture within had long been shrouded in darkness. Anyone
who had known Mathilde could imagine the thick dust that covered the sofas, beds, and wooden tables.

There was no one in the building, or so I thought; I felt the
emptiness as I stood on my aunt's rear balcony. The other balconies were empty, and the fine white tiles with which Madame
Laure had paved her cement balcony looked dusty and old. The
wind had piled leaves, dirt and fine sand in its corners and edges.
Madame Laure's door was closed. I knew I would not hear the
sound of her frying pan suddenly sizzling and then dying down.
I would not see her clean kitchen apron. My aunt would not wait
patiently for the stream of questions the Armenian woman used
to ask her.[11]

And so on. The scene is remarkable for its repeated negations of
life's activities. The repetition of "no one" and the mention of three
persons who left underscore the gulf between present desolation
and former activity. Likewise, images of lock, shroud, darkness,
dust, and dead leaves punctuate the triumph of stagnation over
images of habitation such as furniture, fine white tiles, a sizzling
frying pan, and a stream of conversation. In this way, the passage
establishes the elegiac tone, yearning for youth, and pulsating energy that is characteristic of the ruins topos.

The depiction of decayed and worthless things in the present to
evoke precious bygone times is not a mere wink at tradition but a
way of imbuing the rest of the novel with the shades of nostalgia
for a new purpose. Standing by the ruins in this novel recurs as a
key structural and thematic element. As the narrator reflects on
the building, its very decrepitude ignites his memory and illumi-
nates the novel's thematic interest in the irresistible weight of the
past, alienation in the present and the inevitability of debacle.

Still at the threshold of the novel, the narrator makes a categorical statement— "The building was no longer habitable"—and
then continues:

The dim grey steps were soft and hollowed out from the hard
tramping of so many feet. The black iron handrail was scratched,
and its corners were no longer sharp; the angles indistinct. It

surface looked wet, as though the sweat of all the palms that had brushed it had sunk into it. The iron of the railing was no longer as steady as it had been. The edges of the stone steps were worn, and some had fallen out of place, especially from the upper steps. Not only the steps, but the small balconies which were cut from the same stone as the stairs, and surrounded by the same black railing, looked fragile in the sunny winter light. (5) [12]

Curiously, the narrator is standing in a building that has been bombed to the point, we learn much later, of looking like a "like a hollowed-out aubergine" (173). In explaining why the building is no longer habitable, he makes no mention of the tumbledown façade. Instead, he incongruously invokes a series of images that suggest a space that is domesticated and made comfortable through long use. But for the first sentence, the description could have come from a travel magazine describing a quaint hotel in the south of France. The description sets up the deep irony of a building that is made uninhabitable by decades of intimate use and not by the punctual act of violence that actually destroys concrete and steel. In trying to understand why the building is repeatedly described as uninhabitable, it is necessary to examine not the war, but the decades of life in and around it that precede its fall into ruin.

Daoud's restraint in describing the social pathologies of everyday life in the building microcosm is the novel's tour de force. With a tweak here and there, the indelible horror at the heart of this novel could have overwhelmed the narrative, and its title, *The House of Mathilde*, could have become an Arab contribution to the "House of X" horror genre from Poe to the present. Instead, as the narrator stands in the ruin of the building, he casts his mind back to an everyday life whose normality is itself the cause of horror. This is the novel's bold theme: that the social conditions that lead to rape, murder, dismemberment, and desolation can be found in everyday life.

The Gadijian family is the first to flee the building long before the war. The new house is said to be spacious and gleaming, but it is not for creature comforts that the Gadijians leave since the building at the center of this narrative has an elegance of its own. The narrator describes one of its bathrooms: "The faucet in the Western-style bathroom belonged to an era when artisans invested even the smallest utilitarian things with splendor. . . . It was like something from the pillars of an old citadel. I turned on the faucet, and the water gushed out just as it did many years ago. It rushed out, cold and clear" (6). As a physical structure, the building remains potentially handsome. On the other hand, once the Gadijian family moves from the building, their daughter Alice is "no longer afraid of that mysterious thing that used to make her feel for her skirt all the time, as if afraid of someone suddenly appearing out of nowhere and pulling it down" (6). Within the elegance of the building lurks a potential source of chaos that is figured in sexuality.

The girl's fear of sexual assault and her obsession with maintaining propriety betoken part of a greater tension. In a building/nation that cannot manage the imperatives of change, repression and license are the rule. Mathilde is something of a heroine of repression. The fifty–something widow who lives alone is at one point the object of a man's attention, but as he drives up to the building in an Italian sports car, gossip and innuendo intimidate her until he eventually stops visiting (47–48). Or again, the narrator's uncle falls in love with a schoolgirl but only manages to stare at her from his car with his sister sitting beside him (68–69). Successful efforts to fulfill desire fare little better, replacing repression with license. Bored in the home, the narrator's aunt's husband seeks fulfillment in carousing and ends up unleashing turmoil in the family (60–64). The dual themes of repression and license, established early, mount to climax by the end.

Ideological resistance to change, which is the source of repression, demands a commitment to boredom and conventionality. The building's original owners, the al-Kilanis, set the tone such that even the children interiorize torpor: "Every afternoon, Umm Ibrahim, her children, and her mother-in-law squeezed on to one of the two parallel balconies that overlooked the park. They crowded on to one balcony and left the other completely empty.

There was no room for the children to play on the balcony, or even to move around. They sat, like their mother and grandmother, without seeming ever to get irritated or bored. They gazed at the spacious park, and every so often one of them stood up and raised his head over the black railing, to look down into the street that separated the building from the park" (12). It is not that the building stifles a freedom-seeking human spirit; there is no context in which struggle would even be recognized as anything other than obstreperousness. The horizon of possibility for the al-Kilani family is limited to sitting placidly on the balcony, "in rows, as if they were sitting in a long car" (13). The image of the automobile, traditionally associated with freedom, here vehicles a state of near catatonia. Initiative and energy do infuse the building when the narrator's family moves in, but eventually the new inhabitants are also enervated or, like the narrator's indomitable grandfather, they leave. Men in the building are often sitting silently, facing a wall or leaning against one. Women pack furniture into rooms such that movement from one side of a room to the other is impeded. They visit neighbors according to ritual such as the narrator's mother and Umm Ibrahim al-Kilani (72–73). Even on a picnic, both the narrator's aunts "treated their day out as if someone had instructed them how to behave" (67), Relations in the building and in the family are rigidly predetermined just as, on the national stage in the late 1960s, feudal families dominated a rapidly changing nation through the exercise of age-old conventions.

The isolation and territoriality of its inhabitants reinforce the building's stultifying atmosphere. The al-Kilanis are said to inhabit the building as if they were strangers to it, and the new inhabitants return the favor. Greetings to neighbors become a bone of contention as Mathilde refuses to greet the new neighbors on the stairs. The tension between old and new inhabitants is overlaid with class animosity. When bakers, a milkman, and a watchman move into the building, the long-standing inhabitants gossip and treat them coldly. Activities and events—a wedding on the rooftop of the building and condolences for deaths—counter the generalized retrenchment into the self, but it is arguably too little too late; the weight of precedent is just too great. Neighbors become alienated from each other such that spaces are rigorously partitioned even in individual apartments. The aunt, for example, relegates the narrator's family and their possessions to one side of their common home for years because their arrival in the apartment came a couple of months after that of the aunt's family. The establishment of such demarcation lines in the home, as in the nation at large, ramp tensions to the tipping point.

In the final third of the novel, the demographic, class, and gender tensions hitherto repressed burst into paroxysm. In the building microcosm, inhabitants respond to war according to their wont. Fear forces them into the inner rooms of their living spaces, contributing to even greater isolation and alienation. More flee the building. Squatters arrive, and hostility between newcomers and old inhabitants increases. As the pressures mount, the narrative strand dealing with Mathilde emerges from among the others. Since it is she who embodies both the repression and the license characteristic of society, it stands to reason that the Arabic title of the book is, literally, "Mathilde's Building."

She is the most reclusive person in the building, but it is suggested that she eventually becomes the most sexually transgressive. Successfully dissuaded by gossip from responding to the advances of her suitor in the sports car, the widow's preserved honor does nothing to lessen her misanthropy. She speaks with only one neighbor and refuses to greet new neighbors, much less attend their rooftop wedding reception. Thus it comes as a surprise when during the war she welcomes into her home a young student boarder from south Lebanon. In terms of class, gender, and ethnic-religious identity, the young man represents absolute otherness for Mathilde, and her gesture initially appears refreshing. Yet taking in the boarder betokens no real change on her part, only a tactical move. When it dawns on her that the boarder will take his meals in the house and actually use the bathroom, her resentment of change and otherness resurfaces and she reverts to repression (138). She parcels the apartment space between them just as the nation was being divided during the war, just as the land of Palestine had already been divided, just as her own body will be dismembered. She begins to fear him and in particular his sexuality. She imagines him leering at her legs and is disturbed as he lounges around the house in his pyjamas, but they manage to keep to their respective spaces. During a shelling, however, Mathilde and her boarder shelter together in a safe part of the house. She is sitting on a chair and he on the floor: "She told him to move closer to her, and he crept towards the corner near her own. They were much closer to one another, so close that she drew her foot back to leave him more space" (149). Mathilde's invitation from a position of dominance to intimate proximity dissolves the barriers between them. This moment is pivotal. He sees her in her nightdress; she sees his eyes "confused and wet." Just as the nation cannot implement change without violence, Mathilde and her boarder cannot entertain a shift in power relations. In the pathological context of the building/nation, the momentary intimacy that might conceivably betoken understanding of the humanity of the other is instead framed as a zero-sum power gambit.

Repression segues into license. The boarder and Mathilde become more intimate with each other, and he circulates freely throughout the apartment, even entering Mathilde's room, where it is implied they have sexual relations (161). From there, he begins to explore the apartment, sizing up its contents and spaces with a proprietorial air. Soon he asserts authority in a way that is overdetermined as a return of the repressed Muslim and working-class others. The shift in the balance of power is again gendered and sexualized: "When he spoke to her before returning to his room to sleep, he looked down coolly at her neck and at her feet pressed firmly together on her bed" (162). From this point, which may plausibly be seen as the aftermath of rape, he regards Mathilde with patriarchal disdain for the woman who has witnessed his vulnerability during the bombing and who is now herself vulnerable. The logic of repression and release in transgression that began with Mathilde's rejection of the man in the sports car and was followed by her sexual release with her boarder culminates in her murder and dismemberment as well as the building's near-destruction shortly thereafter.

The irony of the debacle is that decades of repression and stagnation designed to avoid chaos actually ensure it for each inhabitant. Mathilde's standoffishness and alienation lead to the chaos of her death; Madame Khayyat, whose apartment is one of the more hermetic in the building, suddenly abandons it to the narrator's aunt and leaves. The famously dull and ingrown al-Kilani family suddenly finds their apartment gutted and its intimate spaces exposed to all (171). In each case, the best-laid plans for stability come to nothing. Nor, however, does the paroxysm of license bring renewal. The aunt's son and his wife who take over Madam Khayyat's apartment have very little time to enjoy it before the building's destruction. The narrator's aunt herself, who gets exactly what she wants and more—eviction of her brother's family, then control over Madame Khayyat's apartment and finally over the whole building—is even more alone at the end than the generation of Mathilde she replaces. Radical change when it comes in the form of chaos brings only a nostalgia for stagnation.

The narrative ends, as it begins, in the ruins of the present. The standing-by-the-ruins frame has allowed the narrator to explore the microhistory of a building and its causal relationship with the present. More important, the topos infuses the narrator's memory with an elegiac note that blunts the edge of what might otherwise appear to be a radical and self-righteous condemnation of the present. As the narrative draws to an end, it pays implicit homage to the ancient standing-by-the-ruins topos: "My aunt was alone in the building. The interior of her flat had not changed, and she still watered the plants in the tin pots that she had lined up along the sides and front of the big balcony. The building was empty except for her flat. It looked like the abandoned suite of an old beach hotel. She would no longer hear the sound of the frying pan suddenly sizzling on the flame and then dying down. She would no longer see her clean kitchen apron" (179–80). Here the elegiac note characteristic of the ancient topos trumps the thematization of the war. It conveys the pathos of all life, begun in boundless hope, lived however imperfectly, and now past. In his typically understated and oblique way, Daoud illustrates this in a final vignette as the narrator describes his aunt's lawsuit against the landlord and how she hires a young, earnest lawyer who devotes all his hope and energy to the case, "and that was why my aunt was so certain he would lose it" (181).

By this light, the building inhabitants' determination to cling to the way things are, no matter how sullied by chaos and corruption, is ultimately contextualized under the more existential will to retain hope and youth in the face of change. Thus while the text does not hesitate to show, in keeping with the wisdom of journalism and political science, that "mistakes were made," its narrator virtually implores along with the pre-Islamic poet Imru' al-Qays: *"Qifā nabki"* (Halt, let us weep)—over these ruins, over this lost youth.[13]

DECAY OF ELEGY IN *THE STONE OF LAUGHTER* (*HAJAR AL-DAHIK*)

Hoda Barakat was born in 1952 into a middle-class Christian family from Bsharri in north Lebanon and is the sister of the novelist Najwa Barakat. She earned a degree in French literature from the Lebanese University and left Lebanon for Paris to do doctoral work, returning in 1976 as the civil war broke out. During the war, she worked as a journalist and translator, participating at one point on the margin of political activities but soon backing out. She left for Paris in 1989 during the war's final paroxysm and has since worked there for Radio Orient. In interviews, she stresses her attachment to the Arabic language, stemming from her exposure to classical literature in her mid-teens. She affirms; "There is such a thing as a mother tongue. . . . I see the world in Arabic." *Hajar al-Dahik* (*The Stone of Laughter*), her first novel, was written over a five-year period during the war. She regards it today as the basis of her subsequent work, a way of "building a bridge to the external world" during a time in which the "violence of the world made me feel a violence within myself." The novel was also a response to the Arabic novel of the early 1970s, which was highly ideological and foisted on writers "the heavy handicap of a missionary responsibility," forcing them to be "the guardians of Truth." Living in Paris during the Independence Uprising of 2005, she followed the events closely but did not actively participate in them. She admits to a sense of alienation in Beirut: "It is no longer recognizable as the city I knew. . . . I have not made my peace with Beirut and I think it's too late, because the Beirut I need to make my peace with is no longer there."[14]

The act of beholding ruins after the orgy of violence can kindle a range of feelings from elegiac contrition to righteous revanchism. Memorials, too, can evoke such a range of feelings.[15] Hoda Barakat's 1990 novel, *Hajar al-Dahik*, translated by Sophie Bennet as *The Stone of Laughter*, takes advantage of the overlap between ruins and memorials. It was published toward the end of the civil war and is the only novel studied in this chapter set entirely during the war years. It traces the coming of age of a young man, Khalil, who reaches adulthood under conditions of naturalized coercion and violence. He is apolitical, unambitious, androgynous, and temperamentally opposed to the war. By puttering around his apartment, keeping things clean and neat, he attempts to preserve himself from wartime violence. He is fond to the point of adoration of his friend Naji and is close to Naji's mother, Madame Isabelle, who lives upstairs. When Madame Isabelle and her family vacate the building and a sniper executes Naji for his involvement in the war, Khalil is crestfallen but eventually recovers and socializes more with friends from college who have gone on to work at a newspaper. He becomes friends with the family that moves into Madame Isabelle's apartment upstairs and shows a particular fondness for the young man, Youssef. Driven by wartime penury, Youssef joins one of the militias in order to meet the daily needs of his family. Khalil approves of the decision, aware that his own state of isolation is no model for one who must support a family. Youssef, too, is shot and killed, sending Khalil into a depression and illness from which he emerges with the conviction that he must take care of his health at all costs. The third occupant of Madame Isabelle's apartment is a mother who is herself killed by her son when she

learns of his viciousness. Khalil's friends at the newspaper intro-
duce him to "the Brother," a gun-runner and drug dealer with
close ties to a militia. Thereafter, Khalil's involvement with the
Brother deepens to the point where he becomes himself a hench-
man and catamite. The fourth occupant of the apartment above
Khalil's is a widow with her young child. Khalil is friendly with
her until he perceives her standing in the way of the Brother's plan
to store arms in the building. The final pages of the novel depict
Khalil beating and raping the woman and leaving the scene, no
longer an androgynous adolescent but a broad-shouldered man.

This brief summary shows how *The Stone of Laughter* unfolds according to a pattern of Khalil's rising affective investment in a succession of neighbors, followed by sudden bereavement and decline.
Its depiction of a crisis of conscience as reflected in sexuality bears
comparison with that of *The Clown* by Heinrich Böll, *The Lost Steps*
by Alejo Carpentier, and *Waiting for the Barbarians* by J. M. Coe-
tzee. By the end, Khalil adapts to repeated trauma by becoming the
agent of traumatic change himself. I argue that the motor of this
transformation consists in the way social circumstances encourage
Khalil's gradual recoding of ruins from an elegiac morality to one
of retribution. In this focus on the domestic social realm, *The Stone
of Laughter* shows how social attitudes transform memory into a
motor of violence. In the text, three primary instances of standing
by the ruins punctuate the transformation of memory. All are centered on the ruins of Madame Isabelle's home.

The first time Khalil finds himself standing before the ruins of
Madame Isabelle's home conforms very closely to the function of
ruins explored in Daoud's *House of Mathilde*. Khalil enters the
home after the family's departure and after a bomb has exploded
in a nearby street, shattering the windows of the apartment and
scattering dust and debris throughout.[16.] It is an elegiac moment
as the memory of the house is invoked in opposition to the exterior space of the war:

> Madame Isabelle's home contains furniture so heavy and old that
> it seems to have grown into the building, so that the huge dresser

with the curved mirror, for example, has come to stand in place
of the lower half of the wall, blocking the hole that gapes out onto
the empty street . . .

It is a comfortable home, whose owner took his time building it before he died a death as natural as falling asleep, surrounded on his deathbed by his children and grandchildren who
had benefited from his patient wisdom . . . this is what one would
suppose, looking at the starched, winged, cream lace and crochet
coverings, or the dark silk coverings spread over the little tables.
(16, ellipses in original)

The placement of the dresser literally dams the exterior space of
war, and the dust and debris cannot compromise the "wisdom"
that is said to infuse the home. Likewise, the image of hand-
stitched textiles that remain in the abandoned apartment are metonymies of quiet prosperity that expose the rash barbarousness
of the war without. Yet the civility of the past has been desecrated
and exists only as an afterimage evoked from ruins. The sight of
dusty household objects and the abandoned space recall for Khalil
memories of Madame Isabelle's daily habits and the family's last
moments in the home. It is a way of measuring the tragedy of the
present from the standpoint of a peaceful past. Coffee cups left on
a table are ruins, "like a talisman, to repel evil from the new inhabitants. . . . [T]hey left them as a token of faith in continuity and
as a warm welcome for the nervous newcomers" (21) The scene of
ruin is a source of strength for Khalil, a standard of everyday life
existing in memory that permits him to remain aloof from the
war beyond the home.

All other things being equal, ruins and elegiac memory might
serve as memorials and allow Khalil to preserve himself from war
indefinitely. The war, however, is not simply a foreign threat; it
is a part of society and is overdetermined by economic and gender issues. The text stresses that only two visions of masculinity—
young fighter or war manager—are available; one is either a man
and loves war as a fighter or manager, or one is not a man (12).
In his progress toward adulthood, Khalil's temperamental opposition to the war is a self-exclusion from socially valorized im-

ages of masculinity. Early on, he requires a model and looks to his friend Naji, who, himself, tries to sidestep war-related masculinity by playing an intermediary role between both sides to the conflict, but the war entraps him and he is killed. Later, Khalil looks to Youssef, who embraces the war ethos for only just as long as it takes to support his family and get an education, but he too is caught up in it and killed. Since Khalil has no socially acceptable vision of masculinity to set against the war, he remains aimless and dependent, "disgusted at his self-pity and disgusted at the way he behaved like a plump divorcee" waiting for Naji (12). His story is that of a series of failed attempts at forging a nonwarrelated masculinity.[17]

As important as Khalil's quest for an alternative to wartime manhood is, it is part of a greater problem. The elegiac morality implicit is contemplative, not active. The wartime morality of retribution, for all its violence, is active and efficacious. Even the fact that violence never produces anything but pain and the leaders' personal gain cannot erase the fact that Khalil's domesticity is sterile. The narrative stresses that Khalil exists "in a stagnant, feminine state of submission to a purely vegetable life" while other men who accept the linkage between war and masculinity enjoy "the force that makes the volcano of life explode" (12).[18] It is Khalil's task to fulfill his human potential without succumbing to violence, and to this extent, he is something of an antihero. The common fate of Naji and Youssef underscores the enormity of the task; the dominant ideology admits of no compromise such as they attempt.

Khalil also rejects the role of war manager. Nayif, his friend from college and literary foil, is a politically committed journalist in the pay of a war faction. Nayif's wife, Claude, both harridan and moral touchstone, exposes her husband's and others' sentimentalized attachment to progressive politics. Her criticism of the men in journalism and politics who perpetuate the war is also an indictment of the masculinity that is associated with war. At a get-together in her home, she apostrophizes an editor: "If you get off our backs, Abd al-Nabi, you and your shit mistress Beirut . . . you'll reach fifty. Forget about love, get married and have children and you'll solve your problems and ours at the same time." When her husband tries to calm her, invoking the fact that the man is in exile from his homeland because he is opposed to the regime, Claude shoots back: "So let him stop being in opposition where there's no system at all . . . where there's nothing at all . . . he can't sleep at night if he isn't singing the praises of the martyrs . . . of the rose of blood, of the fist raised in the face of this and that" (92, ellipses in original). She, unlike her husband, esteems Khalil's stance and his ambiguous gender identity, but as a woman she is herself marginalized, and her word is dismissed as a rant, which it is, but an incisive rant.

Ruins defined as traces or leftovers from war are scattered throughout the novel, but seldom function as they do when Khalil stands in Madame Isabelle's abandoned apartment for the first time. In most cases, circumstances conspire to baffle the elegiac moment, and instead, ruins simply accumulate in the form of wartime pollution. After a day of a dozen insults, Khalil returns home and muses that the sea overflows with things from the city, with its decaying limbs . . . Then the sea returns them to us as vapors and rains . . . then they come back and . . . we clean with them and water our plants (34, ellipses in original). The literal and figurative limbs, synecdoches of wartime atrocity, simply accumulate and perfuse everyday life. There is no pause before these ruins, only a desire for flight: "Where can the city go to get away from this sea?" and the absurdity of the question reflects the absurdity of escape or purification (35). Or again, a festive evening at the newspaper for which Nayif works takes place during a vicious battle outside, and Khalil walks out the next morning into a war zone. He picks his way through the ruins, but they elicit none of the recentering of the soul that he experiences on his first return to the ruins of Madame Isabelle's apartment. To the contrary, he sees loiterers who watch the ambulances dodge through the debris, noticing that they "had their mouths open in what looked like a grin as if they were saying over and over again, 'we're not in it'" (40). The devalorization of symbolic communication, such as suggested for example by Claude's inability to be taken seriously by the men around her, perpetuates the discourse of violence. Khalil sees pictures of those who died in the battle already plastered up all over the neighborhood. These photographic ruins provoke thought only within the narrow band of redemptive self-sacrifice, never elegiac memory. In such a context of impoverished discourse, martyr imagery replaces language, creating an inflated semiotic economy whereby the quantity of blood shed is proportional to the justice of the cause: "The headlong pace had become so swift that no sooner had the picture been up for the appropriate number of days for passers-by to see than another picture came to cover it and to cover the one it was covering itself" (41). The overheated "debate of blood" is part of a larger public relations economy: "All the parties and organizations used to prepare lists of their martyrs' names every season on programs that were remarkably like the promotional leaflets of tourism companies and hotels" with small portraits or stars peppered on the map to show key points of victory or martyrdom. Accordingly, the party avoids the grief of death and ruin since each death is practically recuperable as a symbolic representation of a sectarian-political value. The avoidance of the elegiac function of standing by the ruins ensures that war never has to be regarded as unredeemable tragedy even if, from the standpoint of those who lack ideological fervor, such deaths mean that pollution continues to accumulate.

The second time Khalil stands by the ruins of Madame Isabelle's home occurs when he returns to it after Naji's death. Unlike the first time, Khalil senses no recentering of the self in personal history: "The breath of the people who lived there had gone, gone from the dry air, disappeared without trace . . . even their things which, with a little effort, Khalil could remember them using, could remember them living with, now seemed empty, neutral, and barren as ordinary things" (59). As if to emphasize the mere accumulation of violence, a stench permeates the house, which "had finally become haunted" (58). Without the elegiac assessment of past violences, pollution becomes abomination.

Accordingly, the overheated, unopposed wartime ethos infuses everything. The parties become increasingly orgiastic and the laughter increasingly hysterical. Khalil comes to consider the famous Lebanese "love of life" as feverish consumerism indulged in while the city burns (85). Likewise, Claude exposes the periodic celebrations of the city of Beirut as empty sentimentalism and crisis denial (92). Even when Youssef is killed, Khalil feels great remorse and even responsibility for the death, but at the same time, he is "like someone whose dead have been stolen away." His grief is not cleansing and does not translate into tears as he remains in limbo, "not man enough to forge his world of dreams and not woman enough to accept" (132).

Khalil's inability to find solace in standing by the ruin of the abandoned home and his impotence to realize his human potential in the world mean that he has nothing beyond his will to pit against the wartime ethos. When the man who ordered Youssef's killing takes over Madame Isabelle's apartment, it is a symbolic breach of Khalil's resistance. The man installs his own mother in the apartment, but after she learns of her son's shady business dealings, he has her killed, leaving her cat as a haunting presence that wanders throughout building. With the war having symbolically entered the building, Khalil realizes that he cannot remain apart from the fray and falls sick. Upon his emergence from hospital, he has an epiphany to the effect that the crime and viciousness he witnesses in the street are a game "to celebrate life," and to the extent that the life of the active combatant reaps rewards, he is not mistaken (172). It becomes clear that when he is offered a benefit to illegally sell what was once Madame Isabelle's apartment after the previous inhabitant's murder, he should do it: "for me to be the only one who sticks to the principle, for me to be the single exception to the rule for the sake of the principle so that I come to scorn and despise and hate myself, must be nonsense" (177). Thus the economic motive fills the now affectively empty apartment.

For a third time, Khalil goes up to Madame Isabelle's apartment and beholds it as a ruin in the wake of the woman's murder. Unlike the first time, when he sees the apartment ruin as infused with the lives of Naji's family, and unlike the second, when he sees it as permeated with evil, this time he enters with trepidation but is surprised to find it inert: "What had he been expecting to find in it? Who was he expecting to find in it? The spirits of those who had lived in it? Who had left it? Who had died in it? Even his sorrow as he walked around the rooms was a slender sorrow, paper thin and superficial" (177–78). Traces are present, but they have become meaningless things that no longer move him. He remembers Naji, Youssef, and their families, but his emotional attachment to the space is broken, precluding any elegiac moment but also freeing him to begin anew. Thus when the new tenant, a widow with a small child, sees the furniture in the apartment and declares that she wants all the junk removed, Khalil raises no objection and agrees to have the apartment gutted for the new tenant.

In sweeping away the ruins of Madame Isabelle's home, Khalil engages in a bit of the creative destruction characteristic of capitalist renewal. He begins to feel affection for the woman, and helps her get settled. Ironically, the one thing that remains of the previous tenants, the murdered woman's cat, brings Khalil into close proximity with the young mother as it wanders between apartments and occasions Khalil's visit to her. The localized renewal between Khalil and the young woman unfolds, however, within the parameters set by war. Having sold most of his possessions, Khalil is drawn by economic necessity into the circle of the local warlord "the Brother" and attends one of his parties. In the orgiastic shrillness of the party, the Brother takes a liking to Khalil and gives him his card. Later, as Khalil leaves the party, a motif of wolf imagery culminates, and he is set upon by militia thugs. Only the warlord's card saves him, and Khalil realizes that his association with the Brother is his means to survival. He concludes: "there is no choice: for you to love yourself means to hate others," (199).

As if to thematize how his new convictions contrast with standing by the ruins, Khalil invokes the great Lebanese singer Fayrouz, whose songs of lost love and elegiac nostalgia are famous throughout the Arab world. He realizes that "this woman's songs had nothing to do with him." She was singing for a loss that he did not know and could not imagine. . . . It was a symbol to the core. A symbol that symbolizes nothing to him.

Fayrouz's songs belong to our families, perhaps, to those who are full of longing for Kfar Hala and the mountains of flint. But the singer does not reach me, nor does she lift me up to skies like those who weep, whenever they hear her voice, who weep for that generation that was over before it began, before it inherited . . . the rites of assuming power. (201, ellipses added)

Like standing by the ruins, Fayrouz's songs foster yearning for something that can never be. Yet at the same time, when the elegiac reverence for the purity of the (illusory) past dissipates, so does the moral brake on Prometheanism.

Khalil agrees to the storage of weapons in the building. When the young widow objects, he returns to the apartment to beat and rape her while her child sleeps in an adjoining room, repolluting the space that had been swept clean of ruins. Returning from the rape, Khalil encounters the cat of the previous murdered tenant: "In the entrance, the *hajjah*'s cat was meowing and rubbing itself against Khalil's leg" (209). As a reminder of a past in which he was opposed to the violence and coercion of war, the cat functions, like a ruin, to expose the debasement of the present. Consequently, "Khalil kicked it viciously and the sound of its meowing shot up like a scream." The cat's anthropomorphic scream is a reminder of the animal's original owner, a mother murdered by her son, and the rape of the young widow who could not scream as her son was sleeping in the next room. The kick, in the narrative present, recalls this past, and we, like Khalil upon his first return to Madame Isabelle's abandoned flat, long for what they represent: a time prior to the infusion of war into Khalil.

Khalil's interiorization of the war ethos is coded as a triumph of patriarchal masculinity. His transformation into a warlord's minion, rapist, and catamite goes hand in hand with his assumption of stereotypical masculinity. The narrator enters the diegesis and remarks on Khalil's departure in a car: "I went up to the rear window . . . Khalil had a moustache and a pair of sunglasses,"

and as the car moves off, she notices, "Khalil seemed broad-shouldered in his brown leather jacket" (209, ellipses in original). At
this point, in the last lines of the novel, the narrator makes an astonishing comment, apostrophizing Khalil as "My darling hero,"
implying her embrace of a Khalil who is no longer present. Since
the object of her affection does not exist in the narrative present,
the transformed Khalil reminds her of what he was. It is a perfect
ruins situation, only this time the ruin is not Madame Isabelle's
apartment or the murdered woman's cat, but Khalil himself, the
"laughing stone" of the title.

RUINS REDEEMED IN *DEAR MR KAWABATA*
(ʿ*AZIZI AL-SAYYID KAWABATA*)

Rashid al-Daif was born in 1945 in Ehden, in the north of Lebanon, one of eight siblings who lived in a single room. He studied
Arabic literature at the Lebanese University in Beirut and traveled to Paris, where he earned a Ph.D. in lettres modernes from
Paris III in 1974 and a D.E.A. in linguistics from Paris IV in 1978.
He taught Arabic literature at the Lebanese University from 1974
until his retirement in 2008 and currently teaches creative writing at Lebanese American University in Beirut. Among the more
prolific of Lebanese writers, he has published three volumes of poetry and fourteen novels, many of which have been translated into
several languages. Early in the civil war, he was a loyal member of
the Communist Party, engaging in propaganda, smuggling, and
armed conflict, but within two years became disillusioned and left
the party in 1979. In 2005, he was an enthusiastic but not uncriti-
cal supporter of the Independence Uprising, remarking that "the
street was transformed into a poem" that brought together Sunni, Shiite, Druze, and Christians. About the Arabic language, he
points out that his pared-down, direct style in Arabic is "perfectly
correct" even if it sounds similar to the spoken Arabic of Beirut.
His aim is to "attain the simple statement, free of the trappings of
classical rhetoric." As it is for many contemporary Lebanese novelists, Beirut is the center of most of his work. He explains that this

is not a political, romantic, or ideological choice, but a fascination with the city's palpable diversity and open-mindedness. About *Dear Mr Kawabata*, he affirms that it was "a genuine attempt at a self-critique" of his and his comrades' wartime activities.[19]

Rashid al-Daif's 1995 novel, *'Azizi al-Sayyid Kawabata*, ably translated by Paul Starkey as *Dear Mr Kawabata*, may be seen as a far-reaching critique of the social function of the ruins topos in Arab culture.[20] In both *The House of Mathilde* and *The Stone of Laughter*, ruins in the form of the building and Madame Isabelle's home, respectively, provide a window at some point for memory to conjure a sustaining alternative to the unbearable present. In both, like the ancient poet longing nostalgically for his beloved, the narrator stands before a ruin and envisions a halcyon past against which the war ethos can be condemned. Even when chaos overwhelms the metonymic equivalents of the nation—Mathilde's building and Khalil's resistance—ruins hearken to an alternative. Yet the consoling vision and hoped-for alternative provided by the ruins topos is not efficacious and can even be debilitating. *Dear Mr Kawabata* responds to the implicit question begged by both of these novels: What if the pleasure of nostalgic vision anesthetizes consciousness of problems in the present? Is not nostalgia a futile projection of desire onto an indifferent world?

The end of open warfare is always high season for opportunism. Al-Daif's novel is set in 1991, some months after the fifteen-year civil war. It opens with the narrator walking along a still shell-pocked street, stopping short as he suddenly recognizes himself trait-for-trait in another man. He recognizes his double as a former comrade-in-arms who has since become a notorious postwar opportunist. The narrator's self-identification with the embodiment of corruption allows this novel to begin where, in effect, war novels such as *The House of Mathilde* and *The Stone of Laughter* end—in a state of normative moral collapse. Its exploration of evil in the self places *Dear Mr Kawabata* in a category along with *A Clockwork Orange* by Anthony Burgess; *Masks* by Enchi Fumiko; *Wonderful, Wonderful Times* by Elfriede Jelinek; and *The Assault* by Harry Mulisch. As if to underscore the un-hypothetical nature of his personal crisis, the character-narrator, one Rashid al-Daif, shares many characteristics with the author, Rashid al-Daif: both were born and raised in a Maronite Catholic village; both obtained doctorates in France and became professors of Arabic literature in predominantly Muslim West Beirut; both were active members of the Lebanese Communist Party, and both suffered grave shrapnel wounds during the war. From a past marked by violence and coercion, his own and that of others, the narrator sets himself the ambitious task of trying to grasp a traumatic past without indulging in nostalgic dreamworlds, fashioning pretexts for revanchism, or, like the opportunist, conferring upon himself a blank slate. An earlier age might have called this a novelistic exploration of evil within the self, which would be fine except that this notion assumes both a self and a baseline of virtue. With no such certainty, Rashid enlists the figure of the great Japanese writer Yasunari Kawabata (1899–1972), to whom he addresses his life story: from his awakening to science and militant Leninism as a youth to his disaffection and disorientation in the narrative present. By the end of his narrative, Rashid does manage to distinguish himself from the opportunist, but his solution to the problem of traumatic history is unexpected and humbling.

In the long letter to Kawabata that springs from this personal and social crisis runs a motif of the sundering of language from the world. He recalls how as a smart-aleck adolescent he stung Sadiq, the village theologian, into spiritual breakdown by showing him the failure of religious discourse to jibe with the empirical reality of Yuri Gagarin's space flight. He recalls exposing the irrationality of his father's lifelong commitment to Christian sectarianism, and he recalls disabusing his mother of her belief in redemption, declaring to her: "There is no reward to be collected in heaven for the suffering you suffer today."[21] The blade of cause-effect reasoning cuts deeply into the legitimizing narratives of religion and clan, and it finally slashes into his own Leftist political convictions. Indeed, no novel thematizes the crisis of shifting from secular to sectarian priorities as scathingly as *Dear Mr Kawabata*. The narrator describes the intoxicating days of secular ideological commitment: "We took words for our mounts, confident that we were riding history! . . . The world, with all its constituent parts, was simply words turned into things. As soon as the word changed, the thing would change: water, earth, air, individuals, groups—in short, all living and inanimate creatures. All that was required was that the masses should learn these word-truths, and perfect their use, for the course of history to be changed. This was our mission" (5–6). Not long after the war began, he recalls the moment when such Promethean utopianism segued into guilt and aphasia: "I realized that my mouth was full of ants, that my lips were stitched together like a deep wound sewn up with strong thread" (6). The young master of demystification thus witnesses the disenchantment of his own doctrines.

His resulting deep suspicion of language leads Rashid to open a veritable indictment of the literature of nostalgia. In much the same way that he demystifies religion and sectarianism, he condemns such literature for betraying the truth of the past. Without quite targeting the standing-by-the-ruins topos by name, he asks Kawabata: "*Do you suppose that tears are what deprive our literature of the capacity to delve deeply into the secrets of its subjects? On the basis that too much sadness deprives a man of the capacity to see and understand clearly and intelligently, as the classical Arabic dictionaries say?*" (11)[22] His denunciation of the literature of memory would include, first and foremost, that of the amatory prelude (*nasīb*) to the classical ode, and, by extension, the elegiac mode discussed in this chapter. Both, the narrator is arguing, feed an emotionalism that perpetuates ignorance and self-delusion. He then implicitly connects literature and the political misfortunes of the Arab world. My "fellow-Arabs," he observes, "are generally fed on memory, on Memory in fact—the Memory that we Arabs were once masters of the earth. It is for this reason that 'Revival' is the objective around which political discourse (and also literature) generally revolves. My fellow-Arabs know the future well, because the image of it is already in their minds. It is the past as they like to see it, and as they would like it to be" (17). The history of ruins literature is thus the history of wishful thinking and vain emotionalism that prevents a society from accurately assessing its place in the world and formulating a program for advancement. According to this view, when the ancient poet dramatizes the link between ruins and memory by anointing his forehead with the ashes of an old campfire before reciting, he is not cathecting the priceless but absent past through the ruins of the concrete present, but deploying primitive shibboleths in order to bamboozle self and other.

The narrator's critique is relentless and uncompromising. Yet at the same time, it is useful to observe how Rashid comes to this insight. He addresses Yasunari Kawabata, an extradiegetic authority in whom he invests a great deal of affective energy:

> Dear Mr Kawabata,
>
> I always used to dream of being appointed king of some distant peoples. I would rule over them with justice, and dedicate myself to their service.
>
> I dreamed that I would be appointed as an arbitrator between warring factions, in some part of the world, to provide a model of fair play. [. . .]
>
> I loved the innocence of the stranger. Perhaps I still do. The stranger's lack of preconceptions to me meant neutrality. Perhaps it still does.
>
> So here I am, Mr. Kawabata, appointing you as the king I dreamed of being myself, the arbitrator obeyed because of his sincerity. (8)

One may be tempted to dismiss Kawabata the narratee as a mere cipher-ideal, a replacement for the God with whom the narrator dispensed as an adolescent. For Rashid, Kawabata is a paragon of virtue, but he is also akin to a lover; Rashid refers to him as a "perfect woman," "a princess, a virgin" (104). Kawabata's ontological distance along with his emotional presence make the great Japanese author function for Rashid very much like the absent lover for the ancient poet. He is known to Rashid only through his books, but precious little content of these books is revealed. They are analogous to ruin-traces: inert objects infused with the significance of another world. The great writer's books are metonymies of the esteemed Kawabata just as the ancient poet's burnt fag ends and discarded tent pegs index his beloved. Kawabata, like the beloved, becomes the projected embodiment of an alternative world and his books, like ruins, become the privileged window onto it. Thus, notwithstanding Rashid's harsh critique of the ruins topos, it is no exaggeration to affirm that he articulates this critique via the ruins topos itself.

Standing by the ruins is not only a structural feature of this novel; it is also prominently thematized. The most remarkable ruins scene in the narrative reveals both the justice of Rashid's critique but also its redemption. Rashid makes a point of associating the bullet-riddled bronze statue in Beirut's Martyrs' Square with the spiritual and emotional center of the Lebanese nation (see Figure 1). This is somewhat surprising since if there is one place that evokes the sentimentalized effusiveness that Rashid eschews, it is Martyrs' Square. Indeed, he reflects:

> I still feel extremely upset when Martyrs' Square is being talked about.
>
> I don't like it when a man tries to achieve greatness for himself too easily.
>
> Film-makers have taken shots there, photographers have taken pictures there, and journalists written articles about the place. Visitors pay visits, tourists travel there and there is now an improvised café at the feet of the statue of the martyrs in the middle of the square. [. . .] *This, despite the fact that a certain modesty and sense of propriety are more usual among us Arabs.* (116–17, italics in original)

This passage epitomizes Rashid's opposition to the ruins tradition but also lends it nuance. His unease with the ruins of Martyrs' Square is not that they are unworthy of emotional investment, but rather that this investment is banal, commodified, and obfuscating. He bridles at the kitsch sentimentality projected onto the square because it allows words to "run away with us wherever they will . . . while he, the poisonous being—history—just goes on" (116). In learning that all language-world links are ephemeral and contingent, Rashid goes from an unreflective enthusiasm for

Figure 1. The war-damaged statue at Martyrs' Square. Photo by Ken Seigneurie.

eloquence to awareness that it can be complicit with violence. He eventually confesses: "I smell in this eloquence the scent of blood, Mr Kawabata" (150). The problem, then, is not with projections onto the past as such but with facile projections that flatten it into pretexts for opportunism, and thus his animus toward nostalgia and opportunism are one and the same. In sum, the problem for Rashid is not the literature of absence but the absence of literature that can mediate the past.

Without falling into prescriptivism, *Dear Mr Kawabata* does suggest two features of what a nonsentimental and therefore non-opportunistic literature of the past would look like. On the one hand, it remains critical. Even though Rashid's world crumbled under the law of noncontradiction, he keeps faith with the method. Crucially, he does not scruple to direct it against his own pieties and self-image, and this is how he comes to distinguish himself from his double, the former friend and opportunist:

> Which of us did not kill with his own hand, which of us did not kill with his tongue?
>
> Except for *him*, of course. My friend. . . .
>
> The smartest thing about him was his suit. A grey suit, with a carefully knotted tie, and a white shirt with a collar that circled his neck without constricting it.
>
> A suit that had only just emerged from the cleaner's, pressed for some special occasion.
>
> And smiling!
>
> As if nothing had happened. (136–37)

Rashid learns that what bothers him most are not the opportunist's deeds, which were no worse than those of others, so much as his selective memory. The former friend fancies himself separate from the scrum of war and postwar. A neck motif concretizes this lack of historical consciousness: "When I was a young man, Mr Kawabata, I saw with my own eyes that blood could bend the neck of a killer. Because blood was heavy. 'There is blood on his neck,' we used to say" (138). Likewise, Rashid's neck, we are told, is twisted from a shrapnel wound. The opportunist's neck, on the other hand, is "smooth as the neck of a virgin, and unblemished—the color of children who hadn't known filth in the streets or the excrement of domestic animals" (139). The neck, for Rashid, carries traces of the war and its attendant responsibilities. In this way, the image of the neck functions like a ruin, a trace and elegiac reminder of the past. The problem with the former friend's smooth neck is therefore the *lack* of ruin-traces. Unlike Mathilde's destroyed building and the transmogrified Khalil and unlike this narrator, here is a man upon whom not a trace of war adheres. The lack of ruin corresponds to the former friend's denial of history. The past for him is not full of shame, humiliation, and guilt as it is for the narrator. He accepts a sentimentalized vision of history according to which he, the former party ideologist who had justified all manner of violence and expropriation, boasts "he'd never fired a shot at anyone" (139). Recall the narrator's problem with the poetization of Martyrs' Square: "I don't like it when a man tries to achieve greatness for himself too easily" (117). The narrator has now come full circle; from his initial hostility to the ruins tradition, he ends by implying that ruins are a necessary means of measuring the pain of history without which human dignity makes no sense.

A second feature of elegiac memory is perhaps surprising given that at the beginning Rashid is so skeptical of the literature of nostalgia. By the end of his narrative, he comes to appreciate the role of affective investment. He begins to cast the same demystifying eye on the automatic rejection of feeling as he does on sentimentality. He notes numerous instances of the former friend denigrating human feeling supposedly in the name of scientific socialism only to belie such convictions by opportunistic behavior. Thus he recalls his former friend who chided Rashid for missing his mother during a wartime training exercise only to later declare that he would marry in order to have a daughter who would be his alone to serve him forever (106–7).

Rashid comes to understand feeling as a means of confirming identity and ratifying a given grasp of history. After being gravely wounded in the street, Rashid is transported to a hospital morgue, where his body is piled among corpses. There he imagines seeing various people, from a nearly forgotten first love to his parents and to the former friend. He is moved by the expressions of grief among these people and his own feelings for them. Other people are also in the morgue, poking through the corpses in search of loved ones. Rashid sees the grief his mother feels for him and contrasts it with another mother's indifference toward him. This specificity confers upon him identity. Seeing his father's sorrow fills him with guilt, which is also a way of giving meaning to his history. By contrast, he imagines seeing the former friend who can only remark that Rashid should now parlay his wound to advantage for sympathy and profit. The former friend's lack of emotional investment allows Rashid to see for the first time a shabbiness in the former friend's clothing that he could not previously perceive. His newfound esteem for the affective component of the human being allows Rashid to sympathize, if not agree, with his parents and the village theologian Sadiq's rejection of science. He imagines seeing Sadiq on the latter's deathbed and admits that this is the first time he had "looked at him properly" since his own father's death (166). By the same token, his embrace of human affect allows him to distinguish himself from the former friend who fancies himself above emotionalism.

Rashid thus condemns the unreflective retailing of standing by the ruins, but at the same time does so via a clever reappropriation of the topos. His replacement of Kawabata for the beloved and of books for ruins reinvigorates the tradition by revealing a role for affective investment in historical consciousness. As a trigger of affectivity, ruins can be marshaled in an effort to resist sentimentalism and opportunism. In sum, the reappropriation of the ruins topos allows Rashid to critique historical critique itself and provide himself with a greater sympathy for human diversity, and thus prepare himself for the challenges of a transition from the postwar to civil society.

ANTI-RUIN IN *YA SALAM* (GOOD HEAVENS)

Writer, journalist, teacher, and novelist Najwa Barakat, sister of Hoda Barakat, was born in 1960 and grew up in Beirut in a middle-class family. As an adolescent and young adult during the civil war, she was "too young to take part ideologically" in the war but was strongly marked by it. She studied theater at the Lebanese University until traveling to Paris at the age of twenty-four, where she completed a degree in cinema studies. She also wrote for several Arabic newspapers and journals and worked on a number of cultural programs for Radio France International and the BBC. Today, she lives in Paris and spends a good deal of time in Beirut. Since 2005, her energy and enthusiasm for literature has translated into leading a "How to Write a Novel" workshop series for young writers from throughout the Arab world. Among the fruits of this initiative are three novels published by emerging writers. She was an active supporter of the 2005 Independence Uprising that "gave renewed hope" to the nation and has shared in the subsequent disappointment of its aspirations. About *Ya Salam*, she notes that it is a book "about human ruins and a city in ruin."[23]

The rule of law ensures a degree of justice and equality, yet rule-flouting expediency brings innovation and change. The Lebanese habitus is marked by a high degree of expediency within sectarian and legal structures whose restrictiveness varies according to social class. Wartime is, of course, the carnival of Promethean expediency. At such times, violence and social mobility threaten the rulers, and the impulse for order fills the air, most often with a quasi-sectarian will to purify and compensate for the excesses of expediency. Purification, done expediently, is violent, which increases the chaos that begs for order and therefore more violence. And so the vicious circle turns, common wisdom has it in fifteen-year cycles, until some new combination of law and sectarian prerogative can be found to ensure stability and the continued prosperity of the rich.

Najwa Barakat's highly compelling 1999 novel *Ya Salam* is a

trenchant exploration of the expedient will as it infuses love, live-
lihoods, and the family during war and postwar. In its relentless
pursuit of the logic of expediency to the point of psychological
breakdown, *Ya Salam* would stand alongside *Querelle of Brest* by
Jean Genet; *The Impressionist* by Hari Kunzru; *Season of Migration to the North* by Tayeb Saleh; and *Perfume: The Story of a Mur-
derer* by Patrick Suskind.[24] Its title, *yā salām* ("oh dear" or "good
heavens") is an exclamation most often used in reference to an unexpected bold initiative that may turn out to be positive or negative. The phrase "*yā salām*" works on other levels as well. Loqman
and Najib are former militia fighters in their early thirties, alienated and disgruntled at having to find a new way to make a living
during the postwar. The literal translation of *yā salām*, "oh peace,"
would also underscore their "war with peace." They long for the
time when the balance of power lay in the strength of arms, and
their frustration is reflected in their wish to inflict violence on
numerous individuals and groups. Loqman and then Najib eventually strike up an interested relationship with a woman, Salam,
whose name adds another layer of ironic meaning to the book's title such that the exclamation *yā salām!* might well be addressed to
her in response to the expediencies she undertakes in the aim of
ensuring her love interest.[25] The motto of all three, Loqman, Najib, Salam, and the world they live in might be summed in a comment Loqman makes soon after he undertakes an act of casual sex
with a woman who literally kicks him out of the car after getting
what she wants. He declares to his sex organ what is in effect the
novel's premise: "That's life, my friend, one day you get it, the next
day it gets you" (26).

A summary of this highly literary novel that features numerous
foil characters, foreshadowing, delayed decoding, and the topoi
of rebirth and catabasis ought to take account of its principal
motifs and themes. Traps are prominent. Loqman, the maker of
bombs, is trapped in postwar peace, but finds a way out when he
meets Salam, the mistress of a wartime militia leader, "the Leper,"
who was a master in torture and who was trapped and murdered
shortly after the war. Loqman is not attracted to Salam, except for

her rump, but she is close to the Leper's senile mother who has a small fortune from her lifelong work as a seamstress. Loqman begins a relationship with Salam hoping to leverage control over, or trap, these resources but soon feels himself trapped by Salam's affections. On a visit to Salam's brother, who is committed to an asylum, Loqman meets another war buddy, Najib, who is trapped as a patient–sex slave in the asylum. Loqman contrives to get Najib released into his custody, and Najib passes along to him an extended study of rats written by a fellow patient who was fascinated by rats and who claimed that rats, the embodiment of expediency in this novel, caused the civil war. Together they come up with the idea to release rats into rich neighborhoods in order to "trap" the rich into paying them to retrap the rats.

Abusive and fetishized relationships are another prominent feature of this novel. Loris, the Leper's mother, adores her son to the point of disregarding the death of her husband and humiliating herself on the altar of her son's happiness. Salam is similarly obsessive, humiliating her brother during the war when he returns traumatized after an evening of observing her boyfriend, the Leper at work. For his part, Loqman uses Salam's affections to obtain capital for the rat extermination business until he meets Cherine, a Franco-Lebanese emigrant who returns to Lebanon to work with UNESCO on the preservation of the downtown archaeological ruins. In Cherine, Loqman sees his ticket out of Lebanon and uses her accordingly. As Salam becomes aware of Loqman's unfaithfulness, she shifts her affections to Najib, who takes to beating her when he isn't ignoring her. Najib has a history of sadism toward women and is himself abused in the psychiatric hospital, but he is passionately interested in rats and converts a room in Salam's flat into a "laboratory" with rats he traps from the neighborhood. All so many psychopathologies of love, perhaps what Barakat is referring to in noting the "human ruins" of this novel.[26]

This novel also thematizes the will to purify. The Leper's torture victims are always naked and made to submit to some parody of religious purification. Loqman longs on numerous occasions to cleanse some person or group of people from the face of the earth with murderous expediency. Najib embarks on a quasi-scientific quest to achieve wholesale rat eradication. At one point, Najib, Loqman, and Salam muse together on various people they would like to see devoured by rats. In the short but important passage on the downtown archaeological ruins, the novel expands the purification theme from the personal to the national level as the authorities decide to fill in the archaeological site in order to provide a clean slate for development. The culmination of purification, however, occurs within the intimacy of the family and is motivated by Salam's relationship with her mentally ill brother, Selim. He is expelled from the asylum when it emerges that Salam gives him the breast to quiet him during her visits. In her turn, Salam is prey to a terror that Najib will reject her if she brings Selim into the home. The personal crisis ends with her locking her brother, bound and drugged, in the basement shelter that has not been used since the war. She then goes about cleaning the house obsessively, but the anxieties of keeping her brother confined and of losing the desultory and sadistic attentions of Najib lead Salam to give her brother an accidental overdose, and he dies. Fearing the stench of the corpse will expose her, Salam seeks the most expedient way to purify the pollution of her crime. She releases a cage full of Najib's rats into the basement to devour her brother's remains, eliminating any trace of him.

The themes of traps, abusive relationships, and purification come together in the last pages of the novel. Loqman's seduction-trap works perfectly, so that when Cherine despairs of saving the ruins of the downtown and decides to return to Paris, she invites him to join her. They marry, and on the eve of his departure for a new life, Loqman decides to say farewell to Salam and Najib. Entering Salam's apartment, Loqman discovers her disheveled and babbling and Najib dead of plague in the adjoining room, each having been "trapped" by their respective desires and expediencies. He manages to leave over Salam's remonstrations, but on his way home, realizes that without Salam and Najib in the way, he could easily make off with the fortune of the Leper's senile mother, so he returns. In breaking into her apartment, he is whacked on the head and awakens to find himself bound and gagged, trapped with the old woman gabbling semi-coherently over him. In the final pages of the novel, it becomes clear that during the war the doting mother had accidentally witnessed one of her son's torture sessions. Traumatized and feeling responsible for her son's behavior, she eventually gasses the devoted son in his sleep, expediently purifying the world of he who expediently purified his victims. Yet Loris is haunted that the circumstances of her son's death precluded his understanding why he was executed. The arrival of Loqman, whom she confuses with her son, gives her the second chance she needs, so after her soliloquy, she turns the gas on Loqman, too.

Thus the thematization of expediency in this text leaves little room for attention to ruins. The "ruin-reminders" of actions are routinely swept away or ignored. We are never invited to witness the ruins of Loqman's wartime bomb-making or to see the victims of the Leper's torture, or to pause over Salam's humiliation of her brother. Yet this is not a novel without memory. *Ya Salam* effectively asks why reflecting on the past should be morally uplifting. The memory of the Leper's wartime torture hangs like a bat over the actions of Loqman, Najib, Salam, and, in a different way, Loris. Najib recalls anecdotally a wartime scene, which is a near-parody of the classical-ruins topos. Whereas the classical poet beholds ruins and conjures images of sensual pleasures taken mutually, Najib, who has no ruins to behold, recalls in near-ecstasy an evening of pleasure with a woman whose nipples he luxuriated in burning. Unlike the classical poet whose conjuring of past joys serves to mediate his reintegration into a harsh natural world by intensifying its minimal pleasures, Najib's joys increase his alienation and trump the harshness of nature with gratuitous violence. His acts are a parody of consumption; he even stresses the joy of "tasting" the victim's seared flesh, *ṭaʿm* (68). While it is not clear that the presence of ruins, a rediscovered piece of costume jewelry perhaps, would bring to Najib's mind the woman's existence as a once-autonomous being whose torture and subsequent suicide would be recognized as such, it is surely the case that without a ruin-trace, Najib's mind freely projects as it will and depicts the events as harmless fun. Thus when he hears her rummaging around in the kitchen the next morning, he is pleased at the thought that she is preparing breakfast for the men and is astonished when it dawns on him that she is looking for a way to hang herself (68). In a world of unbridled expediency free of normative human dignity, it is difficult to argue that torture is worse than other expedients. Concrete ruin-traces recognized as such may brake the free play of semiotic expediency and foster a cultural value around the autonomy of the nonself.

Ya Salam is therefore a novelistic experiment in life without ruins; indeed, it is a novel of "anti-ruins," rigorously thematizing the elimination of ruin-traces in its privileged symbol of expediency, rats. An extract from a rat-master's journal on the Norwegian rat reads: "It lives on carrion, human or animal, small living prey or plants. It gnaws everything to maintain its strength: paper, cloth, rubber, even metal. The males are violent and engage in struggle with their own kind, cannibalizing each other at times if hungry enough" (75–76). Rats are the principal means of conveying the culminating image of expediency as Salam releases them into the basement where her brother's corpse lay. With her mind at ease now that the problem of Selim spoiling her relationship with Najib has been solved, she turns back to listen on her way out of the basement: "Tomorrow, she'll forget. Tomorrow, no trace will be left of the secret she'd been hiding in the basement. When the rats gather around it, they'll tear, bite, gnaw, rip and consume everything to the point of completely concealing it, as if it had never been there or as if it had never been at all" (163), Thanks to rats, the wheels of expediency turn unencumbered by ruin-traces.

Even in the archaeological ruins of the downtown, the one thing rats do not devour—stone—is deactivated as a functioning ruin. A member of Cherine's team of archaeologists notes that it is precisely in the middle of the ruins that the rats have their biggest nest (122). When the authorities, like Loqman, see no point preserving nodes of memory in the form of ruins, the point is

driven home that ruins have no place in the postwar world of expediency. They decide to curtail the archaeological project and fill
in the site, replacing the exploration of history with a commercial
venture. An exchange between the UNESCO team members underscores the stakes in burying ruins:

> "What do you expect from a country that doesn't respect its his-
> tory . . ."
> "They've lost their memory to the point of having no roots!"
> (145)

The term *aṣl* translated here as "roots" does not refer simply to cultural identitarianism but rather to an origin or source that includes
moral principles. The disregard for ruins connects to the disregard
for history and morality, another of Barakat's thematic interests.[27]

Another scene tailor-made for standing by the ruins but stu-
diously avoiding the topos has Salam stumbling in the darkness
in the basement where her brother lay among boxes of the Leper's war booty. She stops as if to begin a ruins scene, declaring:
"God have mercy on your soul, Leper. You stole piles of this stuff
and what good did it do you when you left this life?" Yet she does
not go on to invoke the times she and the Leper shared together
as in the traditional ruins topos, or to consider the morality of
the past as in the new humanist reappropriation of the topos, or
even to muse on the brevity of life and human vanity as in the
Western tradition. Instead, she continues to grope in the darkness
and concludes: "Salam, why don't you sell this stuff and get some
good money out of it?" (153). Expediency and liquidity are almost
synonyms.

Yet, like most objects of repression, ruins, too, stage a return. In
the normally functioning topos, such as in *The House of Mathilde*
when the narrator stands by the ruin of the destroyed apartment
building, it is almost as if the ruin has absorbed the evil that has
occurred in the building, permitting him to contemplate it as an
object. In *Ya Salam*, in the near-total absence of ruins, characters
behold horror directly and, as in ancient myth, the resulting pollution of the spirit transforms characters into human ruins. It is

suggested that Salam's brother, Selim, the "madman in the basement," loses his sanity upon the horror of his parents' death by explosion. Loris, the Leper's mother, is even more clearly a ruintrace after witnessing one of her son's torture sessions. Salam, entering the basement where she has bound and gagged her brother, lights a candle, and suddenly "strange shadows dance on the walls," prefiguring the shadow world of insanity into which she will fall after murdering her brother and as she waits for her beloved, and dead, Najib to wake up (153–54). In addition to the corruption of sanity, in the absence of ruins to "draw off" evil, it infects the body as well. Salam's bruised and bleeding flesh, which she is proud to display, is a ruin testifying to both Najib's and her own psychopathologies. Loqman's corpse is a ruin testifying to his greed. Najib's corpse is a ruin-culmination of the text's theme of expediency: indeed, his crusade to cleanse the world of rats counts him as its first success.

One passage does present a perfect scene of standing by the ruins. Loris, the Leper's mother, wanders almost automatically into her long-dead son's bedroom. She opens the closet, remembers his real name, Elias, and begins pulling out his clothing. She piles it on his bed and begins pressing her face into the clothing until mothballs fall to the floor and the sound brings her back to herself. At this point, "Loris stopped and considered her actions with great interest. When the little white balls stopped rolling, she furrowed her brow and turned, wondering what she would do and what could have made her pile up all these clothes" (107). She almost throws the clothes out the window but resumes her reverie, going back in time to when her son was a boy. Occurring very near the middle of the narrative, this passage reveals with great economy the fetishized relationship between Loris and her son, the militia leader. The passage also reveals, as if the germ of all that follows, Loris's self-abnegation when her son feels shame at her status as a seamstress. His later life as a torturer and collector of war booty may be seen as a way of radically leveling this class disparity that shamed his mother and him as a child. The importance of this ruins scene, however, goes beyond the glimpse it provides of the Leper's motivation. Standing by the ruins of her son reveals that for Loris, an affective center exists beyond the self, and this provides a moral framework for her actions. As insane as she doubtless is and as criminal as her act is, her soliloquy at the end shows that Loris understands the evil that her son commits and that she commits in killing him and in killing Loqman. In this scene of standing by the ruins of her son, she is by turns the doting mother who buries her face in her dead son's clothing and also, as she ponders throwing the clothing out the window, the society that judges. By comparison, Najib, Loqman, the Leper, and Salam never take stock of their actions as anything other than more or less successful expedients in obtaining the objects of their desire.[28] Yet Loris's standing by the ruins of her son is not an instance of the ruins topos within the new humanist aesthetic explored in this book. Instead, the scene takes place within the framework of the "righteous violence" characteristic of the mythic utopian aesthetic described in the introduction.

Be that as it may, this novel's mission to plumb immorality through an aesthetic of anti-ruins ends up vividly illustrating the potential role of ruins in mediating history and memory by showing what happens in their absence. It suggests through counterexample that one way of exiting the vicious cycle of expediency, chaos, and purification is to remember the iterations of the only-apparent cleansing violence that engenders chaos. Ruins, as the traces of violence, can structure memory and steel consciousness against "cleansing chaos" for those who contemplate them. To stand by ruins, I have tried to show, is to remember the victims of expediency, to be conscious of the will to purify and to defend nonfungible human dignity.

Excepting the exception of Loris standing by the ruins of the Leper's clothing, the novel has only one example of standing by the ruins. In the brief frame narrative that envelops the action of the novel, we are invited to take a cloud's-eye view of the city. In the opening scene, a cloud comments that the people below have lost the ability to weep. After the intervening events, the clouds in the last chapter "stand" over the moral ruins of the city and

its inhabitants. The novel ends in rain, suggesting that while humans have become stonelike ruins, their woes move dumb nature
to tears.

LIMITS OF ELEGY IN *BERYTUS: MADINA TAHT AL-ARD* (BERYTUS: CITY UNDERGROUND)

Rabi' Jaber was born in 1972 in Beirut. He earned a degree in
physics from the American University of Beirut in 1993 and has
served as editor of *Afaq* (Horizons), the cultural supplement of
the Arabic daily *al-Hayat* since 2001. In his relatively short career,
he has written some seventeen novels, among them *Taqrir Milis*
(The Mehlis Report), published shortly after the assassination of
the former prime minister Rafik al-Hariri in 2005 and which provides a glimpse of Jaber's sympathies with respect to the Independence Uprising.[29] In *The Mehlis Report,* he traces the life of a man
who postpones a medical check until the all-important report on
the assassination of the former prime minister appears, but the
man dies before the report is published, and the novel ends at that
point. The poet and critic Abdu Wazen notes that the reader is invited to imagine that the last chapter of the novel is written by the
late prime minister in the other realm and that his text ends at the
moment of the explosion at 12:50 p.m. on 14 February 2005.[30] As
for *Berytus: Madina taht al-Ard* (Berytus: City Underground), Jaber prefers to let the text speak for itself.[31]

The catabasis trope is not uncommon and has been used for numerous purposes.[32] Rabi' Jaber's untranslated 2005 novel *Berytus:
Madina taht al-Ard* (Berytus: City Underground) employs it principally as a way of exploring consciousness of class. This theme,
if not the catabasis per se, unites this novel with *Woman in the
Dunes* by Kobo Abe; *Half of a Yellow Sun* by Chimamanda Ngozi
Adichie; *Destroy, She Said* by Marguerite Duras; and *To Live: A
Novel* by Yu Hua. For a Lebanese Arabic novel composed in 2004
and published in 2005, such a theme is unusual. In retrospect, it
was in 2003–4 that Lebanon enjoyed the closest thing to a national

life well lived since prior to the civil war in 1975. True, the nation was burdened with a $30 billion debt, corruption, and Syrian military occupation, but it was still arguably the best of recent times. The expulsion of the Israeli Defense Forces in 2000 and the influx of investment, tourists, and foreign students seemed to poise the nation before a renewal of its prewar status as the cultural, financial, and touristic hub of the Arab Middle East. The makers of literature, film, and popular culture were shying away from war and postwar subject matter, so Rabi' Jaber's dystopic exploration of war memory in *Berytus: Madina taht al-Ard* was an exception. It was also an exception among exceptions in that dystopias generally try to dispel the innocence that accompanies prosperity, while this one, I argue, seeks to vindicate a degree of willful self-deception.

The novel opens with a group of friends dining on a summer evening in the upscale open-air café-restaurant located on the roof of the Virgin Megastore in downtown Beirut. The evening is clement, the menu eclectic, and multilingual chit-chat clue a Levantine impulse to bury the euphemized "events" of 1975–90. As the group complains about the traffic and the humidity, it dawns on the narrator that a gaunt eccentric picking his way between tables is approaching them and sending a ripple of incongruity over the gathering. The odd man stops and addresses the narrator, Rabi' Jaber, and reveals himself to be a reader of the well-known author's books. His gleaming eyes and "subterranean" voice put a merciful end to the diners' desultory small talk, and we learn that the emaciated man, Butros, was once a fat security guard at the narrator's place of work. He wants to tell his story that begins in the ruin of the City Palace Cinema where he once worked, a stone's throw from the restaurant in downtown Beirut (see Figure 2). He recounts how one night he heard a strange sound and glimpsed a wraithlike intruder. Bounding off in pursuit, he chases the will-o'-the-wisp into the bowels of the ruin until an instant's decision, or indecision—it is never clear which—propels him into a hole beneath the foundation. It is the beginning of a rough catabasis that ends in numerous broken bones, a coma, and a year-long conva-

Figure 2. City Palace Cinema ruin, 2010. Photo by Ken Seigneurie.

lescence among quiet, pale-skinned people with enormous, beautiful eyes. Denizens of a dark maze of stone, soil, and stalactites
known as Berytus, they speak in whispers, make almost no music in order to avoid echoes and cave-ins, make their soup, bread,
candles, and even shoes from fish, and spin their clothing roughly
and arduously from bleached roots. Ignorance, myths, and half-
truths are rife among this population of some one or two thousand souls who live in constant fear of real and imagined threats.
Yet despite breathing bad air and drinking water polluted by an
aboveground garbage dump, they enjoy a stable politically and
ecologically responsible society. Boutros lodges with the kind-
ly Shaykh Isaac and becomes attached to a father-figure, Falaky
"the astronomer." He falls in love with a woman, Yasmina, and is
loved by another, Rahel, Shaykh Isaac's daughter. He learns that
this somber, insalubrious city is populated by refugees or their
descendants from the waves of war and famine that periodically sweep over the region aboveground. They eke out an existence
among perils that include a corpse-vomiting river, batlike birds

that attack sex organs, and a perceived threat from the "mud people" who live on the edge of the city as refugees among refugees. Entire neighborhoods have been abandoned or eradicated by disease, and one consists of a petrified forest of people flash-frozen for eternity in their last gestures. By the end of the narrative, it becomes clear that despite their assiduous efforts, the vitality of the community is waning and all will die of an epidemic that bleeds the joy out of life. Boutros, living among these victims of history, comes to examine his own repressed past, reliving wartime memories not all of which are traumatic. He recalls a family idyll in addition to the death of loved ones and the kidnapping and disappearance of his childhood friend and cousin, Ibrahim. While it is clear that he suffered much and shared in little aboveground prosperity and happiness, Butros's memory whets his longing for life aboveground. Yet at the same time, he also feels the tug of inertia and psychological security underground as others come to consider him a part of their society as a "hunter" (ṣayyād), which is to say a border guard.[33] In the end, between an exploited life as a security guard aboveground and a relatively privileged life in Berytus, Butros summons the initiative to flee Berytus only when he stumbles upon his lost cousin Ibrahim languishing as a blind beggar in Berytus. His narrative ends as he emerges into the shining bright black night of Beirut and exults in its raucous vivacity.

Evident even in this brief plot summary is an almost endless ripple of topological and intertextual resonances. Among the numerous catabases, resurrections, and epiphanies that index a wide range of literary antecedents from the New Testament to *Alice in Wonderland*, the standing-by-the-ruins topos stands out. It structures the plot and vectors the primary theme of the narrative. Butros's story begins in the ruined movie theater that lies like "the head of a fantastic giant."[34] The image is appropriate. This narrative will explore images of the Lebanese nation as they are projected on the screen of Butros's changing mind. And like the "head" of the Lebanese body politic, these images and the cinema ruin itself are shot through with traces of violence. Butros stands not by, but literally in, this ruin, spending nights contemplating its war grafitti and hearing the wind hiss through its artillery-shell-sized breaches: "I heard it blow gravel down the metal stairs and onto the splintered wood, and I couldn't push the sound from my mind. It was as if someone had pierced and scrambled my conscience with a dinner fork" (18). As his mind becomes mixed up with that of the "giant," the ruin draws him into the past: "On that long, cold night with rainwater streaming down from the high white dome propped on pillars and spiked all over with re-rod, I remembered the war, the building we lived in behind the bridge, the roar of cannon from each half of the city, and I thought about the demarcation line between 'West' and 'East.' When thunder boomed in the sky and lightening streaked over the wide empty square I was scared. It was as if I'd become a child again, hearing bombs and seeing from a dormer window flashes over the same bridge, unable to sleep" (19–20). This scene's deployment of the ruins topos serves as a maieutic to draw memories into consciousness that Butros would just as soon leave repressed. The process leads to a preternatural overlap between past and present, and the ruins topos is the connection between them. As the ruin draws Butros into Beirut's shadow city of Berytus, he embarks, not on a trip to the past, but a trip to the present that is infused with the habitually disavowed past.

The City Palace Cinema ruin is the portal to a world whose dystopic spaces are a refracted image of the unbearable history that subtends aboveground prosperity. The deft superimposition of traumatic history and contemporary prosperity is the formal tour de force of this narrative. The Beirut of the frame narrative is famous for rising from the ashes of its periodic devastations and sloughing off memory of its violences. Berytus is neither contemporary Beirut nor a historical slice of the city, but an amalgam permitting historical consciousness in the present. In its fearful, rumor-ridden people, its musty air, polluted water, and funereal streets, Berytus wears Beirut's historical traumas as if it were the city's Dorian Gray–like portrait. The character of Butros and the ruins of the City Palace Cinema suture the fragmented realms of traumatic wartime and postwar prosperity into a single narrative.

Butros's passage from one realm to the other and back makes him the reluctant apostle of a strange gospel. It is Butros—"Peter" in Arabic—who has seen marvels, faced horrors, and emerged the wiser. He undergoes a transformation from one who dully endures cold, boredom, and loneliness in order to protect private property into one whose insight penetrates the contradictions and exploitations of contemporary society yet who, in the end, embraces it all. Butros's metamorphosis from fat security guard to disabused yet joyful seer unfolds along three axes that allow him to both assimilate responsibility for wartime history and yet suspend consciousness of that responsibility enough to live fully in the present.

The first transformative axis consists of "de-interpellation" as Butros distances himself from his role as guardian of the status quo. In the City Palace Cinema at the beginning, he zealously performs his duty of keeping vagrants from sheltering in the ruin. On the cold, rainy night when he glimpses the intruder who is wearing what appears to be a flimsy galabiya, Butros recalls: "I leapt down the stairs after him, a red light still glowing in my eyes (the taillights of those cars on the stormy evening). I ask myself how I knew that it was a boy even though he was wearing a dress. That's something we work on in our business. In this profession we learn things. I could tell by the movements of his body even though I couldn't see his face in these first moments. I knew it was not a girl. Anybody but me would have been fooled by the dress, but not me. I said to myself, 'That's a boy' and followed him" (24). From the red light in his eyes, which plausibly indexes his intemperate ardor for the chase, to his certitude that the intruder is a boy, Butros is an enthusiastic, unreflective defender of the reigning economic system whose sway extends even to its own ruins. Though he notes how cold and wet the evening is, his commitment to guarding the ruin blinds him to regarding the intruder as anything other than one who infringes on private property. He will later learn that the vagrant he is so set on apprehending and expelling into the storm is not only not a boy, but Yasmina, the woman he will come to love.

As the smugness of his comment above suggests, Butros at this early point in the novel takes the given world as normative. Orphaned of his mother when he was six and of his father when he was a young man, Butros does not complain about his lot. Later, as he remembers his youth, he recounts deaths and humiliations matter-of-factly. Likewise, his account of spending the days of his childhood from 1983 to 1990 in a porn movie theater, drinking wine and eating snacks is remarkable for its deadpan. Or again, though he states that he does not like guarding the City Palace ruin, he avoids complaining about his lack of personal connections that would land him a better posting. He is a good, gray guardian of a system he accepts at face value.

His energetic pursuit of the intruder according to the security firm's rules of engagement leads Butros to Berytus, where life underground brings into question his role and his second-nature stoicism. He becomes aware of other parameters that govern human life. For months he is helpless and cared for twenty-four hours a day, enjoying celebrity status as he meets and speaks with more people who come to visit him than at any time aboveground (138). He is given precious gifts of dried figs and an egg and is seated in a "president's chair" for what passes as a sumptuous dinner underground. He falls in love and, apparently for the first time, leads a rich affective life. Experiencing a different social status allows him to acquire a critical distance toward his place aboveground. Thus, toward the end of his stay underground, the once-officious night watchman who one might expect to be a hunter-guardian as diligent as he was a City Palace security guard, swiftly abandons his role when he deems it is time to leave.

The second axis of Butros's underground transformation consists of reconstellating his wartime experiences. From listening to the stories of fantastic happenings underground, Butros begins to shake out his own memory. When he hears about the underground river that projects corpses from its depths, Butros's mind subsequently "projects" to consciousness the memory of thirteen corpses that his adolescent brother Nizar once discovered on the bank of a seasonal river during the war (141). He recalls Nizar's blank, traumatized look every time he would tell the story "as if waiting for someone to save him." This, in turn, leads Butros to reflect on his brother's participation in a wartime massacre that, again, leaves some thirteen corpses. More memories follow: Butros's witnessing the death of a comrade in the same region where he once picked pears with his father; his cancer-afflicted mother; and the sight of his father gazing at a flock of doves (141–44).[35] The miscellany of these memories, ranging from war violence to family idyll, suggests that in de-repressing consciousness of the wartime past, Butros is finally able to reconstellate hitherto disparate memories into the same fabric of experience.

The stakes in this process are implied by the fate of his brother Nizar, who, by contrast, is never able to integrate the trauma of discovering the thirteen corpses to other aspects of life. Nizar incessantly repeats the story of discovering the corpses as if he were "drowning" in the "corpse-bloodied water" (141). Perhaps as a result of failing to assimilate the memory of violence, he reproduces it, eventually mimetically repeating the slaughter of a similar number during the gruesome night raid at the Beshara al-Khoury intersection (216). Even long after the war, the shadow of the original trauma falls on the intersection where Nizar, the bus driver, passes daily. By associating traumatic experience with everyday events, Butros defetishizes them, providing a richer, less polarized view of history.

The underground space of Berytus contributes to this process of assimilation. Though Butros is not a fearful person by nature, the fear of being buried alive recurs throughout his narrative: as a boy, when he is trapped in a tunnel and when he is afraid to enter his first basement cinema; as an adult, when he falls down the hole under the City Palace and when he recalls the fate of a fellow security guard who was trapped underground for three days. Conjuring in his mind all these "burials" in dark, tomblike Berytus where he, nevertheless, lives a relatively privileged existence allows him to de-repress and reintegrate the traumatic memory of burial.

Butros is aware that the maieutic process of associative recall is a hit-and-miss affair fraught with error and psychological pro-jection. His narrative thematizes its own arbitrariness as when he engages in a metafictional discussion with his narratee, "Rabi' Ja-ber," about "true stories," or wonders, "Why am I telling you this now?" or admits the possibility of alternative narratives by begin-ning several sentences with, "If I were in a story . . ." (15, 32, 38). Butros concedes also, "The more I talked, the more I learned I'd forgotten" and finds himself repeating in anaphora, "How can I tell you about . . ." as if to underscore the presence of things be-yond the horizon of understanding (178). At times, it is not clear whether events actually occur in the diegesis or are the products of Butros's imagination (39, 68). Indeed, the entire stint under-ground occurs while Butros is drowsy and perhaps dreaming, a possibility reinforced by the *Alice-in-Wonderland* intertext. The difficulty of ascertaining truth is thematized in the plot also as myths and fearmongering proliferate in Berytus such that it is never clear whether dangers are real or ideological bogeymen. Yet while admitting that his memory is open to considerable doubt, Butros refuses to renounce the maieutic process, and he endeav-ors to ground memory in perception through the motif of "I saw . . ." and recursively narrates numerous events in the effort to circumscribe them. He returns incessantly, for example, to the story of his cousin Ibrahim's kidnapping and disappearance dur-ing the war.

The third axis according to which Butros undergoes trans-formation consists of his reinterpellation as a desiring subject. Spending his war years in an inebriated stupor watching porn films is a survival tactic for the young Butros, but it is also alienat-ing. Likewise, his working as a guardian of someone else's prop-erty affords him a living in the postwar, but it also alienates him from realizing his human potential in the world, what the young Marx would call his "species being." The motifs of sleep and cor-pulence convey this protective alienation. Lying comatose under-ground for weeks in Berytus figures Butros's lifelong affective im-poverishment. Upon awakening from the long sleep, the erstwhile fat man is thin and ready to emerge from the chrysalis of alienation into desire. His love affair with Yasmina is the best index of this process. At the beginning of the diegesis, he is virtually un-aware of his own desire, convinced that in pursuing the wraith-like Yasmina in the City Palace ruin, he is simply doing his duty and denying even that the object of the chase is a woman. In dark and underprivileged Berytus, he ironically experiences the free-dom to feel love. Hearing about Yasmina's grief at the loss of her husband conditions his view of her before he lays eyes on her up close. He describes his first meeting with her: "I, who lay on a bed underground for months, felt joy in my heart, like the release of a dove in the air. When a beautiful woman smiles, anyone within eyeshot feels joy. And if she's sad, your joy is doubled. Despite her sadness, she laughs for you, for your pleasure. So how can a man not but be doubly happy?" (63). Butros's desire is kindled here as much by the image of the Grieving Widow as by the person be-fore him. Afterward, when she comes to him in the evenings, the sound of weeping heralds her arrival and, presumably, his arous-al. Yasmina jolts him to life, not by her beauty or by anything she says—she seldom says much—but by her tragedy and suffering. From her pain, Butros relives. This affective transformation is lik-ened to a Lazarus-like revival as Butros marvels at Yasmina's re-moval of the bandages that wrap him before they make love (100).

Butros's desire unfolds in tandem with his imaginative recon-struction of life aboveground. Before Yasmina comes to him for the first time, his senses are in a state of high alert, his ears feel-ing as big as those of an elephant even if he is unsure of what he is hearing. He imagines hearing restaurant noises, which establishes the consistent association in his mind between Yasmina and the aboveground (99). On other occasions, he stares at a blank white wall while waiting for Yasmina to arrive. The wall, like the porn movie screen of his youth, is the screen of his projected desires. On both occasions, Butros stares at the wall while waiting for Yas-mina, and his mind eventually travels back to the porn theater (117–18, 159, 166). The blank wall imagery culminates in Butros's realization that his identity is itself blank and therefore his to build: "My eyesight is filled with gold spots dancing before me in the darkness. . . . I'm lost in the emptiness of the cold cave, lost in the emptinesss and no longer know where I am. . . . I'm lost and don't know my place. I don't know who I am" (159). Butros's desire for Yasmina is the key to his integration to aboveground society. With her, Butros's libidinal desire overflows into longing for life aboveground. Cathexis passes back and forth from Yasmina to the home for which he increasingly longs. Hearing its music in reality or projection, he vividly imagines its streets and sites as if the city could be conflated with a lover's body (68–75). The most ambitious articulation of this nexus occurs on his last night spent in the home of Shaykh Isaac (156–66). The passage begins and ends with Butros waiting for Yasmina in the bed where they habitually make love. He is particularly anxious, sensing what might well be the last time he sees her. At the same time, the aged Isaac plays the flutelike naï before an open sarcophagus, deepening consciousness of his own mortality. Hearing the music, Butros, by contrast, yearns for his beloved all the more poignantly. After Shaykh Isaac goes to bed, Butros, like the poet of old who stands by the ruins of lost love, feels the need to weep out of desire (157). Then he hears, or imagines hearing, music and laughter from above and longs at this point not for Yasmina, who will not come, but for home. Yasmina and home shimmer before him as interchangeable signifiers of desire. Longing exceeds its mark, releasing memory like a search engine gone awry, and Butros recalls "swarms" of miniskirted women milling around delicacy-laden tables and beautiful people sliding into their imported automobiles while he sits on duty eating a sandwich. He does not regard these memories in bitterness as examples of class exploitation or pleasures he will never share although they are arguably both, but instead wonders repeatedly, "Will I ever see this again?" Likewise, he recalls everyday scenes from the war: children playing among ruins and stagnant pools, open fires, street vendors, human bones bleaching in the sun, a vendor making a falafel sandwich, and over it all, crucially, a flock of doves swinging from one horizon to the other in implicit benediction of it all (163). His love and longing for Yasmina mediates his longing for life in all its forms and distinguishes him from old Shaykh Isaac, who readies himself for death. In this flood of longing, Butros is not unlike the ancient poet whose yearning for his beloved passes into the otherwise indifferent world. And just as the poet reconciles himself with an unjust and alienating cosmos, Butros's attachment to Yasmina passes into longing for home and the determination to embark on the arduous return to it. Love for her is the motor of anamnesis, but she is no longer its object.

If the passage, indeed the novel, were to end here, a valid aesthetic purpose would be served in tracing Butros's sentimental education and reintegration into a society that is not particularly welcoming. Yet his attempt to come to terms with his past is not simply an exercise in self-discovery and the awakening of desire. In his encounter with Ibrahim, Butros, like his namesake "Peter," bears testimony to both weakness and transcendence. He remarks at the beginning of his narrative: "My story is sad; it breaks the heart, and I'm afraid to begin it, so you see me stopping before its threshold. Yet I have to cross it. It's up to me—quite precisely— to descend. If I don't go down who will rescue all of them from the death that awaits them? And if I do descend, what will that change?" (23). Since he has already returned from Berytus and is about ready to launch into his narrative, to "go down" in the present tense can only mean to tell the story of misfortune that goes unsaid and forgotten in phoenixlike aboveground Beirut. To tell this story is somehow to "rescue all of them," the assumption being that knowledge of harsh facts lends dignity to those who suffer and might just forestall further suffering. This is the eminently reasonable logic of transparency: genuine reconciliation can only occur in the frank acknowledgment of the truth of injustice.

Yet in the same passage, Butros immediately adds: "And if I do descend, what will that change?" In other words, can the knowledge of history really have any effect? And if so, is that effect necessarily salutary? While the obvious Christian typology stresses the salvific aspects of Butros's descent into Berytus, a counternarrative stressing the necessity of ignoring painful history insinuates itself. Butros admits that he finds Yasmina's effort to make him happy while she is aggrieved by the loss of her husband irresistible, but he is unable to work up much sympathy for her plight (63). Both she and Shaykh Isaac's daughter, Rahel, ask him to take them with him back aboveground, but he does not. He is fascinated by the misfortune wreaked upon the underground city but remains unimplicated. He marvels at the city which "like ours is called Beirut. All these lives filled with poverty! All these homes on the verge of collapse! And the sight of all this sadness! It's true that I found their white, wan faces captivating . . . and it's true their wide, black eyes are splendid and charming . . . but despite everything I found them sad" (191). Butros seems equidistant between sympathizing with suffering and appreciating the physical beauty of the troglodytes. If it is the case that Butros learns to desire underground, it is also the case that desire comes at the price of having to almost ignore suffering. Indeed, at times, such as when Yasmina weeps before lovemaking, suffering positively kindles Butros's desire.

The inverse relationship between desire and consciousness of painful history culminates in Butros's response to the fate of Ibrahim, his cousin who was kidnapped as a boy during the war. The disappearance of this friend and close relative from childhood is established early on as the most traumatic event in Butros's life. Thus when Butros finally finds himself face to face with a blind beggar whose voice he recognizes immediately as Ibrahim's, the stage is set for a recognition scene of deep pathos. The blind Ibrahim is among numerous other blind people languishing near a fountain who beg Butros for a drink. Butros does not understand why they cannot simply get a drink for themselves but complies with the request, offering this modicum of charity to all who ask, including Ibrahim. Reminiscent of the Christian story of Jesus at the pool of Bethesda, the sight of all this suffering evokes pity in Butros. He is especially touched by seeing his cousin Ibrahim, but in a radical departure from his intertextual equivalent, Butros pointedly avoids speaking to Ibrahim in order not to be recognized. He leaves his cousin where he lies and decides at one and the same time to quit Berytus (230–31). Yet Butros's refusal to play the Christ role of miraculously saving one who suffers secures him within the ambit of another Christian intertext, that of his namesake Peter's denial of Jesus. Leaving Ibrahim to die next to the pool, he departs as swiftly and ignominiously as Peter leaves Jesus to face his fate alone.

Butros's response to Ibrahim dramatizes the dilemma between solidarity and fulfillment. To be sure, the catabasis awakens Butros to the forgotten suffering that subtends aboveground prosperity, but it also brings into question the commonsense conclusion that "something should be done about it." Underground, his fortunes are reversed: he is cared for instead of caring for the property of others; he attracts the attention of women instead of watching them from his guard's perch; and he is the object of generosity instead of exploitation. Seeing life from the other side of the guard shack, as it were, kindles his desire for fulfillment, which by definition cannot be realized if he is attending to the pains and sacrifices of others. The narrative, therefore, specifically rejects the notion that fulfillment comes in self-sacrifice. Indeed, the more Butros sympathizes, the more it looks as though he becomes a connoisseur of pain. Especially with Yasmina, Butros falls in love with her widowhood before he even sees her and is arguably aroused at the sound of her weeping and the sensation of her tears in the dark as he makes love with her. The climax of the novel, his abandonment of Ibrahim, punctuates the willed ignorance of suffering he must acquire in his search for fulfillment.

It is almost, but crucially not quite, a zero-sum game. If Butros stands in solidarity with suffering, he blinds himself to desire; if he fulfills desire, he blinds himself to suffering. The text suggests that both modes of consciousness are necessary and almost mutually exclusive. Sleep and corpulence, metaphors for self-oriented ignorance of the wider world, are specifically cited as saving Butros's life during the war and during his fall underground. In Berytus, the sight of the inhabitants' suffering repeatedly prods his memory into expanding awareness, which forces him to emerge from the chrysalis of his ignorance. This consciousness of suffering, especially in his relationship with Yasmina, equivocates into desire, which supplants solidarity and, in turn, congeals into ignorance anew, presumably until another reawakening to suffering jogs it awake. It is a frustrating serial exchange of blindnesses, but without it, Butros would live in a state of obese torpor, or—the upper-middle-class equivalent—poke at his steak and complain about the humidity and traffic as do the frame-story narrator and his dinner companions.

The dilemma is irresolvable but not unmitigable. In the narrative climax, when he sees Ibrahim, Butros's speechlessness betokens an unwillingness to sacrifice his own fulfillment, to be sure, but it also suggests a sudden realization that if he speaks with his lost cousin, he may reindulge in the same connoisseurship that elsewhere permits him to enjoy Yasmina's tears or to remark on the poverty of Berytus while enjoying the beauty of its people. By this light, Butros's silence before Ibrahim is not so much cold-hearted as a refusal to fetishize his cousin's suffering. The best he can do for his cousin, who stands in synecdochic relation to the suffering of all others, is to perform the almost perfunctory gesture of giving water. In this culminating scene of the novel, Butros stands in silence, poised between consciousness of suffering and fulfillment. It is an elegiac moment as he stands by the ruin of this once playful, ebullient boy, keeping faith with what his cousin once was and recognizing the limits of his initiative in the present.

Thus to his question: "And if I do descend, what will that change?" the answer is: "very little," yet perhaps that little, symbolized by the giving of water and elegiac consciousness, is the essential sliver of difference between barbarism and civil society. It signals a level of awareness of suffering and solidarity superior to crass ignorance albeit far short of heroism. Butros's consciousness of his lack of solidarity in behalf of those who live underground is about as close as this text comes to redemption. When he states, "I remember things I don't want to remember," he places himself on the line between recognizing suffering and willfull denial (211). When he declares: "I wanted to talk about my cousin Ibrahim. Now I don't," he admits his incapacity to maintain solidarity (225). And when he repeats what he had already said before, that the day he fell into Berytus was the worst in his life, it suddenly becomes clear that the reason is not the hardships he undergoes in Berytus but the knowledge he gains there of his inability, like that of his namesake Peter and like the postwar city of Beirut itself, to maintain solidarity with suffering in the face of human desire (225).

CONCLUSION: LEARNING TO YEARN

Butros, like the narrators of *House of Mathilde*, *Stone of Laughter*, and *Dear Mr Kawabata*, harbors no utopic vision. Their elegiac grasp of history seeks to overcome the illusions of dreamworlds and the temptations of polarization. In each case, it is a question of learning to yearn for the absent within the present. In *House of Mathilde*, the narrator comes to yearn for the beauty of life lived under the shadow of chaos and corruption. In *Stone of Laughter*, the narrator comes to yearn for her "hero" Khalil despite his having become a garden-variety thug. In *Dear Mr Kawabata*, the narrator yearns on his deathbed for his benighted parents and the village theologian, all of whom have passed away. Almost as if to present a control group, *Ya Salam* thematizes a thoroughgoing rejection of yearning for the past. In its depiction of unanchored lives spinning into the madness of absolute expediency, *Ya Salam* is a cautionary tale about lives lived without imagined centers. In *Berytus: Madina taht al-Ard*, a central topos is the notion of rebirth; the narrator who comes to recognize his exploitation learns to yearn for the very society that exploits and marginalizes him. In four of the five novels examined here, learning to yearn expands the narrator's affective horizons to include an imperfect world; in the fifth, *Ya Salam*, they collapse into narcissism. Like the ancient poet who yearns for lost joys and ends up integrating himself into a harsh cosmos, the narrators' learning to yearn has the effect of forging links of common humanity during a time when war, opportunism, and socioeconomic relations sunder them.

CHAPTER TWO

"Speak, Ruins!"

The Work of Nostalgia in Feature Film

Nostalgia and Lebanese film have gone together since 1929, when Jordano Pidutti depicted an emigrant's homecoming in the first Lebanese film, *Mughamarat Ilyas Mabruk* (The Adventures of Elias Mabruk).[1] Cinema was ideally suited for capturing nostalgic feelings in a country of emigrants. Slow pans, point-of-view shots, and cross-cutting in time formally coded the poignancy of the past. In return, nostalgia offered the new medium meaningful pauses in kinesis as the hero stops to take stock, build psychological capital, and tie the present to the past before returning to action. This symbiosis between film and nostalgia is manifest in the forms and topoi associated with nostalgia. The first Lebanese talkie, the 1934 *Bayn Hayakil Ba'labakk* (Among the Temples of Baalbek), elaborated a *nasīb*-like plot of an Arab prince falling in love with a foreign woman and then being forced to forsake her.[2] These early films, each in its way, thematize perennial Lebanese concerns about dealing with the other, with the past, and with the pain of separation.

The development of nostalgic fantasy culminated in 1964 with Yusef Maalouf's film adaptation of Gibran Khalil Gibran's auto-

biographical novel *al-Ajniha al-Mutakassira* (*The Broken Wings*).
Hardly a scene in this melodrama goes unendowed with nostalgia.
It begins with a frame narrative of the middle-aged poet/protago-
nist looking back on his life and literally opening the first pages of
the Book of His Life. Within this first level of historical regress, we
see the poet at eighteen reminisce with a friend about the halcyon
days of their childhood. Gibran then meets a venerable shaykh
who immediately falls to musing over the friendship he shared
with Gibran's father in their youth. Nothing can stop the nostalgic regress. Even Gibran's first meeting with his beloved Salma
prompts the poet to declare joyously that he is sure they have already met. Indeed, even before meeting her and without seeing
her picture, Gibran sketches Salma's portrait and throughout the
film gazes at it longingly, suggesting that their love is otherworldly
and beyond time. The film emplots the contrast between an idealized past and a present debased by class and economic concerns.
Salma is the daughter of a wealthy man and therefore cannot wed
the comparatively poor poet Gibran but rather must marry a rich
scoundrel and womanizer. This ensures a tragic present and an
always unattainable bliss over which Salma and Gibran can pine.
Salma eventually dies in childbirth, and Gibran's mourning seeps
back into the frame narrative and the closing of the book, remind-
ing the viewer that the whole story was itself an instantiation of
nostalgic memory. By the end of this chapter, it will be clear how
far contemporary filmic representations of memory have come
since this 1964 movie.

   The 1960s heyday of nostalgia continued in the folk fables of the
Rahbani brothers' musicals featuring the Lebanese diva Fayrouz.[3]
These films adapted from the stage—*Bayya' al-Khawatim* (*The
Ring-Merchant*), 1965; *Safar Barlik*, 1965; and *Bint al-Haris* (*The
Guard's Daughter*), 1968—tend to reinforce a fantasized vision of
Lebanese heritage at the expense of grappling with the challenges
of modernity.[4] While it would be churlish to indict these delight-
ful films for purveying the "false consciousness" of nostalgia, it
is no less the case that their refracted images of tensions within Lebanese society are thoroughly celebratory.[5] Yet if nostalgia

is mystifying, its absence is of course no guarantee of social relevance. Many 1960s Lebanese films were Hollywood derivatives produced and directed by Egyptians who worked in Lebanon to escape Nasser's crackdown on the the arts.[6] The industry thrived economically at least for a time on fare such as the 1965 James Bond knock-off *al-Jaghwar al-Sawda* (*The Black Jaguar*), featuring a Beirut of international intrigue and exoticism, but like their Hollywood models, these films avoided serious treatment of the problems they referenced.

If Lebanese cinema of the 1960s and early 1970s was steeped in fantasies of nostalgia and adventure, by the late 1970s, Lebanese filmmakers, like their counterparts working in the novel, effectively reappropriated the aesthetics of yearning in an effort to face the violence and anomie of ethnic-sectarian war. This chapter argues that, wittingly or not, they redeployed the ruins topos, thereby introducing a new function for longing distinct from that of *The Broken Wings* and the Rahbani musicals. They forged a new idiom that highlights the ethical dimension of history and that remains prominent in Lebanese cinema to this day.

The new aesthetic emerged from a particular social and political context. The pan-Arab defeat of 1967 made it increasingly difficult for Arab cinema to distill social, political, and economic problems into idealized essences as in *The Broken Wings* or to flatten them into background décor as the action films tended to do. The industry found itself between an imperative to engage social and political problems and an engrained mercantilist aesthetic. The result was that numerous early 1970s Lebanese feature films tried to do both and ended up trafficking in representations of wish fulfillment to real social problems.[7] The mixed political and mercantile priorities managed only to index the bad conscience of Lebanese cinema. The outbreak of civil war in 1975 put paid to such fashionable commitment. Filmmakers began taking stances in opposition to the war ethos. Some returned to the nostalgic mode: "The movies portrayed the role of the neutral citizen who does not want details of reality beyond their appearances, one who clings to traditional heroic morality as well as to emotional and sentimental values. This tendency was reinforced by the daily wartime anxiety to recover whatever belonged to the near past: the rule of law, beauty, and the previous status quo."[8] This vein of Lebanese cinema exhausted itself, but an afterimage of longing for the return to the rule of law and beauty remained.

Enter the generation of young filmmakers schooled abroad and steeped in the revolutionary consciousness of 1968 Paris.[9] With a background in socially committed cinema and faced with the outbreak of civil war in Lebanon in 1975, their work transformed the moribund nostalgic and mercantile aesthetics and heralded a return of the long-repressed social consciousness. Burhan ʿAlawiyya, Maroun Baghdadi, Randa Chahal Sabbag, Jean Chamoun, Samir Habshi, Jocelyne Saab, and Heini Srour, working on shoestring budgets and depending on European coproductions, rejected facile optimism about the Arab situation to directly thematize the war.[10] Challenging the mood of the nation, their documentary and feature films eschewed fantasy in depicting psychological trauma. Burhan ʿAlawiyya explains the rationale for such a step by recalling the early 1970s Arab cinema establishment: "We had the impression they were engaged in total falsification. . . . After the first shot in the war, those films disappeared."[11] The new filmmakers also split from their mentors in the French New Wave. Longing for a return to peace and civility found its way into Lebanese war films in both form and in subject matter.[12] Thus, for example, while filmmakers experimented liberally with camera, lighting, plot construction, endings, and wry humor, their work also often included a sober ruefulness about the past that sharply distinguished it from the French New Wave most had studied in their youth. The result was a cinematic practice that corresponded to a structure of feeling deeply rooted in Arab culture.

Lebanese films from the late 1970s also tend to be more ideologically circumspect than committed. Most of the directors had Leftist backgrounds and had learned their trade in Paris, Brussels, or Moscow, but their work reveals critical irony toward any programmatic agendas. These films also distinguish themselves from foreign productions filmed on Lebanese soil such as Volker Schlondorff's powerful 1981 *Die Fälschung* (*Circle of Deceit*), which tend to explore the effects of war—it could almost be any war—on the psyche of foreign observers. Instead, the Lebanese films trace the war's impact on everyday life in a local context. Maroun Baghdadi's *Bayrut, ya Bayrut*, finished just before the outbreak of war in 1975, set the tone for much that followed with a protagonist whose impatience with smug rectitude is equalled only by his sense of responsibility.

Burhan 'Alawiyya notes that local critics and the public were not altogether eager for an Arab cinema that sought "to act in the world." These films' critical treatment of ideological self-deceptions and complicities with war brought a good deal of bad press. Moviegoers habituated to cop shows, musicals, and melodramas found films about the war an impertinence. So did the state. Cinema conceived of as anything beyond idle distraction was perceived as a challenge, which it was, and thus censorship dogged the filmmaking process.[13] Eventually, the press and audiences warmed to the antiheroes, anticlimaxes, open endings, and scenes of everyday life during war although the authorities remained wary, as evidenced by the cutting of forty-seven minutes of Randa Chahal Sabbag's ninety-seven-minute 1999 film, *Civilisées* (screened in English as *A Civilized People*).

Today, the pioneering work of 'Alawiyya, Baghdadi, Chahal, Chamoun, Habshi, Saab, and Srour constitutes the tradition according to which young Lebanese filmmakers measure themselves. The early war films by Baghdadi and 'Alawiyya, for example, established a veritable iconography of the war survivor that endures to this day in films such as Ghassan Salhab's 2006 *Atlal* (Ruins; screened as *The Last Man*). Characters in these films interiorize the shocks of war and endure its intense but desultory psychological violence. In directing an uncompromising eye on the war and its post-traumatic stresses, these films from the late 1970s through the first years of the twenty-first century seem determined to compensate for decades of cinematic irrelevance and official obscurantism. Indeed, Lebanese film to this day remains generally provocative on moral and social issues thanks in part to the wartime pioneers.

The filmmakers of the war revolutionized the themes, techniques, and narrative structures of Lebanese cinema. In this effort, they reappropriated Arabic literary topoi for their own purposes, jarring viewers out of the moral certitudes of ethnic-sectarianism without abandoning Arabic aesthetic frames and their associated structures of feeling. In particular, the reappropriation of the well-known standing-by-the-ruins topos reinflected the responses traditionally evoked by the ruins topos to bring into question the ethnic-sectarian pieties that fuel the ideology of martyrdom. Their films became part of an undercurrent of moral and cultural renewal that flows even during times of chaos.

Not all that many war and postwar Lebanese feature films exist, but the job of choosing a few to work on is not easy. Most represent ruins at one point or another, and standing-by-the-ruins scenes are frequent. This book's priority of exploring the range of ways in which the ruins topos has been deployed means that numerous relevant films must go unanalyzed here. Note especially in this regard, *al-I'sar* (*The Tornado*) by Samir Habshi (1993); *al-Shaykha* by Layla Assaf (1993); '*An al-Awan* (*The Time Has Come*) by Jean-Claude Codsi (1993); *Civilisées* (*A Civilized People*) by Randa Chahal (1999); and *Atlal* (*The Last Man*) by Ghassan Salhab (2006).[14]

RUINS OF CONVIVIALITY IN *BEIRUT: THE MEETING* (*BAYRUT, AL-LIQA'*)

Filmmaker Burhan 'Alawiyya was born in 1941 in Arnoun, south Lebanon, and moved to Beirut in 1956 with his family. In 1959, he began working nights at the Télé Liban, the national television station, to help pay household expenses. He studied political science in Beirut at Lebanese University before going to Europe, where he took part in the Parisian student revolt of 1968 and adopted a Leftist revolutionary ideology. He graduated from the Institut National Supérieur des Arts du Spectacle (INSAS) in Belgium in 1972 and returned to Lebanon. During the Israeli invasion of Lebanon 1982, he went to Europe but has since returned and makes

Figure 3. Haydar contemplating ruins from his balcony window in *Beirut: The Meeting.*

his home in Lebanon. In the wake of the antagonisms that have resurfaced in the country since 2005, he speaks of the Lebanese as living in internal exile: "Beirut is no longer the place that can gather everyone under one vision. The Beirut that remains is geographical, but geography is not everything."[15] About the reception of *Beirut: The Meeting*, he notes the importance of patience, acknowledging that the vituperation which met this film upon its release in 1981 for daring to depict wartime mentalities among militia members and civilians alike took a long time to be transformed into esteem and vindication of the artistic consciousness.[16]

The opprobrium directed at ʿAlawiyya's 1981 feature film *Beirut: The Meeting (Bayrut, al-Liqaʾ)* at its release for supposedly fanning sectarianism is today almost incomprehensible.[17] The film does deal frankly with the war and even thematizes its sectarian dimension, but it would take the ingenious bad faith of wartime passions to make a case against it for sectarianism. A more plausible cause for controversy would lie in the film's sustained effort to trace the war's psychological effects on citizens since this brings into question the nation's capacity to remain morally unaffected by war. Though it depicts little overt violence, the plot of *Beirut: The Meeting* is steeped in the violence of the wartime everyday. In depicting this theme, ruins are the metonymic traces of war that characters read, contemplate, and suffer under.

The film opens with a brief montage of detritus rotting on a beach, heaps of garbage in an alley, and tangled wires spliced illegally into municipal lines—all so many indices of civil entropy. The sound track of screaming seagulls and busy flies suggests that even nature partakes in equal measures of futile complaints and profiteering. The camera cuts to the interior of an empty flat and a disheveled man framed in deep focus at one end of a long hallway. It is the time in the narrative when viewers expect either the entrance of a hero or a victim, but the scene resists such clear-cut coding. The man limps toward the camera and stops before a sliding glass door and makeshift curtain, looking like a forlorn victim. Stepping out onto a sunny balcony, he gazes blankly at sanitation workers below shoveling rubbish and raises his eyes into the glare (see Figure 3). Looming before him is the most famous ruin of the war, the enormous Holiday Inn, proudly completed just prior to the outbreak of hostilities in 1975, soon gutted and then transformed into a militia stronghold (see Figure 4). On this morning in Beirut, circa 1979, the camera shot from below gives the ruin an aura of implacability, the antagonist of the man who suddenly appears heroic.

Haydar, standing on the balcony before the ruin, is silent and pensive, partaking of neither the seagulls' futile indignation nor the flies' profiteering. As a recent refugee from the south with his brother, sister-in-law, and their baby, he appears to be biding his time. He wanders back from the balcony, and a newspaper headline grabs his eye and triggers the plot: phone service has been reestablished between predominantly Muslim West Beirut and Christian East Beirut. Haydar limps purposefully from the house and finds a shop with a phone and calls Zeina, a fellow student he hasn't seen in two years. She lives on the other side of the city in

Figure 4. Holiday Inn ruin, 2010. Photo by Ken Seigneurie.

East Beirut and is set to emigrate to the United States the next day. With less than twenty-four hours to see each other, they agree on a time and place to meet later that day.

Haydar makes his way to the meeting in Christian East Beirut through artillery-pocked buildings, smoldering fires, and piles of rubble. His determination contrasts with the aimless shuffle of the odd vendors who wander among the ruins as if entranced. He smiles slightly at a pitiful tout who leers and beckons to him from a dark basement, and remains silent in response to a taxi driver who relishes telling anecdotes of human venality. He observes impassively from the window of the taxi as a militia fighter intimidates an elderly passerby for his insufficient piety before the death of a militia fighter who "gave his life" for the unknown old man. The unwitting inversion of Christian soteriology from death and redemption to death and humiliation emblematizes the film's representation of everyday life during the war. Through it all, Haydar remains laconic, as if husbanding his energy for a yet greater ordeal.

The day, which had begun with a hero-victim standing before war ruins—or rather taking a stand before them—unfolds against them as well. Ruins are not only traces of war; they also possess agency in this film. In the taxi to meet Zeina, Haydar gets stuck in a cacophonous traffic jam awash in midday light. Suddenly, the camera cuts to silent and empty, ruin-lined streets whose perspectives are blocked by yet more ruins—the excreta of war. The brusque cut comes as nondiegetic commentary reminiscent of French New Wave technique. The silent ruins suggest that the city's vast no-man's-lands and chaotic transport situation are everyday consequences of the war.

As Haydar works his way from Muslim West to Christian East Beirut, the camera periodically cuts to Zeina as she energetically engages in a dialogue of the deaf with her militia-member brother. Like Haydar plodding through the estranged city, she, too, suffers a similar alienation, affirming that she hasn't spoken to anybody in two years. Indeed, the great victim in this film is communication. Haydar and Zeina have never been lovers but once shared a prewar intimacy that embodies a vision of prewar Christian-Muslim relations. Their planned meeting plainly allegorizes the hope for national reconciliation. Haydar's patient progress toward Zeina is hindered in numerous ways. Zeina, too, waiting for him in a café, faces impediments. She listens as idle young men marvel stupidly at stories of coercion and treachery and eventually leaves in fear for her safety. Shortly afterward, Haydar arrives.

Undaunted by the aborted meeting, Zeina and Haydar decide to each make a cassette tape for the other and to meet at the airport the following morning to exchange them before Zeina's flight. Yet if the war's physical ruins prevent their daytime meeting, psychological ruins emerge in the evening. Haydar alludes to the war's effects on communication, beginning his tape with a question: "Do you think we can still talk the way we used to?" As if invoking the muse of transparent language, he wishes his words would arrive directly and "without distortion," and that he not be "carried away." His fear is not unfounded. Since they last spoke before the war, he notes, "the dictionary has changed," and his words must now be filtered through sixty thousand dead bodies, garbage dumps, bullets, and "millions of slogans scrawled on walls." All so many ruin-traces that reroute human concerns through themselves. Thus Haydar tells of Umm Kassem, a sixty-five-year-old refugee from south Lebanon who lives a "suspended" life as she awaits the moment when she can return to her home. As he speaks, the camera pans the ruins of a home, presumably Umm Kassem's, indicating that her longing for home will be fruitless. Haydar's deadpan comment, "We're all a little bit dead," glosses the suspension of everyday life during a time of war.

From her side, Zeina's tape tells the story of George, her brother, who as a militia fighter is party to torture and the mutilation of corpses. She asks George why such a policy exists, and again ruins are a central heuristic as the camera cuts to George running into a ruined home searching through empty rooms. As Zeina recounts in voice-over how the question bumps higher up the militia hierarchy, George continues searching from room to ruined room as if to dramatize the fact that the answer to his sister's question lies in the ruin. As he climbs the staircase of the empty building, Zeina reports the answer: "If we don't cut throats, torture or mutilate the corpses, the fighters at the front won't have the courage to shoot at those who are in front of them even from far away." Ruins here and in Haydar's account are obstacles to everyday life, but these obstacles are also the site of revelation about the war.

The characters' separate monologues gradually leave actual stone ruins to explore psychological ruins. Haydar tells of an aborted love affair he had with a village girl who, like all girls, was not allowed outside the home once armed men infiltrated the village. Haydar, deprived of the company of women, tells of the resulting psychosexual consequences, feeling uneasy around his sister-in-law and being unable to look her in the eye or speak to her. Zeina, too, sees the psychological effects of war in sexual terms. Recalling a dispute with a professor in class, she declares that the war is castrating, "violating men so they are willing to participate in it." She stresses that the linkage of war and sexuality is historical, not natural, and that otherwise the country would be called "Impotence, not Lebanon." By this time, it is almost as if the two are speaking to each other as the camera has Haydar facing left and Zeina facing right in consecutive shots under similar lighting. The effect underscores the congruity of their separate man/woman, Muslim/Christian monologues.

As each explores psychological trauma, selfhood breaks down. Haydar admits to having reached the point of dreaming despite himself about eradicating a neighboring village and later muses: "What does 'despite myself' mean? Do you know what you want and don't want in the same way that you know that snow is white and blood is red? Many things have happened and I've said, 'I don't want them' . . . but it's not so sure." For her part, Zeina admits to feeling an objectless sense of guilt. She stops her tape and goes to bed but sees in a dream the great nineteenth-century Lebanese patriot Yusef Bey Karam, who runs her through with a sword, perhaps in implicit punishment for choosing to emigrate. Each is forced to confront unavowed weaknesses and guilt as part of their inquiry into the psychological effects of war.

By the end of the evening, the separate monologues apparently achieve something of a catharsis. Yet Zeina awakens to a new day and is immediately thrust into the world of her brother's militia

Figure 5. Driving through the ruins in *Beyond Life*.

connections, which will supposedly smooth her departure but actually hinder her. On his side, Haydar goes to the airport, where he meets a well-meaning former student who blithely endorses forgetfulness as a way of dealing with the misfortune of war. He also runs into a man with a beatific grin who pitifully tries to persuade emigrants not to leave the country. The willed forgetfulness of one and the delusions of the other suggest the futility of Haydar's heroic struggle against the war's corruption of dialogue. His inability to connect with either of these compatriots and Zeina's inability to connect with her brother mean that each counts on the tape of the other as a last hope. Not altogether surprisingly, Zeina gets caught in a traffic jam on the way to the airport, and the meeting never takes place. The allegorical resonances of this abortive meeting spring to the fore when Zeina finally arrives and realizes that despite their best efforts, she and Haydar will not see each other. She collapses in the airport and is picked up and comforted by her brother, the militiaman. For his part, Haydar in the taxi on the way home calmly pulls the tape from his cassettes and drops it out the car window. The camera focuses for a long moment on the wind-driven tape as it joins the Holiday Inn, the empty streets, the piles of rubble, Umm Kassem's home, and myriad other ruin-traces of a once convivial nation.

RUIN AND DE-EDUCATION IN *BEYOND LIFE* (*HORS LA VIE*)

Maroun Baghdadi, one of the most promising Lebanese film-makers of the twentieth century, was born in 1951 in Beirut and died accidentally in 1993. From a middle-class family, he studied law and political science at Saint Joseph University in Beirut and traveled to Paris to continue his studies but abandoned law at the University of Paris to continue his higher education in cinematography. He returned to Beirut in 1973 and began working in the French-language press as a critic and at Télé Liban, where he laid the foundation for his work on documentaries, making eight between 1976 and 1980. In 1982, he left for Paris, where he worked on several movies and returned nine years later to produce *Beyond Life*, his last complete project. Politically, Baghdadi placed himself on the Left early in his career, supporting the "National Movement," a coalition of Leftist forces and Muslims who supported the armed Palestinian presence in Lebanon. Later he distanced himself from programmatic politics. He envisioned a unique role for Beirut in the region by virtue of its cosmopolitanism and openness to new cultural forces, and retained a faith in the potential for film to bring change to Lebanon.[18]

In his 1980 documentary *Hamasat* (Whispers), Maroun Baghdadi begins with images of a man and woman strolling among war-ruined buildings, stopping from time to time to reflect on the vanished past of prewar Lebanon. She is the poet Nadia Tueni, and her expressions of nostalgia and hope make of this sequence perhaps the purest wartime update of the ruins topos that exists on film. It also establishes Baghdadi's commitment to the nation and his faith in the power of film.

Which makes his 1991 feature film *Beyond Life* all the more surprising. Loosely based on the experiences of Roger Auque, a French hostage held during the war, the film's subtle but caustic irony dissolves any impulse toward nostalgia. A scratchy recording of the paean "Bayrut, ya Bayrut" begins the film, but a voice-over litany of war casualty statistics ironizes the song's nostalgic vision. Whether this suggests a cause-effect relationship between the prewar idyll and wartime atrocities or simply that the prewar is irrelevant to current events, the scene effectively inoculates the viewer against nostalgia for antebellum Lebanon. Before the end of the credits, the viewer will have seen numerous atrocities, abject grief without solace, and a photographer who puts down his camera to help carry the wounded and is among the first to charge through the breach of a building under attack. This same photographer, shortly after this participation in wartime activities, chooses to end his association when witnessing soldiers vaunt over the dead for a photo. He refuses to take the gruesome photo and strides away jerking the film from his camera and throwing it on the ground. As the credits end, so does the photographer Patrick Perrault's faith in representing the war. Yet, as if to deny him the prerogative of choosing to quit the war, an Islamic militia unit the next day accosts him in the street, bundles him into a car, and speeds away through a labyrinth of ruins in what has become a veritable topos of the Lebanese war film: driving through the ruins (see Figure 5).

In *Beirut: The Meeting*, we recall that Haydar's standing by the ruins of the massive Holiday Inn dramatizes his will, which might as well be called "indomitable," to pit himself against the immensity of wartime degradation. He eventually fails, and this moment is underscored by his ripping out and throwing away the casette tape. Such a loss of hope is essentially the starting point of *Beyond Life*. From the moment Patrick rips the film from his camera, *Beyond Life* begins exploring the implicit question, "What are the way stations to submitting to the wartime ethos?" By way of response, on numerous occasions throughout the film, a car-mounted camera drives through endless tracts of ruins. These scenes allegorize the coercion of consciousness that Patrick undergoes as the plot unfolds. In the moving automobile, traces of violence in the form of ruins funnel one after another into the viewer's perceiving eye, overwhelming the mind, which cannot gain the psychological purchase necessary for contemplation and thus ends up glutted by traces without content.[19] Driving through the ruins, therefore, is emblematic for the viewer of the anticognitive force-feeding Patrick undergoes in his life as a hostage.

The process of scrambling Patrick's sense of identity and autonomy is an overlapping three-stage ordeal as he realizes his vulnerability, accepts the hostage regime, and finally renounces willful activity. Nothing pushes Patrick along the hostage learning curve faster than the dawning awareness that everybody involved in the war is hostage to it. All are vulnerable and infantilized. "Eat!" his captor shouts as he pulls Patrick from the getaway car and crams a sandwich under his nose. When Patrick demurs that he is not hungry, they command: "Eat when we feed you!" Later, in his cell, he overturns his meal with an air of almost childish petulance and is scolded: "You'll eat the same as we do. You're no better than us." Likewise, urination and defecation are sources of "accidents" between the recalcitrant hostage and his captors. Their insults and patronizing comments are akin to those of a sadistic parent such that when he speaks outside his cell, a jailer claps a hand over his mouth, commanding him to just "shut up and obey." More rarely, they also soothe him in baby-talk voices: "Everybody is calm here. Nobody shouts." The regime encourages childish vanities on the part of captor and hostage alike. Thus Patrick worries about whether he smells bad and whimpers when he finds no mirror in the bathroom whereas his captors croon around a freshly painted car before the camera cuts incongruously to children flying a kite as if to stress a "boys with toys" topos.

The various cells in which Patrick is confined reinforce the notion that he is being "de-educated" to be a good hostage through a process of progressive degradation. The first cell is a school classroom where his captors teach him the regime. Later he spends time in a stable like livestock, and then chained, as he notes, "like a dog," and then, having in some but not all ways been "broken," Patrick finds himself in a children's nursery. Finally, they move him to a pantry closet along with inanimate objects of everyday use. Paralleling Patrick's infantilization and dehumanization, his captors, when not frenetically violent, are themselves often as bored as children on a rainy day or idle as inert objects.

Among the means of de-educating Patrick, his captors impose consciousness of vulnerability through emasculation, which is often coded as feminization. Among the first things he hears shortly after being kidnapped is that he is *manyūk* (fucked), and the last thing his captors do before releasing him is to dress him head to toe in a woman's black veil. In between, they treat him with patriarchal harshness but also with patronizing smiles as if his complaints were mere peevishness. When a militia commander and a jailer visit him, Patrick demands an interrogation to prove his innocence. In response, the jailer coos in his ear: "You don't need anything. You're *still* pretty. Pink and cute. You've got woman's hair" and attempts to stroke it. Patrick jerks away and warns him: "Touch me and you're in for trouble!" The commander, who does not speak French, asks the jailer to translate Patrick's comment into Arabic, and when Patrick asks him what he said, the captor teases: "I told him you're bored" as if Patrick were a capricious mistress.

The captors' own emasculation is coded in homosexual tendencies such as the jailer who tries to touch Patrick and also in numerous instances of interrupted contact with women. A man on a boardwalk wooing his girlfriend is hailed from a passing car and has to leave immediately on militia business. Another is chatting to a woman on the phone before his chief grabs and slams the receiver for a war-related call. This same chief himself watches a television program featuring young people dancing in a nightclub when his wife passes and declares, "I envy them," suggesting the frustration and affective aridity in their own lives.

The most vivid testament to wartime emasculation comes in the exception that proves the rule. At only one moment in the film does Patrick symbolically recover his virility, and that is when one would least expect it. In his last cell before being released, he spends much time trembling in a fetal position, terrified of leaving the dark closet. Apparently broken in spirit, he nevertheless soothes a child who lives in the same house and who wanders into his closet, frightened by the shelling. In gratitude,

Plate 1. Lebanese Leftist civil war poster: "Against Imperialism and Zionism." Image courtesy of the American University of Beirut Archives.

Plate 2. Sunni Muslim militia commemorative poster: "On 21 March the Murabitun destroyed the symbol of the fascist temptation and vowed to carry on their mission whatever the cost." The building in the center is the Holiday Inn hotel ruin. Image courtesy of the American University of Beirut Archives.

Plate 3. Nasserist party commemorative poster evoking Delacroix's *Liberty Leading the People* over ruins: *top,* "Fifth-year anniversary of the power of the organization"; *middle,* "The United Arab Nasserist Socialist Organization"; *bottom,* "Our people have determined to rebuild their lives on their land with freedom and justice, with struggle and truth, and with love and peace." Image courtesy of the American University of Beirut Archives.

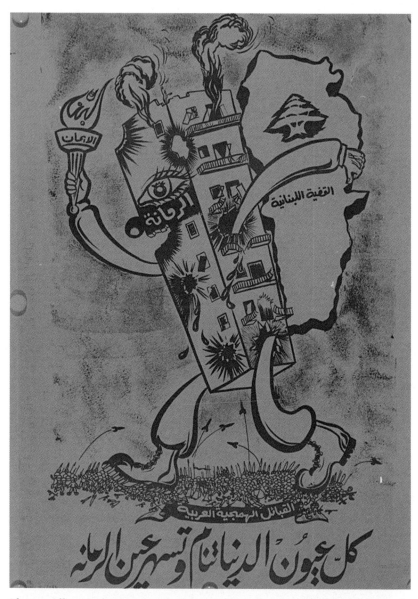

Plate 4. Allegorical ruin in a Christian militia poster: *in the flame of the torch,* "Lebanon"; *in the torch,* "Faith"; *on the map,* "The Lebanese cause"; *banner underfoot,* "Barbarous Arab tribes"; *bottom,* "All eyes of the world go to sleep, but Ain al-Ramaneh stays awake." Image courtesy of the American University of Beirut Archives.

Plate 5. A slogan for whisky in the service of a political message. Image courtesy of *al-Balad* newspaper.

Plate 6. Frame 1 (*right*): God bless the opposition. / I'd die for the opposition. / I'm going to be an opponent in Jordan! Frame 2 (*left*): Forget it! / I take back everything I said! / Forget I even mentioned anything! This image, created by a Jordanian caricaturist, depicts the temptations faced by a non-Lebanese Arab student in Lebanon, particularly during the Uprising. In addition to the obvious contrasts between political freedom and authoritarianism, social-sexual liberation and patriarchal repression, the drawing also contrasts cosmopolitanism and nativism in a caricatural depiction of linguistic difference contained in the background signs of both frames. The word for "opposition" in the poster depicted in the first frame, *mu'arada*, conveys a typical Western mispronunciation of the Arabic ḍ, while the same word is depicted as *mu'araza* in the second frame, a mispronunciation that exaggerates the "arabity" of the sound. Compare the difference in English between "oppposission" and "opposichun." Source: www.mahjoob. com. Image courtesy of Emad Hajjaj.

Plate 7. Advertisement for a plant nursery inspired by the Lebanese flag. Image courtesy of Exotica.

Plate 8. After the Independence Uprising appropriated Johnny Walker for its purposes (see plate 5), the whisky-maker returned the favor, putting politics in the service of selling whisky in the wake of the 2006 Israeli-Hezbollah war. Photo by Hala Daouk.

Plate 9. Poster of Hassan Nasrallah and Hezbollah martyrs: *top,* "You are the people and you are the leaders. You are the honest promise"; *large type,* "Martyrs of the Leaders." Photo by Ken Seigneurie.

Plate 10. One of many commercial recuperations of the 2006 war. Photo by Ken Seigneurie.

the child's mother, chaperoned by Patrick's guard, comes to him and gives him two small tangerines. Accepting the gift of symbolic manhood, Patrick peeks under his blindfold at her feet and ankles, remarks that they are slender, and asks the woman if she is pretty. She smiles and answers in the affirmative while the jailer's implausible claim that she is fat and cannot speak French only exposes the war's corruption of sexuality. Patrick's brief flirtation ends there, but the scene is crucial to establishing the hostage's resilience even within abjection. The scene also contrasts with another between the woman and her affectively retarded husband. She complains to him that his toddler son, who has cottoned to Patrick, fears him and that she is fed up with their life, voicing most clearly what nobody else dares: "we are all hostages just like the poor devil rotting in there," pointing toward Patrick.

The violation of personal integrity extends beyond emasculation. Patrick's captors break into his apartment and take personal items. They constantly assure him that they know what he thinks and what he needs. When he asks for a newspaper, one smiles at the preciousness of the request and promises to give him some tangerines. They claim to know "all about" him and, in lieu of a solution to his predicament, urge him to pray to God for forgiveness. The guards reveal some anxiety about their own enforced ignorance. When Patrick demands to know why he has been taken hostage, a captor responds:

"You journalists always want to know why."
"And you don't? Why are we here? You, me, all this?"
"God knows."
"God doesn't know why I'm here. Neither do you. No one knows."
"If you're here, you must have done something evil."
"What have I done?"
"Think. You've got nothing else to do."

The assumption of sin applies to captor and captive alike. Thus when a jailer—the one Patrick calls "Philippe"—confides to him that he wants to go to France to study, Patrick encourages him, saying he is "free" to do it. Philippe only laughs, but his aspiration is serious enough to attract the attention of the militia leaders, who find out about the plan and reprimand Philippe. A fellow jailer, "Frankenstein," remarks at the futility of the effort: "He thought he could change his life through studying. As if a Shiite could get anywhere here." Patrick's residual commitment to personal freedom exposes his captors' own submission to the hostage's life they lead.

Patrick's internalization of the hostage regime is never complete. Early on, he tries to escape, and as punishment, his captors wrap him head to toe in packing tape and transport him to another cell. The "package," however, declares that he is a journalist, not a spy, and that his name is Patrick Perrault, not "Naoum." The name is a bone of contention Patrick never releases. The kindest of his jailers, the one Patrick calls "Philippe," gives him a new name out of affection, but Patrick bridles at the willful manipulation of his identity. His jailer responds gently that everybody in the place has changed names for the needs of the war, and he himself manifestly does not mind being called Philippe. He justifies his treatment of Patrick, citing an Arabic proverb: "He who treats you like himself is not unjust toward you" and, indeed, Patrick's humiliation is not all that different from the everyday state of his captors. Every once in a while, even after being "broken," jailer and captive alike recover their spirit, Philippe in his desire to go to France and Patrick in his attempt to escape and his flirtation with the woman.

By citing infantilization, emasculation, and psychological intrusiveness as parts of the hostage regime that both captor and captive suffer, the point is not to minimize the obvious differences between the two, but to show how the "hostage ethos" conditions all who are involved in the war. Enforced ignorance also unites hostage and captor. In the middle of the film, a new jailer bursts into Patrick's cell doing shadow karate and ranting in idiomatic American English. Calling himself "DeNiro" for his imitation of the Travis Bickle character, this jailer claims to have been a Hollywood actor, and, indeed, everything about him is affected and stagy. DeNiro, a bundle of behaviorist performances, embodies the impossibility of fathoming appearances much less anything beyond them.

DeNiro takes Patrick unblindfolded to a stable full of horses, from where it would seem Patrick could escape. DeNiro admonishes him along the way: "Don't listen to the devil. He tells you to take a horse and run!" Suddenly, he shoves Patrick unblindfolded outside the stable to a sandbag wall declaring, "I'm here to protect you from yourself!" He releases a horse into a deserted alley where an unseen sniper promptly shoots it dead, and DeNiro crows: "This is Lebanon, man! Don't trust your eyes. Things are never the way they look. There's always a snake behind the rock!" This demonstration punctuates Patrick's de-education as it terrorizes him into submission. At the same time, the realization that one is never more blind than when one's eyes are wide open brings a consciousness of the war's complexity that Patrick, the war photographer who has captured it in eyewitness testimony, never could have fathomed.

With no hope of establishing cause-effect relationships behind events, one-answer-fits-all ideologies provide the illusion of understanding. DeNiro assures him: "You know about drugs, you know about Lebanon." Frankenstein muses, "Today, with Islam, we're going to change the world" after admitting that he had previously fought for a half dozen other militias, each with presumably its own truth to die for. Others declare simply that only God knows all and that therefore Patrick should pray. Such "explanations" beg for their own explanation. A jailer reads a classical French text that allegorizes the general opacity of wartime: "And didn't you see that my wild fits of passion meant that my heart refuted my words in every way?" In this film, everybody's words and fits of passion are refuted, but not by any identifiable "heart." Patrick is told his capture was a mistake and yet he is kept. He asks why he is being held and is promised tangerines. He is told there will be a prisoner exchange, and there is no exchange. He is told that Philippe has been executed, and then Philippe appears. Language is as divorced from events and yet as symptomatic as the roles DeNiro assumes.

The jailers' own predicament is in some ways even more hope-
less than that of Patrick. Both the gentle Philippe and the sadistic
Frankenstein come from the same poor Shiite village in the south
with no realistic hope of ever escaping the war, much less achieving a modicum of prosperity. Frankenstein has lost a son, doubtless as a result of the war. Another jailer muses innocently on his
desire to have a family and to be a "man of justice"—just before
trudging off to one of the more depraved wartime occupations as
a sniper of hapless civilians. On Patrick, the war has a severe but
limited effect on the exercise of freedom; on the others, it pre-
cludes any concept of autonomy as such.

The process of compromising Patrick's dignity under the hostage regime culminates with his renunciation of willful activity.
When he begins responding to his environment with the same
passivity and desultory violence that his captors display, his hostage training is complete. As he becomes aware of his vulnerability and incapacity to act autonomously, Patrick begins a frenetic
shadow karate, pathetically defending himself against he-knows-
not-what, mirroring DeNiro's karate travesty.[20] Like his captors,
he also takes to praying. Even the décor around him underscores
their kinship; when he is finally released, he wanders into a hotel,
and a billboard in the background announces the chance to win
big in the Lebanese Lotto, suggesting that the mere good fortune
of his passport, not prowess of any kind, has freed him.

The integration of Patrick into the hostage regime leads to one
of the great peripeteia of Lebanese cinema.[21] He has been "force-
fed" awareness of his vulnerability and weakness, but rather than
eliminating his capacity for autonomous action, the ordeal confers on him the capacity to understand the humanity of his captors. At the beginning of the film, his observer status preserves a
distinction between him and the militia fighters even as he charg-
es through the breach of a building along with them. This becomes evident when at the sight of the fighters' savagery, Patrick
exercises his prerogative to rip the film from his camera and stalk
off, effectively weary of war-slumming. Throughout his ordeal, he
comes to understand his captors' situation such that once freed

and in France, he finds himself dialing their number, effectively demonstrating his solidarity with them and his alienation from his French social context. After months of figuratively "driving through the ruins" as a hostage and being forced to interiorize a multitude of images he would not have chosen, Patrick grasps the common predicament of his captors. As the phone rings, the camera moves from Paris to Beirut as if Patrick transports himself in imagination there to assume the subject position of standing by the ruins of an abandoned kitchen. The slow pan over the ruins of the fighters' apartment and then a car-mounted driving-through-the-ruins shot formally quash the distance between Patrick and the world of war he left behind. He remains a part of the war and it of him. The final shot ends as the car, passing through an endless vista of ruins, meets only one other car on the long road. Like the other instances of driving through the ruins, this one also funnels the war's desolation into the viewer's helpless eye but with the difference that now the viewer, like Patrick, feels not only the coerciveness of the war but also some solidarity with the driver of the other car who also endures it.

LIVING AMONG THE RUINS IN *THE PINK HOUSE* (*AL-BAYT AL-ZAHR*)

Both Joana HadjiThomas and Khalil Joreige were born in 1969, in Beirut, to middle-class families. They studied at the University of Nanterre Paris X and have written for the press. Today, in addition to filmmaking as a husband-wife team, they also do installation art and teach at the Institut d'études scéniques, audiovisuelles et cinématographiques (IESAV) at Saint Joseph University in Beirut. Too young during the war to have taken part in it, the couple describe themselves as resolutely nonsectarian. During the Independence Uprising of 2005 they were in Paris editing *Yawmun Akhar* (*A Perfect Day*), a film symbolic of Lebanon dealing with a compulsive sleeper, and, as HadjiThomas remarks, "during this time the nation awoke." Their work has often been oriented toward shedding light on the nation's obscured past, "integrating the history of the war into memory, not in order to stay in the past but to live in the present." About *The Pink House*, their first feature film, HadjiThomas affirms that they chose to show how wartime tensions continue to exist in a postwar situation. She adds, the film's exploration of "memory, traces and ruins continues to nourish our work" to the present day. [22]

To the extent that civil wars may be said to end, the Lebanese conflict is most often said to have ended in 1990. People watched in a spirit of exhaustion and disbelief as world-famous Lebanese warlords morphed from one day to the next into politicians and businessmen. Yet it was the plan to rebuild the Beirut downtown district devised by one of the few leaders who did not carry arms during the war, billionaire Rafik al-Hariri, that sparked long and open controversy. For some, this man of modest origins who spent the war making a fortune in Saudi Arabia, was a savior for his generosity to numerous nonsectarian charities. For others, his plan was a carpetbagger's gambit to seize the nation's urban heart for the benefit of international big business. A few claimed he was both. The downtown reconstruction plan was eventually adopted and implemented, becoming at one point among the largest construction projects in the world. Again ruins were at the center of Lebanese preoccupations. The reconstruction company that goes under the acronym Solidère razed many acres of ruins, arranging to evict those who lived among them, often refugees pushed from previous homes during the war. A vigorous debate ignited over the role of ruins in conditioning memory. Some argued that Solidère tried to expunge war from memory in the interests of global capital; others claimed that the renewal was necessary for the well-being of society.[23] Joana Hadjithomas and Khalil Joreige's 1999 film *al-Bayt al-Zahr* (*The Pink House*), was among the first to explore this specifically postwar situation.[24] Focusing on attitudes toward ruins, *The Pink House* provided a nuanced vision of the often conflicting imperatives of memory and change.

The opening scene of the film dramatizes the impact of postwar change on social structures and desire. A boy hawks a big, glossy picture of idyllic prewar Beirut in the din of a dusty, congested street. The bright image of palm trees and since-vanished prosperity indict the ambient monochromatic scrum. The camera cuts to another part of the street, and another boy with an enormous megaphone calls out above the street noise to a girl in an upper-floor apartment. Middle-aged men shout at him to shut up as a radio voice-over announces the ongoing reconstruction of Beirut. Walid, the lovesick boy with the megaphone, vows never to give up as if aware that the Beirut reconstruction project and patriarchal oppression are in league against desire. By the end of the film, he is still calling out to a Zeina who never appears or responds. Considered as bookends, these scenes embrace a narrative of truncated desire and implacable economic and social forces characteristic of the Lebanese postwar.

The house is associated with desire from the outset. It appears for the first time through the binoculars of Abdallah, a young man watching Layla Nawfal, the woman he loves, through an open window as she goes about her chores. In this modest neighborhood, the Adaimi and the Nawfal families, one Muslim the other Christian, have taken refuge for eleven years in the abandoned but once-august "Pink House." Abdallah's binocular view pans to another window, where a young man, Munir, gazes at a veritable picture shrine he has erected in homage to Farah Nawfal, who fled home rather than endure his attentions. For Abdallah and Munir, the Pink House, whatever else it may be, is a node of futile longing and affective impotence.

Futility is not limited to the younger generation's ill-starred loves. All the Nawfals and Adaimis indulge in various fantasies at the same time that they endeavor to maintain the appearance of conventional lives. Omar, the father of the Adaimi household, leaves in the morning to go to "work" and then spends the day gambling while his wife, Samia, daydreams of playing the elegant hostess to Lady Fortune, the *deus loci* of the Pink House. Their son Maher venerates photocopied images of fallen militia fighters, and their other son, Suhayl, transforms rationality itself into a fetish as he obsessively measures and catalogues every trace the war has left on the house. Naji, the father of the Nawfal household, mulls constantly over the indignity of having his daughter Farah run away from home while her suitor, the hapless Munir, remains. Naji's wife, Nawal, like Samia, exists in a fantasy world as she communes with religious figurines all day long. Their other daughter, Layla, longs with flagging hope for feckless Abdallah to initiate a serious relationship. The motto over the Pink House front door, "Fortunae Domus" (House of Good Fortune), mocks them as they live like mice among its once-elegant statuary and friezes. The house, in fact, does harbor a mouse whose symbolic kinship with its human inhabitants endures to the end. While critics generally viewed the Pink House as a symbol of Lebanese heritage, this crucial thematization of futility and impotence is sometimes overlooked.[25]

The Pink House might seem at first blush an ideal setting for standing by the ruins inasmuch as there is no shortage of lovelorn souls around it, but its habitation changes the dynamics of longing. For the ancient poet, as for the pining young man Mounir, to stand by the ruins of past joys deepens the feelings of love and longing for the absent loved one. The same applies, to a large extent, to all those connected to the Pink House who indulge in fantasies of desire. All yearn for what what will always remain beyond their grasp. In the case of the ancient poet who finds no flesh-and-blood object of desire, his cathexis passes to the ruin-context that once permitted his love. He gazes fondly upon the weed-grown paths and burnt fag ends, and in his state of heightened affect, signifiers slip as cathexis passes metophorically from the loved one to the worthless ruins that are associated with her and thence synecdochally to the world of which the ruins are a part. This two-stage deflection of desire mediates the poet's—and the engaged listeners'—integration into an otherwise indifferent world. For the Adaimis and the Nawfals, however, since they inhabit the ruin, they are dependent on it and cannot freely contemplate it as a ruin. The past of war and suffering clings to the house they inhabit; they love it for the shelter it offers and hate it for what it represents: violence and expulsion from their previous home. This ambivalence prevents them from letting it mediate their integration into the postwar. Unable to separate themselves from the ruin, they reject its associations with pain and yet embrace it as a refuge.

Within the legacy of trauma represented by the Pink House, the inhabitants' fantasies function as psychological havens. Samia hosts her make-believe tea parties; Nawal worships her religious figurines; Maher venerates images of dead militia fighters, and Suhayl contemplates and catalogues the house's every war-trace. All so many ways of trying to shut out or digest the war legacy. Among these responses, Munir's shrine to Farah stands out. He may appear pitiful and bordering on insane, but his admission that he has lied and passed himself off as a fellow refugee in order to be near Farah suggests not so much his weakness as his faith that love can flourish even within the memory of trauma. When he senses that a man is mocking him to a group assembled in a café, Munir enters the café and begins to tell his own story. A tracking shot takes him and nobody else deeper into the café so that as he speaks, others are left in background silhouette against the bright light from outside. His bearing is saintly as, backlit, he stands alone telling of his devotion to Farah, and one wonders whether her flight had to do with his so-called madness or with her reluctance to see her suitor throw himself against the traumatic war legacy.

Munir's foil, Abdallah, who loves Layla, is unable to buck the humiliation of the war legacy that reminds them all that they were victimized with impunity. Caught between desire and the impossibility of realizing it, he hovers. When Layla remonstrates with him for his lack of initiative and declares that she no longer wants to see him, he lashes out symbolically against the postwar disorder and corruption that prevent the refugees' status from being equitably resolved. In the middle of the night, he steals up an electric pole and cuts dozens of electricity lines that are illegally spliced into the municipal line. Like the Pink House that offers the temporary solution of living space while perpetuating the legacy of war, the wires temporarily solve the problem of electricity by perpetuating the wartime weakness of the state. To cut the wires is thus to symbolically cut the wartime umbilical that has outlived its purpose.

The standoff between the inhabitants and the house is broken when a suave developer arrives to announce that he has bought the Pink House and that the families have ten days to leave in return for three thousand dollars in state compensation per family. Small merchants in the neighborhood rejoice, seeing takeover as an opportunity to rejuvenate the neighborhood while the Adaimis and the Nawfals are incensed, seeing their eviction as an insult added to the injury of living a squatter's life in Beirut. Having striven, mostly in vain, to transform the ruin into a home, the Adaimis and Nawfals receive the eviction notice as a denigration of that effort. They perceive their imminent expulsion as another trauma on top of the one that forced them from their original homes.

The rest of the film turns on how they extricate themselves from the memory of wartime coercion embodied in the Pink House without submitting to the postwar reconstruction project. Neither the developer nor the neighbors appreciate the dilemma caused by this dual signification of the house as simultaneously both marker of shame and of dignity. The merchants view the families' emotional investment in the Pink House as sentimentalism in the face of necessity. A motif of imploding ruins, heard in the distance and viewed on television screens, underscores the "creative destruction" whereby ruin, reconstruction, and perhaps war itself are necessary phases of late capitalist development.[26] A member of the merchants' party claims at one point in a heated discussion that all the talk about the families' "honor" and "respect" is old-fashioned and was even a cause of the civil war. It is a strong indictment, evoking the tit-for-tat sectarian killings, kidnappings, and bombings that occurred throughout the war whenever one party deemed that it had been disrespected by another. The Pink House inhabitants even have a green line painted on the sidewalk in front of the house, ostensibly "the color of hope" but inevitably reminiscent of the Green Line that divided the warring halves of Beirut during the war.

The Adaimi sons take two paths of action in response to the eviction notice. Maher, the militia partisan, hopes to meet the developer's intimidation and physical force with that of the local militia. His brother Suhayl, the intellectual, passes around a petition, counting on legal means to stop the developer's plan to gut the house and leave only the façade as window dressing for a garish commercial center. The proposed compensation eventually reaches twelve thousand dollars for each family, which the small merchants' party finds entirely acceptable because for them the fundamental problem is simply finding the best price for a commodity. It does not, however, solve the families' dilemma of how to extricate themselves from the humiliation of wartime history as represented by the Pink House without succumbing to the postwar humiliation of arbitrary expulsion from their home.

They eventually intuit that their honor lies in the responsibility they have long exercised in caring for the house whether they actually own it or not, and that dishonor therefore lies in the forced removal of that responsibility. The solution is to maintain somehow a modicum of responsibility for the space, so they take the initiative to destroy the house themselves and thereby deprive the developer of the façade. This prevents the Pink House, the symbol of their pain, from being transformed into a pastiche of "oriental charm." More important, destruction transforms the Pink House from a refuge for squatters into a full-fledged ruin that can be freely contemplated as such (see Figure 6). Undertaking the demolition themselves also permits them to memorialize the ruin by capturing its fall on video, which they then bury in what will be the foundation of the new building. In this way, they take charge themselves of burying the war's legacy and thereby break its hold over their lives.

The Pink House inhabitants and the small merchants' party gradually come together when it becomes clear that the building project means the elimination of the surrounding small businesses as well. At the same time, the inhabitants acquire something

Figure 6. Standing in the ruin of the Pink House.

of the small merchants' will to commodify by accepting the compensation that is offered and holding a street sale of the house's
contents. More important, the resolution to the problem of the
Pink House implies an affective reconciliation among inhabitants
as well. The dithering Abdallah manages to obtain and repair the
power shovel that is used to demolish the house. Naji, the father
of the absent Farah, finally buries the hatchet with Munir and
speaks about the hitherto taboo topic of his daughter's flight from
the home. In a farewell dinner, the entire neighborhood sits down
together before the ruin of the Pink House in a standing-by-the-
ruins scene of postwar closure. Their celebration and contemplation includes viewing a video of the Pink House as it appeared in
its glory days long before the civil war—or after a previous one.
Those, too, "were the days," now closed off and commemorated
just as they are closing and commemorating theirs. Like the poet
of old, the inhabitants have managed to convert their misfortune
into a genuine ruin that mediates their integration into the harsh
economy of the postwar world. If the house embodies the weight
of the war on the present, its destruction at least partly on their
terms symbolizes the lifting of that weight.

The proactive transformation of the Pink House into a ruin is not without ambivalence. When an elderly woman sees the young people wreak damage on the house with the power shovel, she mutters, "It's not right." While she is doubtless referring to the illegality of destroying property, she may also be unwittingly recoiling from their active resistance to fate. The proactive creation of ruins contrasts sharply with the traditional role of ruins in the ode. Indeed, the pathos of standing by the ruins lay in the poet's inability to change what fate had ordained. Circumstances beyond the poet's control—marriage, migration, time—conspire against the lovers meeting again, and it is the resulting yearning for what fate forbids that lends the ode its affective weight. *The Pink House*, on the other hand, like the globalizing, postwar world, is resolutely historical, transporting the ruins trope from a world of stoic endurance to one of property rights and civic action. Reconstruction and globalization are human, not natural, phenomena, and the inhabitants' fashioning of their own ruins introduces empowering elements of control and performativity. From the elderly woman's point of view, such initiatives lack the quiet dignity of the ancient poet's resignation to fate, but they do offer a vision of how ruins and memory may be redeployed in the postwar.

RECYCLING RUIN IN *IN THE SHADOWS OF THE CITY* (*TAYF AL-MADINA*)

Jean Chamoun was born in 1944 in Beirut to a middle-class family with roots in the Beqaa Valley. He earned a degree in dramatic arts from the Lebanese University and went on to study cinema at the University of Paris VIII, Vincennes, where he experienced the student movement that continued in the wake of 1968. He earned a degree in cinematography as well as another in editing from the Louis Lumière School at Paris II before returning to Lebanon, where he lived during the civil war. Between 1976 and 1983, he taught cinematography in the Institute of Arts at the Lebanese University. He claims an "independent and patriotic" political allegiance and has never been affiliated with a party. Along with his wife, Mai Masri, he has directed numerous documentaries on the Palestinian and Lebanese situations. He affirms that cinema fulfills "an important role in understanding the history of the country." He is currently working on a film that deals with the still-open question of seventeen thousand people who were kidnapped and disappeared during the civil war. About *Tayf al-Madina*, he notes that it was not made from the standpoint of an outside observer but of one who lives it "from within." He notes also that the role of Siham is based on a well-known Lebanese actress's response to the actual kidnapping of her husband.[27]

In the first scene of Jean Chamoun's 2000 feature film *In the Shadows of the City*, a man drives through a sunny landscape of urban renewal, preoccupied by a recurrent image. Rami sees himself as a corpse, stripped and dumped behind a house. The film flashes back from this point to his childhood, and we eventually learn that Rami's father was kidnapped during the war and doubtless met such a fate. His musing is neither angry nor bitter but empathetic, which is surprising as we later learn that at the time of the events and long afterward, Rami was obsessed with retribution. The plot therefore essentially traces the waning of his wrath as the narrative works its way forward from his childhood to the present. It is also the case that this transformation is mediated by an exceptional encounter with a woman and a ruin.

A film can, of course, be full of ruins and even thematize "ruin" without having anything to do with the standing-by-the-ruins topos. Most of *In the Shadows of the City* is replete with ruins imagery that indexes trauma but bears little relevance as object of longing or nostalgic contemplation. Early in the film, Rami as a boy of twelve in 1974 is carving a wooden doll at home in the south of the country before Israeli bombing forces the family to flee to Beirut, leaving their home presumably a ruin. In order to escape penury, dislocation, and family strife, Rami takes work at a café whose patroness and clients are for him "the soul of Beirut," but a militia attack leaves the café, too, a ruin. Still a child, Rami develops a lifelong love for Yasmine, a Christian girl, to whom he gives the wooden doll he made, but war forces her family to flee West Beirut, leaving their home to ruin. Rami's father is then kidnapped while junk-collecting in war ruins. The crime sparks Rami's cold rage, and he quits his job as an ambulance driver to join a militia unit. During a raid, Rami rescues a woman, Siham, and her child who are trapped in a ruin. Later, Rami takes a hostage who is slated for execution to safety across the ruins of no-man's-land in symbolic redemption for his participation in the war, and the film closes, somewhat neatly it must be said, with Rami having returned to the south of Lebanon and to his early talent in art as he teaches painting to children in what may well be the recovered ruin of his childhood home.

Despite the omnipresence of ruins in this film, they seem only incidentally relevant to the arc of Rami's development. They seldom trigger the deep yearning that is associated with the standing-by-the-ruins topos. Indeed, the film evokes nostalgia only ambivalently. Even when Yasmine, the long-lost sweetheart of his youth, returns as an adult to her childhood home in a textbook standing-by-the-ruins situation, the topos is completely deactivated when she hams a pose for a snapshot next to the house as if it were a Disneyland background. Rami, who happens (implausibly) to witness the scene, is only briefly wistful at the sight although his gaze does linger on Yasmine's daughter clutching the doll he had carved as a boy and given to her mother many years before. The doll functions as something of a ruin, momentarily drawing forth the puppy love he had felt as a child, but the narrative drive, and the significance of the doll, lie elsewhere, and therefore the scene's poignancy is ephemeral. Again, when Salwa the café patroness leaves the country after the murder of her lover, the café is simply reoccupied by the militia. Rami returns to it after twelve years and finds the murdered man's oud strung and dust-free. Nor do the old songs playing on the radio in the disaffected café seem to move him all that much; his contemplation of the scene is almost perfunctory, suggesting that military occupation of the once-happy place may be grim but not tragic. Finally, even the Lebanese war film motif of driving through the ruins conveys in this film nothing so much as an overload of despair—the storm before the calm, as it were—since by the end of the film, the car-mounted camera breezes through newly built cityscapes where once ruins had loomed. In each case, ruins in this film enter an economy of reuse and recuperation that removes them from contemplation. It is as if the film resolves the conflicting imperatives of memory and reconstruction thematized in *The Pink House* by simply denying any role for memory. Reuse and resignification eliminate the evocative power of ruins. If, as Henry Ford is said to have remarked, "history is bunk," by the same token, ruins are junk.

Ruins are therefore synonymous with a Heideggerian "standing reserve" of ulterior use and exchange values that can be plowed back into life in the present.[28] The depiction of Rami's and Yasmine's childhood homes, Salwa's café, the dead man's oud, and Rami's father's poking around in the ruins all reinscribe ruins as new use values. Reuse and resignification eclipse the evocative power of ruins by reinserting them into the forgetfulness of everyday life in the present.

All this is deeply congruent with the militia morality Rami embraces. Just as he has no patience for the counterfactuals of nostalgia, the militia fighters have none for ideological visions: When Rami's militia unit leader announces: "The Revolution's dead. . . . It's all hot air. Everyone fights to save his own skin," he epitomizes the historically widespread rejection of utopic secular ideologies in the first years of the war. This disenchantment has its spatial correlative in the erasure of ruins and wartime memory.

In the Shadows of the City thus plumps unproblematically for the creative destruction of war until, almost by accident, Rami encounters Siham and her child in the ruin. He eventually learns that her husband, like Rami's father, has been kidnapped, but it soon becomes clear that each responds differently to tragedy. When Siham leads a delegation of women to the militia barracks to learn the whereabouts of their loved ones, the militia leader finds the scope of the women's interest and their refusal to let go of a lost cause bordering on absurd. He gently tells them to for-

get about the past, to get on with their lives, and to raise their
children. At this point, the film suddenly and vividly draws the
logical conclusion of its own thematic thrust. What had appeared
to be perhaps a refreshingly unsentimental and expedient "creative destruction" of ruins and fruitless memory suddenly reveals
a sinister callousness. Just as the ruins are forgotten and recycled
for new building, the militia leader urges the women essentially to
forget their loved ones in order to build new lives. The film, which
up to this point has exposed the hypocrisy of commitment and
leaned clearly toward the expediency of ruin reuse, suddenly very
deftly exposes the logical consequences of this policy.

Others have already remarked that the sequence with Siham is
an oddity in the film. 'Adnan Madanat finds it a weakness: "Although the screenplay tries to incorporate the wife [Siham] and
her mission within the plot, the effort seems somewhat forced into
the dramatic narrative structure as a whole. As a result, the relationship between the protagonist and the wife is to a certain extent implausible. Directors are often driven by their good intentions to say too many things at the same time, so they fall into the
trap of stylistic error and narratological imbalances."[29] Madanat
clearly sees that Chamoun is trying to accomplish something distinct from the rest of the film in this passage but misses the essential point. The film entices viewers into accepting moral expediency throughout and then suddenly confronts them with the
consequences of this acceptance. Expediency—and the viewer's
complicity—are exposed at the same time as the militia commander's cynicism.

The "redemption" of standing by the ruins comes when Siham
visits Rami's new apartment and senses that the fully furnished
home is not his (see Figure 7). She accurately supposes that it had
belonged to a kidnap victim and rebukes him for his reuse of the
space: "I'm looking for the missing and you're burying them and
occupying their homes." He retorts, "Living in the past will bury
you alive." Both employ the figure of burial, Siham using the more
elegant form *dafana* to accuse Rami of essentially burying people
who are not yet dead for the sake of expediency, Rami using *qaba-*

Figure 7. Siham and Rami facing off in the recycled ruin.

ra to accuse Siham of burying herself alive for the sake of keeping faith with what is forever gone. It is the singular achievement of *In the Shadows of the City* to so vividly juxtapose the two dominant and mutually exclusive attitudes toward the past. Siham's reverence for the unknown person's apartment testifies to her refusal to sanction human instrumentality: "I'm no fool. I know they might all be dead, but I want to believe the opposite for the truth to come out. . . . I just want the truth."[30] For Siham, the acceptability of reuse turns on knowing the truth about the missing in order to keep expediency from overwhelming humanity under an ever more pressing imperative to destroy and rebuild. The missing man's home must remain empty—a ruin—in order to mark his nonfungible dignity. Humans and ruins are therefore strangely linked such that keeping faith with absent loved ones requires the ruin-metonym.

Rami never acknowledges but implicitly accepts the validity of Siham's claim. He breaks with the militia by conveying across the no-man's-land a nameless hostage slated for execution according to the needs of wartime expediency. From this moral fulcrum, Rami plunges back into the world of reuse and expediency but with a change. At the end, which mirrors the beginning, he drives through the rebuilt cityscape teeming with postwar opportunists, and we recall that earlier occasion on such a drive when he imagined himself a naked corpse dropped in an untidy place. The thought now reemerges in its full significance as not simply the remembrance of his assassinated father but as a conscious sense of solidarity with the missing in a society of forgetfulness. The conflict between memory and forgetfulness has not been resolved, but he has found a way to survive it. Unlike the protagonists of *Beirut: The Meeting* and *Beyond Life*, he is not torn and alienated in a world of wartime expediency. Rather, like the Nawfals and Adaimis at the end of *The Pink House*, he finds a way to invest ruins with memory and noncontingent meaning even as they are erased. Amidst this properly tragic consciousness of ineffectual remembrance, his childhood artistic talent reemerges. In the final scene, Rami is teaching painting in what looks for all the world like his childhood home—yet another recycled ruin. Such art, however, like a ruin, potentially bears no use value but can be invested with traces of memory and therefore provide a palliative to the historical necessity of creative destruction.

IF THESE RUINS COULD SPEAK IN *WHEN MARYAM SPOKE (LAMMA ḤIKYIT MARYAM)*

Filmmaker Assad Fouladkar was born in 1961 to a family active in printing and publishing in Beirut. He spent his childhood in Beirut during the war, but was never a participant and generally shunned political involvement. He narrowly escaped with his life when his family's apartment building was shelled during the Israeli siege of Beirut in 1982. He studied theater in Lebanese University before going to the United States to study cinematography at the University of Boston, where he directed several short films including one based on his war experiences, *Kyrie Eleison*, which

won several awards upon its release in 1990. He was not supportive of Rafik al-Hariri's policies, but when the former prime minister was assassinated, Fouladkar felt compelled to participate in the
Independence Uprising. He has also worked in radio and written
for the press and is currently an adjunct professor at the Lebanese
American University in Beirut. He notes that music, and in particular the Rahbani brothers' musicals featuring the diva Fayrouz,
enticed him into cinema as he imagined filming the plays that
never made it to the screen. He notes that he made *Lamma Ḥikyit
Maryam* after the failure of a more ambitious project. Drawn from
close observation of his own Muslim background and culture,
the film is based on a story that "happens throughout the Middle
East." Today, Fouladkar is working on a successful Arab sitcom,
Ragul wa Sit Sitat (A Man and Six Women) while planning a new
Lebanese feature film.[31]

Assad Fouladkar's 2004 film *When Maryam Spoke* is among the
first contemporary Lebanese films unrelated to the civil war and
postwar concerns, yet its topic is no less explosive. In outline,
When Maryam Spoke recounts the story of lovers, Maryam and
her husband, Ziad, who are happy for three years together before
Ziad's mother begins to press in earnest for a grandchild. The couple initially disregard the mother's obsession but eventually try to
conceive before Maryam learns that she is infertile. They decide
to adopt, but Ziad's mother objects on the grounds that adoption
is against Islam. She urges her son to divorce or to simply take a
second wife while, from her side, Maryam's mother campaigns for
her daughter to see a mystic who specializes in solving infertility
and other marital problems. Pulled by Ziad's mother and failed by
Maryam's, the couple eventually divorce at Ziad's insistence. He
takes another wife, but when his second wife catches him in bed
with Maryam, he is forced to break definitively with his first wife.
They see each other one last time two years later, after the death of
both their mothers; Ziad is unhappy, and Maryam secretly lives in
an asylum. The story ends with Ziad's grieving response to Maryam's suicide.

Figure 8. Ziad beholding the ruin-trace of Maryam in *When Maryam Spoke*.

While the story of this film is simple, its plot is complex, consisting of three intertwining film sequences. The first is a face-on soliloquy of Maryam in which she tells the story of her relationship with Ziad. The soliloquy begins and ends the film and is spliced at various intervals into two other film sequences, one lyrical and one narrative. The second, lyrical strand is filmed in medium close-up and consists of water trickling from a spout over bare skin and a slowly caressing hand. Only at the end of the film is it clear that the body under the water is Maryam's corpse and the hand Ziad's as he washes her. Up to that moment, the sensuality of the gestures and the fact that the body has nothing of death's pallor make the sequence equally suggestive of lovemaking. The third narrative strand constitutes the majority of the film and depicts the key events in their relationship, though not necessarily chronologically. The triple-strand film serves to contrast distinct subject positions. The body-washing sequence is focalized through Ziad and counterpoints Maryam's soliloquy, whereas the realist narrative sequence is an aggregate of Ziad's and Maryam's individual lives along with, crucially, their social contexts.

As in *Beirut: The Meeting, Beyond Life,* and *The Pink House,* sound and visual recording technology play an important role in this film (see Figure 8). Maryam's soliloquy is a videotaped suicide note, but this becomes apparent only in the very last scene of the film, after her death, when the camera draws away from the video screen and we see Ziad watching. He is visibly moved with longing and regret. The final shot of the film has his hand extending toward the screen to touch Maryam's image, but at that moment on-screen she lifts a remote control and stops the recording. The television screen goes to snow, and the film ends. The insertion of video-recording technology in the diegesis obviously permits the pathos of this scene. As the vivid trace of a loved one who is forever gone, the video is itself a ruin, and its effect on Ziad, like the effect of campsite ruins on the ancient poet, is profound. Like a ruin, Maryam's video jogs Ziad's memory to moments of bliss and rue, but unlike campsite ruins, this ruin speaks. For this reason, it is also distinct from the use of sound and video-recording technology in the other films discussed in this chapter. Haydar in *Beirut: The Meeting,* Patrick in *Beyond Life,* and Suhayl Adaimi in the *The Pink House* all destroy the tapes they make. Even the title, *When Maryam Spoke,* refers to her videotape and implies that her speaking is a departure from a norm of silence.

In order to better gauge the effect of the speaking-ruin trope, it is useful to briefly compare this film to another of lost love and ruin. In terms of its examination of how patriarchal authority can split the most ardent of young lovers, this film bears comparison with *The Broken Wings* from forty years earlier. The temporal frame of both takes place after the death of the female lead, who, in both cases, dies unhappily and alone. In both, the male pines disconsolately over the ruin-image of the beloved, in the case of Gibran, a drawn image. Both films also posit relevance beyond their historical and social settings; *The Broken Wings* indexes a cosmic standoff between Innocence and Corruption, *When Maryam Spoke* a generalized Middle Eastern Muslim predicament. One can enjoy *The Broken Wings* without thinking too much about whether Salma might have a point of view distinct from that of her lover, Gibran, but the talking-ruin topos in *When*

Maryam Spoke thrusts Maryam's viewpoint to the fore, enabling a more complex view of the relationship.

To give voice to ruins transforms the topos. In the traditional ode, the poet weeps for irrecuperable past joys but eventually gets a grip, accepts fate, and returns to life and activity. The poem thus ratifies both the desert poet's capacity for deep feeling and self-control. Maryam's speaking activates the otherwise occluded side of the relationship. Through Ziad's lyrical sequence, we see him, like the ancient poet, weeping for lost joys. Through Maryam's soliloquy, we see that Ziad's misjudgment, not fate, bereaves him of his wife. Her video shows how Ziad bends his will not to the implacable cosmos but to conventional thinking, so his tears index not only yearning but also guilt and regret, and his suffering undergoes no conversion into inner strength. Maryam's video thus injects ambivalence into both the primary narrative account of her descent into clinically diagnosed madness and into Ziad's sensual-lyrical reminiscence. Had the ruin been mute, the film would correspond more closely to the traditional ruins topos and Maryam's fate would glow with the pathos of unavoidable misfortune. The speaking ruin provides an alternative subject position that outflanks both Ziad's lyricism and the realist narrative's illusion of inevitability.

When Maryam Spoke also differs from the war and postwar films by deploying the ruins trope less to reaffirm values against anomie than to engage with social issues. The narratively embedded ruin video is key to this effort. Hamid Naficy, noting the prevalence of letters, notes, videos, and e-mails in non-Western cinema, writes: "Epistolarity appears to be less a function of plot formation and character motivation than an expression and inscription of exilic displacement, split subjectivity and multifocalism."[32] In this film, Maryam's video does indeed inscribe her displacement from the patriarchal norm. This "epistephilia," according to Naficy, "often involves a burning desire to know and to tell about the causes, experiences, and consequences of disrupted personal and national histories. As such, they are films of social engagement."[33] Likewise, embedded video vividly conveys a critical stance toward dominant social attitudes in *When Maryam Spoke*. This faith in the power of representation to intervene in the world is foreign to the traditional ode but also, to a lesser extent, to the war-related films. Consider in this regard the fate of recording technology in the other films studied in this chapter. Cassette and videotape in *Beirut: The Meeting, Beyond Life,* and *The Pink House* tend to point to always absent ideals: cross-cultural communication, pure moral commitment, social justice. Consequently, the destruction of recording tape in these films betokens the renunciation of idealized values. The careful presentation and valorization of Maryam's suicide-note video endorses the critique contained in it and, consequently, posits a more socially critical role for the ruins topos.

This film's critique of dominant gender roles in Lebanese society focuses on romantic and utilitarian attitudes toward love and sex as expressed in Maryam's and Ziad's strands of the film. Maryam's underscores the choices that lead to the breakup of the marriage; Ziad's evokes with longing a world of tragically truncated bliss but with no attention to causality. Her monologue assumes the unproblematic transparency of free agency; his lyric springs from a vision of absent joy and present misfortune. The realist narrative depiction of these characters in their social contexts is thematically opposed to the soliloquy and lyric. While Maryam's monologue and Ziad's lyric twine around this realist narrative, each glossing the lopsided core conflict between romantic and utilitarian attitudes toward love and sex, the realist narrative continues its implacable march forward to what it does not even deign to suggest might be "tragedy."

In its depiction of social expediency's priority over romantic individualism, the realist strand deploys image motifs, secondary characters, and a subtext of capitalist modernity. An image motif of water contrasts to that of other liquids. In the body-washing sequences interspersed throughout the film and also in the water that Maryam's friend, Noura, gives her after a bitter quarrel with Ziad's mother-in-law, water is always associated with the simplicity and sensuality of the couple's relationship. By contrast, characters drink tea, orange juice, and rose water during the complex mediations associated with popular religious beliefs and superstitions. Tea, especially, heralds Maryam's entry into the faith healer Shaykh Abu Faraj's world of spells, spirits, and exorcisms. Her grimace at the taste of his fertility philter is also a token of her initial revulsion at a world in which human agency is subordinate to the will of spirits. Against the bright yellow orange juice, the red rose water, and the strong tea, the clarity of the water Maryam drinks and which flows over her body is no match.

Other imagery also highlights the lopsided struggle. Maryam's mother, her only champion in the struggle with her in-laws, wears a garish blue and black polyester blouse early in the film. Later, the same garment hangs inexplicably near the door of Abu Faraj's home, suggesting that the mother is on intimate terms with the venerable quack. The blouse underscores the role the mother plays in mediating her daughter's entry into Abu Faraj's primitive spirituality, which stands opposed to the simple cotton dress Maryam wears in her monologue. Through the image motifs of liquids and clothing, the film contrasts the simplicity of romantic love with the factitiousness of the patriarchal bargain whereby a woman's worth is dependent on her status as a baby-maker.

Secondary characters are also arrayed against the young couple's commitment to romantic love. The shaykh's seed-munching receptionist completes Maryam's initiation into the world of folk superstition. Her conviction that men are "a low grade of human" and that the sexes are locked in a state of perpetual war is no advance over patriarchy for its reversed polarity. While this comment initially vexes Maryam, who exclaims: "I don't have a problem with my husband!" the receptionist's pithy reply, "If he loved you, he'd take you as you are," points to how far the young couple already interiorize the patriarchal bargain. The receptionist boasts of Abu Faraj's capacity to cast and break spells as if he were patriarchy's most dangerous menace, but her comment: "Nobody gets away from Abu Faraj," turns out to be an ironic reversal in that the desperate women who come to him are the only ones who never get away. Maryam's increasing dependence on the shaykh is signaled first in her drinking his herbal tea. He then becomes "the other man" Maryam sees secretly, sealing her dependence on him when he persuades her to breathe into the mouth of a corpse in order to take the spirit of the once-fertile woman. Maryam's convulsions resulting from the morbid act suggest that whatever spirit she may have gained, she has lost her own to Abu Faraj, the surrogate lover. Indeed, the only time that Maryam is seen to break down is when she crumples to the ground and weeps as a wife would at the news that Abu Faraj has been sent to prison for fraud. Other secondary characters also condition the triumph of utilitarianism over romantic love. In Maryam's social circle, her mother upholds the notion that a woman's worth depends on her capacity to bear children and rejects her daughter's alternative vision. Even Maryam's best friend, Noura, can talk of little else than children and is constantly surrounded by babies. Kittens frolic around her, never around Maryam.

While the rage for babies that grips everybody in the narrative is coded as a dictate of traditional Islam, modernity is also in league against the young couple to the extent that it, too, subordinates the individual. When Ziad's mother claims that Maryam is "dysfunctional" and that her son should "get another one," Ziad tartly retorts that his wife is not an automobile, which disturbs her not at all. The question of human commodification recurs when Ziad's second wife fails to conceive after three months. His mother again begins to grumble, and Ziad suggests acidly, "Maybe I should just lay four women and marry the first one who gets pregnant." Yet Ziad himself finally comes to the conclusion that he needs a genetically related child as he stands in the print shop where he works, contemplating the mass production of text in front of a printing press. Maryam may be a unique individual according to a liberal humanist paradigm, but Ziad's brand of Islam, his mother, and his occupation all apparently interpellate him as a maker of copies. It is what God wants, what his mother demands, and what his employer pays him to do.

Faced with engrained patriarchy, superstition, and reproductive Fordism, Ziad and Maryam have only their personal com-

mitment to each other, which their antagonists easily dismiss as
naïve. Even in the realist narrative, however, a motif valorizing
romantic love does appear in the background "noise of culture."
Early in the primary narrative when everything is apparently fine,
the couple watch *Annie Hall*, a story of love and separation that
serves as a cautionary tale against taking love for granted. Media representations provide numerous other implicit warnings to
Ziad's deaf ear. His wedding to his second wife is thrown into
a funk when Maryam shows up unexpectedly and dances to an
Arabic song whose lyrics include: "We gave you water to drink
from a brunette's palm," revealing again the link between water
and romantic love in this film and contrasting his relationship to
Maryam with the "baby contract" he enters into with his second
wife. The song also voices a desperate plea as if from Maryam:
"What more do you want? It's easy for you to forget me and love
somebody else. I'm asking you to swear not to waste our time together." Again, after the divorce, Maryam calls Ziad on the phone,
and a popular song playing in the background, *"Khali Balak min
Zuzu"* (Take Care of Zuzu), from the 1970s Egyptian box-office hit
of the same title, in effect warns Ziad to "take care of Maryam,"
who is on the verge of an emotional breakdown.[34] These contra-
puntal discourses point to the disjunction between the values represented in art and mass media and those of traditional Lebanese
society. Ziad fails to heed or even to fully understand until it is
too late the warnings implicit in Arab and Western pop cultures.
Only when he has seen and heard the ruin of Maryam's videotaped monologue does the weight of these warnings crash in on
him. At that point he understands the ironic accuracy of her gently chiding refrain that he is *"majnūn"* (crazy).

If this were all to the film, *When Maryam Spoke* might be considered ideologically unsubtle. Yet at the same time that the film
reflects on the affective impoverishment of Lebanese Muslim patriarchy, it also demystifies the ideology of romantic love by de-
constructing its distinction from patriarchy. The important first
scene of the realist narrative opens on a birthday party into which
a beaming Maryam enters, carrying a cake with candles. As ev-

erybody sings "Happy birthday!" she places the cake with doting attention on a very low coffee table. The viewer may be forgiven for being surprised when the camera moves to the birthday boy and reveals the bearded face of an adult male, Ziad. Spliced into this already curious scene are brief flash-forwards of black-clad mourners at Maryam's funeral, suggesting that the ultimate tragedy of this couple begins with such uxorial indulgence. Maryam's absolute priority on love is itself indistinguishable from female abasement in patriarchy albeit without the practical compensations the patriarchal bargain confers. While Maryam's fetishization of her husband at the birthday party is only mildly curious, it becomes pathological when she sees the quack Abu Faraj in order to fulfill Ziad's wish for a son and eventually agrees to mouth-to-mouth a corpse. Likewise, her agreement to an amicable divorce and to her husband's second marriage are further way stations to her abasement in the name of romantic love. Even when—again on Ziad's birthday—she lets herself be taken as a concubine to the same house she was thrown out of as a wife, she continues to indulge her ex-husband by offering the "cake" of her body. She bestows it in the name of freely chosen love, but Maryam's devotion is indistinguishable from submission to patriarchal prerogative even if she makes none of the demands a woman is entitled to make in patriarchy by way of compensation.

If the film exposes reproductive Fordism as the aim of patriarchy, it reveals a fetishism of the beloved at the heart of Maryam's romantic love. During the early birthday party scene, Maryam is taking plates back into the kitchen when Noura, her chubby and multigravida friend, sticks her finger into some cake frosting and licks it langorously. Maryam notes primly: "It's that extra that makes you fat," to which Noura replies: "What do you know? This is the good stuff!" Maryam's concern to avoid the "extra" outside romantic love sums up her behavioral economy. Her horizons are defined by her husband whereas Ziad, whose very name means "extra," is interpellated by family, friends, and his occupation to crave more. Early on, he argues to his mother that the couple has waited to have children in order to save money; later,

he splurges on a honeymoon for his second wife. Indeed, only after this superabundant investment does his second wife conceive.
Maryam points out that she never complained about not having had a honeymoon, which, like children and her own dignity,
came far behind her love for Ziad. Psychologically, her infertility
is a manifestation of her unwillingness, more than her inability,
to compromise her total devotion to Ziad. In this way, Maryam's
rejection of the patriarchal bargain is paradoxically also its apotheosis: she gives everything and takes nothing in return.

Yet Maryam is genuinely heroic, sacrificing everything for Ziad
even after the romantic ideal betrays her. This heroism, however,
would remain invisible were it not for her soliloquy. On the evidence of the realist narrative and Ziad's lyrical sequence alone,
one could be excused for considering her simply mad. The ruin-
video of Maryam's soliloquy inflects both the lyrical and realist
strands with tragedy. Maryam's talking ruin also allows this film
to distinguish itself from its historical antecedent, *The Broken
Wings*, which rigidly upholds the distinction between patriarchy
and romantic love. Ziad's standing by the ruin of Maryam's suicide video binds the film's separate formal elements and directs
its thematic complexity to an emotion-laden point as he seeks to
touch his wife's image on the video screen. Whereas the Gibran
character of *The Broken Wings* feels pain before the drawn image
of his beloved, he has no way of knowing her view of the tragedy.
Thanks to Maryam's monologue, Ziad comes to understand his
role in that loss. The ruins video gives Ziad the knowledge that he
has finally been capable of love but only after it is too late and his
lover dead.

CONCLUSION: ELEGIAC SELF-CONSCIOUSNESS

This chapter began with the claim that Lebanese war and postwar
feature films break with the tradition of diffracting the representation of social conditions by refurbishing another tradition, that of
the ruins topos. The analyses of films showed how they draw from
the underlying modes of expressing feeling in Arab culture to of-

fer an elegiac grasp of the past during a time of war and postwar. Specifically, I argued that the elegiac mode is not inert but an effective means of thematizing social crisis. This rather counterintuitive function of elegy depends on the way the reappropriation of the ruins topos sets in counterpoint two different ways of regarding history. Through the representation of sound- and video-recording technologies, these films present counterdiscourses that permit the film to explore ambivalences about history. In the one film studied here that does not foreground recording technologies, *In the Shadows of the City*, an incongruous character, Siham, voices these ambivalences. At the same time that they do justice to complexity, these films employ the ruins topos to evoke a sense of the past in which human dignity is normative. In this way, these films are both alive to the contradictoriness of life yet unimbued with anomic relativism. They are an important constituent of the broader aesthetic practice that I describe in the introduction as elegiac humanism that grew and flourished throughout wartime and postwar Lebanese culture in opposition to a dominant aesthetic of redemptive self-sacrifice.

Each of the films studied here contributes to the development of the elegiac humanist aesthetic in a different way. The act of standing by the ruins at the beginning of *Beirut: The Meeting* infuses Haydar with the heroic spirit to cross battle lines in an effort to communicate with the ethnic-sectarian other, and though he fails, the ethical impulse behind the quest remains unimpeached. Driving through the ruins in *Beyond Life* dehumanizes Patrick but also testifies to his resistance as he imaginatively chooses to drive through the ruins in the last scene of the film. In *The Pink House*, the home-ruin embodies the coercions of the postwar consensus but also resistance against it as the residents create, and defiantly stand before, the home-ruin in the final video sequence. In *In the Shadows of the City*, Rami's occupation of a missing person's home-ruin is the moral nexus between remembering and forgetting war victims. It is only when Rami learns to separate himself from it—stand beside it—that he can come to terms with wartime death. In *When Maryam Spoke*, when Ziad stands before the video-ruin of Maryam, he is able to gauge the extent of the

tragedy of her death. By making ruins "speak" in all these different ways, these films make use of the tradition of nostalgic longing to acquire consciousness of conflicted pasts. They expand the
object of longing and imaginative identification from the absent
beloved to include consciousness of justice and self-responsibility.

CHAPTER THREE

Elegiac Humanism and Popular Politics

The Independence Uprising of 2005

In the first two chapters of this book, I argued that the aesthetic of elegiac humanism that emerged in the late 1970s grew from within a structure of feeling stretching back to the known roots of Arab societies. These culturally conditioned feelings are associated with the topos of "stopping by the ruins" (*wuqūf ʿala al-aṭlāl*), and are as keyed to history as the topos itself, which waxes and wanes, morphs, and is reconstituted according to circumstances. Such topoi and structures of feeling suffuse popular culture as well and provide an alternative to the dominant ethos and aesthetic of redemptive self-sacrifice. This chapter concentrates on the popular cultural manifestations of elegiac humanism during the winter and spring of 2005, when a popular uprising led to the resignation of a Syrian-sponsored government in Lebanon and precipitated the withdrawal of Syrian troops from the country.[1] Although the chapter examines a sliver of material from a period lasting only a few months in one small country, the characteristic features of elegiac humanism plausibly subsist to various degrees at other times and in other societies imbued with classical Arabic culture.

In the introduction, I distinguished elegiac humanism from the dominant mythic utopian aesthetic and its associated practices of redemptive self-sacrifice. In the first two chapters, I showed how the new aesthetic, formulated shortly after the outbreak of civil war in 1975, flourished modestly in the novel and feature film. Then came the year 2000, when the Israeli Defense Forces unilaterally withdrew from the south of Lebanon. It was a watershed moment that apparently vindicated the mythic utopian discourses of self-sacrifice and especially that of the Shiite resistance movement, Hezbollah, which had taken charge of armed resistance to Israeli occupation since the late 1980s. Yet the victory also posed the age-old problem of what to do with a military force and its attendant culture of martyrdom after war. To turn it onto the other occupying force, the Syrian army, was out of the question even if the victory over Israeli occupation did focus attention on this second and more complex occupation. With political, economic, and military hegemony over wide swaths of Lebanon since 1976, Syria looked increasingly like a colonial power and the military arm of Hezbollah like a militia without a mission.[2] The Party of God's discourse of redemptive self-sacrifice seemed increasingly beside the point in an economically and culturally globalizing world.

Likewise for elegiac humanism. If Lebanon were to take its place in the community of nations, it was no longer enough to simply shield the flame of civil society as if the war were still on. In the challenge to bring the nation from a postwar to a peaceful footing, Hezbollah's "pious modernity" and the humanistic discourses associated with the democratic Center and Left were not necessarily incompatible.[3] Ideologically, both sought a way out of sterile nativism by engaging with a modern cosmopolitan world and employing contemporary cultural forms.[4] Both professed openness toward alternative ideologies. Yet despite numerous similarities between them and despite currents within each that seek to maintain openness to the other, humanism and Hezbollah's pious modernity have clashed in an ideological struggle that continues to this day.

This chapter explores the struggle through the cultural representations that embody it and not principally through the content of political speeches, debates, and articles. Since numerous scholarly studies have been devoted to Hezbollah, I focus primarily on the pop-cultural manifestations of elegiac humanism that flourished for a brief ten-week period around what has come to be known as the 2005 "Independence Uprising" (intifāḍat al-istiqlāl).[5] This method may seem strange to those accustomed to keeping the realms of Arab politics and culture separate, one presumably real and efficacious, the other esteemed but decorative. Such a split regards power as the expression of unmediated interests and rigid identities. This chapter takes it as axiomatic that cultural productions are not epiphenomenal but rather a moiling mediator of political debate.[6]

The humanistic discourse of personal moral autonomy is a constant, usually small voice in confessionalized Lebanese society. It is invoked with varying degrees of success in many political debates but seldom tips the balance away from the preponderant weight of sectarian identitarianism. By the first few years of the twenty-first century, students, journalists, and intellectuals invoked human rights and national autonomy in a growing murmur of opposition to Syrian occupation, yet this activity, often undertaken at great personal risk, failed to find a mass audience.[7] By mid-2004, the preconditions for a broader, popular movement began to line up. The Western powers gradually reversed their support for Syrian domination of the country, and at the same time, the Syrian regime itself managed to alienate many of its supporters such as former Prime Minister Rafik al-Hariri when it refused to modify its grip on the nation in response to changing conditions.[8] Yet the atmosphere of generalized and unfocused frustration was arguably nothing more than business as usual in a volatile country.

Then, on 14 February 2005, a massive explosion in downtown Beirut destroyed former Prime Minister Hariri's motorcade, killing Hariri along with 22 others and injuring 135. Some considered the unacknowledged crime a punishment for Hariri's plan to take

Lebanon out of the Syrian fold and his putative role in promoting U.S. and Saudi domination over Lebanon. Others, citing more oblique motives, pointed at Israel or al-Qaeda as the culprit. At any rate, what the explosion represented was at least as important as the practical effect of assassinating the most powerful figure in the country. Targeted assassinations in Lebanon have always had a semiotic function. This one functioned as street theater announcing the vulnerability and subordination of Lebanon in the Middle Eastern hierarchy. More theater followed. Within hours of the explosion, a videocassette was delivered to al-Jazeera showing a young man, the putative driver of the bomb-laden truck, wearing stereotypical martyr's black and claiming responsibility for the crime in the name of an Islamic extremist group. It later emerged that the man did not know how to drive, strongly suggesting that his actual role was that of a talking head claiming responsibility for the murder before, in all likelihood, being himself executed.

It is common wisdom that a traumatic event during a time of tension can raise social frustrations to the boiling point, but without a discursive embodiment, discontent remains unfocused. In the case of Lebanon, the enormous sense of loss and injustice felt by many found a ready means of expression in the ritual of national mourning. To stand in reverence before a tomb or its representation is akin to standing by the ruins and the elegiac humanist aesthetic. As a literary topos, standing by the ruins is a "lyrical symbiosis of love and grief" that goes back to the amatory prologue (*nasīb*) of the pre-Islamic ode.[9] As a mourning ritual, standing by the ruins is surely much older. In spring 2005 in Lebanon, mourning was a powerful means of focusing grief and inchoate political frustration. Thus the three-day mourning period for the former prime minister "naturally" employed traditional forms similar to those associated with standing by the ruins.

A GRAMMAR OF GRIEVING

A "grammar of grief" spanning plastic, dramatic, and discursive representations has come to characterize political assassinations since the civil war. As a rule, shortly after the event, dignified pictures of the victim, often with a brief eulogy, appear throughout the communities he or she served. Candlelight vigils bring friends and supporters together for quiet commiseration while the media toll with eulogies and denunciations of the crime. The funeral is usually held in the deceased's ancestral village and unfolds according to the rites of his or her religious community. Periodic religious-political gatherings follow, commemorating the death and reinforcing the sense of shared sorrow and protest. With little chance for any serious investigation into the crime, there is little hope for justice and the aggrieved settle for such dramatic transformations of slaughter into tragedy as mourning can offer. In this way, standing by the picture, standing with comourners, or standing before the deceased's corpse become ritualized ways of reaffirming human dignity in its manifest absence.

From the standpoint of Hariri's assassins, mourning was doubtless perceived as a bit of harmless theatrics on the part of an impotent people, yet it provided the initial structure for the movement that would eventually emerge. Black-banded images of the assassinated prime minister soon adorned the windows of homes and businesses, walls, lampposts, and automobiles. They proliferated well beyond the deceased's Sunni Muslim and West Beirut turf, popping up across the country and throughout all class and sectarian divisions. Graffiti spread, most of it expressing sorrow and not sectarian rage.[10] Laments often linked the man and the nation in synecdoche: "All of Lebanon died with Hariri," "The country is collapsing for sure."[11] The nearly unanimous grief at the former prime minister's death does not diminish the fact that many, perhaps a sizeable majority, had been sharply critical of his policies as a political leader: "The very man whose person and whose plan divided us in life became the source of our unity in his death."[12] The assassins had succeeded in fashioning a national insult in a country in which nothing was more contested than the concept of nation as such.

The crime beyond the pale led to the idea beyond the pale. A shred of graffiti epitomized it. The name "Hariri" scrawled in Latin letters began to appear with a cross and a crescent dotting each "i," a wild and blasphemous metaphor if taken literally, but acceptable during a time of sorrow. To say that Hariri's murderers killed hope for interfaith reconciliation was to transform the sense of loss into national tragedy. Yet this meaning was unstable. Since the end of the civil war in 1990, the sight of crosses and crescents together had always signified starry-eyed idealism. The common sense of loss, however, temporarily leveled this highly fragmented, individualistic society such that the unthinkable—national interfaith unity—was experienced before being conceptualized. The name "Hariri" with a cross and a crescent dotting each "i" slipped from meaning "hope expunged" to "hope reborn," and the media marveled at the semiotic transformation, declaring that Hariri was not dead.

The notion that interfaith solidarity in the face of injustice could redeem the nation from its 1975–90 sectarian civil war quickly caught on. The Hariri funeral, which is not diminished by recognizing that it was also a staged dramatic representation, drew upon the grammar of grief only to exceed it as a national spectacle. First, the organizers chose not to have the funeral in the slain man's ancestral city of Sidon, where it might have been perceived as a clan or sectarian affair, but rather in Beirut, the nation's capital. Second, the organizers opted for a popular rather than a state funeral, thereby excluding members of the compromised Lebanese government and reinforcing the link between Hariri and the people of all communities. Third, Hariri and his companions were to be entombed next to the massive mosque that Hariri himself had endowed adjacent to Martyrs' Square, a place steeped in national history where the first Lebanese patriots were publicly hanged by the Ottomans in 1915. Finally, church bells and Muslim calls to prayer throughout the country were coordinated in a show of unity. All of these unusual measures served to transform the funeral from what could have been a stodgy tribute into a 250,000-strong dramatization of standing by the ruins. This largest of public funerals in Lebanese history placed grief and mourning for tragedy, not political confessionalism, at the foundation of national conscience and interfaith reconciliation.

The popular actualization of the funeral agenda continued the semiotic reversal of Hariri's death and formed an elegiac core for the events of the following weeks. Although political parties participating in the funeral brandished their own flags, calls to replace them with the Lebanese flag made sense to the majority, who were commemorating the death of a national leader, not that of a party, clan, or sectarian chieftain. The number of participants also contributed to transform the sense of despair and helplessness into popular empowerment. Here, for the first time since the end of the war, masses of all stripes dared to publicly chant slogans against the Syrian occupation.[13] It was also at the funeral that the powerful images of Christians and Muslims praying together in common grief cemented the conviction that unity might be possible. In these ways, the masses who participated in the funeral themselves transformed it into a national movement based on humanistic principles, not sectarian identities.

The following days were crucial. The mourning period was drawing to a close, and so was its capacity to structure opposition. Standing by the ruins can be elegiac, nostalgic, or commemorative but not programmatic. The ephemeral unity provided by grief would eventually wane to be supplanted by a resurgence of sectarian and class interests. The authorities' patience with open opposition would also wane. Nobody doubted that the funeral itself had been infiltrated by informers and the surveillance apparatus. Beau Rivage, Hamaysh, Villa Jabre, and Anjar, names representing places that only private whispers could describe, were still operational interrogation centers. Yet grief was still too great to be weighed against self-preservation, and the reinscription of the tragedy was beginning to inspire more with the will to pass from mourning to some as yet unclear notion of resistance.

The size and oppositional profile of the funeral were astonishing, but the nation's overlords doubtless bet that the status quo would soon return. After all, the Lebanese are known for their political cynicism as well as for being faddish, fickle, and easily influenced. In the past century alone, under far less pressure than nations that were officially colonized, significant sectors of Lebanese society adopted the French and English languages and cultures, Leftist and nationalist ideologies, advanced capitalism, and, more recently, Iranian political-religious doctrine. This nation of fewer than 4 million counts far more than that in the diaspora and is also home to numerous foreign communities, among them some four hundred thousand Palestinian refugees, thousands of Filipino, Sri Lankan, and Ethiopian workers, all of whom are closely monitored, and tens of thousands of Syrian workers, almost none of whom are monitored.[14] The question of national identity and whether it exists at all is always open and burning, so the postcolonial paradigm of liberation struggle followed by indigenization has never set altogether well in Lebanon. From the occupiers' standpoint, rage over a politician's death and tensions over the presence of so many Syrian workers and fifteen thousand Syrian soldiers might well be considered the growing pains of inevitably successful colonization, so the regime declared after the funeral demonstration that it would not withdraw its troops.[15] In the absence of a political program, the spirit of elegiac humanism that moved the mourning period seemed at a dead end.

RECODING MOURNING, POPULAR CULTURE, AND POLITICS

Yet it may be precisely their "faddishness" and an apparently weak sense of shared national history that gave many Lebanese the flexibility to make the key transition from mourning to a new kind of resistance movement. During decades of Syrian and Israeli occupation and war, the Lebanese became accustomed to standing by ruins of various kinds, structural, institutional, and human (see Figure 9). Beholding the ruins of everyday life with little hope for change in the present, it was comforting to recall an ostensibly halcyon past. This knack for seeing solace beyond ruins is a kind of recoding of the world that can be differentially directed. Indeed, as citizens of a small nation located on numerous cultur-

Figure 9. Part of a photo-information exhibit in downtown Beirut devoted to learning the truth about those who disappeared during the civil war. Photo by Ken Seigneurie.

al and political fault lines, the Lebanese have always been adept at swiftly recoding into a local idiom everything from foods and consumer products, dances, and music to languages and corporate structures. This second-nature cultural *bricolage* is at the root of the recoding that transformed mourning into a popular uprising.[16] When in late February 2005 people began entertaining furtive hopes for change, they joined forces with the existing political opposition, which was able to swiftly mount a campaign of cultural recoding aimed at freeing the nation of Syrian dominance.

The Independence Uprising emerged as a reading and rewriting of mourning, recent history, and semantically frothy popular culture. Young people transformed the traditional practice of filing in front of the deceased's tomb—itself a standing-by-the-ruins scene—by taking a page from east European "color revolutions." They circulated a petition calling for an impartial investigation into the assassination that eventually garnered eighteen thousand signatures. Others began camping at Martyrs' Square, renaming it "Freedom Square" and preferring the colors of the national flag over those of their party and sectarian affiliations. Thousands took advantage of vast plywood surfaces around downtown building sites to scribble multilingual messages of resistance. The widespread recoding of spaces and practices was part of the general *zeitgeist* that viewed this as no ordinary mourning period even if that was how it began.

Commentators began to categorize this uprising along with numerous pro-democracy movements in eastern Europe and central Asia. Several features, however, distinguished Lebanon's Independence Uprising from Serbia's "Bulldozer Revolution" of 1999, Georgia's "Rose Revolution" of 2003, Ukraine's "Orange Revolution" of 2004, or Kyrgyzstan's "Tulip Revolution" of 2005.[17] Cases of election fraud generally sparked the east European and central Asian movements, and in Lebanon too, the unconstitutional 2005 reappointment of Emile Lahoud as president arguably triggered subsequent events. But the Lebanese democratic system, as flawed and in need of revision as it doubtless is, was never itself the primary object of the Uprising's reformist fervor; the Syrian manipulation of the Lebanese presidential election was. Indignation at corruption also motivated the east European and central Asian revolutions, whereas Lebanese ire aimed at the Syrian corruption of Lebanese institutions and wartime misdeeds. Thus, without denying Lebanon's many and deep domestic woes, the Uprising specifically targeted the Syrian role in exacerbating them.

The former Soviet-bloc pro-democracy movements also benefited from heavy infusions of support from Western-funded international organizations such as the Organization for Security and Co-operation in Europe, Freedom House, the U.S. Democratic Party's National Democratic Institute, the U.S. Republican Party's International Republican Institute, the National Endowment for Democracy and the George Soros–funded Open Society Foundation.[18] None of these or other Western organizations have admitted to funding the Uprising, although the movement did depend on diplomatic support from the West and much of the Arab world. The east European and central Asian movements were therefore more clearly a theater of a high-stakes proxy struggle between the United States and Russia. In the Syro-Lebanese conflict, Russia is indeed an ally of Syria, but its interests in Lebanon are not perceived to be vital as they are in its neighboring former republics and Slavic Serbia. The United States favored the Uprising, but its interests in Lebanon pale by comparison to its interests in Israel, and since no element of the Uprising displayed any warmth toward Israel, American support would remain perforce limited. Even France's support for the Uprising had to remain within the parameters set by the U.S.–Israeli axis. Thus excepting Iran, for which Lebanon has been a high foreign-policy priority since the 1979 Islamic Revolution, great power support for the Uprising was primarily diplomatic and symbolic.

Its birth in response to violent crime and its growth into a national movement made the Uprising actually two movements, one after the other. The cultural productions of the mourning period differ in key ways from those of the subsequent independence movement. Along with graffiti, popular songs produced in the immediate aftermath of the explosion were elegiac in tone, essentially elaborating riffs from the standing by the ruins tradition.[19] The mode of expression was typically lyrical or oratorical, employing an intimate form of address that assumed the passage of discrete concepts from one clearly distinguished will to another through language conceived of as a transparent medium.[20] This communicational paradigm often hyperbolically equated the person of the assassinated prime minister with clearly conceived ideals whose expression had been frozen during three decades of war and occupation. Ballads such as "Is Such Injustice Possible?" ("Maʿqūl ẓulum al-bashar" by Walid Tawfiq) personified injustice and linked hope for a just future with the slain former prime minister:

Is it possible that injustice would kill our dream?
Would stones cry from the harshness of this injustice?[21]

Another song by a group of artists brought together for the occasion, "The Story Isn't over Yet" ("Lā mā khulṣit al-ḥikāya"), conflated the nation and Hariri:

> The story isn't over yet,
> No, no, this isn't the end.
> We have not forgotten.
> You're still within us,
> And the nation is still the goal.[22]

Yet another song, "Source of Love," ("Nabʿ l-maḥabbeh") by Majida al-Roumi, originally about Jesus Christ, was remixed with words from a speech by the assassinated Sunni Muslim, lending a sacrificial and interfaith significance to the former prime minister's death. The first three lines of the following quote from the song are taken from a speech by the former prime minister; the last two are the singer's address to Jesus:

> I entrust to God
> This beloved country, Lebanon,
> And its good people.
> Don't leave us.
> Keep watch over our nation in these difficult days.[23]

These songs do not age well as they assume a great degree of emotional unity between speaker and audience, which inevitably dissipates as emotions settle. Soon enough, the message begins to sound hectoring. Likewise, the apostrophe in Ahmad Qabur's song "Say Allah, Stand up Yalla" ("Qūlū allāh, qūmū yalla") depends on a preexisting unity of feeling without which it sounds bullying.

While the call for justice would unify the movement from beginning to end, the mode of address soon became more complicated. Intertextual references became more discursive and less hortatory. A televised "theme" demo in support of the protestors in Martyrs' Square featured a fragment of Ahmad Qabur's famous 1982 song "I'm Calling on You" ("Unādīkum") that contextualized resistance to the Syrian occupation as a new stage

in the modern Arab struggle. Originally a poem by the Palestinian poet Tawfiq Zayyad, Qabur's song gained fame in 1982 as one
of the most powerful appeals to resist the Israeli invasion of Lebanon that summer. The clip's bold and public linkage of the Syrian and Israeli occupations broke a lot of china in the Arab Taboo Shop. For three decades, the Syrian occupation could only
be considered within the framework of Arab solidarity and was
conflated with Arabism. To recode the Syrian occupation as a colonialist gambit on a par with those of Israel or the United States
was a major public demystification of Syrian designs. By making
it look as though history itself is the subject of the appeal, the song
permitted a degree of interpretive agency on the part of the listener that is absent in the personalized appeal. It is also important
to note that the clip in which "I'm Calling on You" appeared was
broadcast by Future TV, the station owned by the Hariri family.
One of the most important factors in the Uprising was the genuine diversity of media sources in Lebanon that permitted an ongoing and productive debate. The fact that the controversial former
prime minister owned radio and television stations and a newspaper ensured that at least these would support the movement. As it
turned out, other media sources did as well.

As the source of address, message, and addressee became less
self-evident in the transition from mourning to resistance, the
oratorical discursive regime whereby a discrete message is transparently passed from one will to another faded without ever disappearing. Jacques Rancière notes that the oratorical mode of
address is characteristic of a hierarchical relationship between
speaker and listener such as that of a lyric poet, orator, or pop star
and audience.[24] It is ideally suited to situations of release of widely
shared, pent-up feelings, but is less effective in contexts requiring
persuasion and negotiated positioning where its ipse dixit authority is perceived as coercive.

In the movement's transition from mourning to activism, the
ethos and aesthetic of elegiac humanism had to become less elegiac and more open to dialogue without betraying its humanistic, as opposed to sectarian, commitment. In the weeks following

the funeral, there emerged an addressee-oriented communicational paradigm characterized by irony, humor, and indirection. It avoided the "hierarchies of the representational system" in favor of horizontal reading practices.[25] Rancière adds that the "democratic" nature of this communicational paradigm lies in the fact that "meaning was no more a relationship between one will and another. It turned out to be a relationship between signs and other signs."[26] Using Rancière's analogy from paleontology, just as rocks and pebbles "speak" to anybody who knows how to read them, so discourse in this regime makes no direct appeal to the authority of the speaker but depends on the reader's capacity to read symptomatically. As a result, readers drawing different conclusions discuss the object under study, not the personal authority of the speaker.

Such a reading practice was necessary to respond to the dynamic and multipolar nature of the Uprising. Even the name of the movement was the product of jostling signifiers, not an injunction from the apex of hierarchy. Some referred to the "*intifāḍat al-istiqlāl*" (Independence Uprising), borrowing semiotic resonance from the widely respected Palestinian Intifada. Others referred to the movement as the "Beirut Spring" in homage to the anti-Communist Prague Spring, or ironically as the "Gucci Revolution" in reference to the striking presence in it of educated middle-class women. The U.S. State Department made a bid for the "Cedar Revolution," which sounded a little namby-pamby compared to the others, but it, too, gained currency in the omnivorous Lebanese news market. In each case, however, meanings were products of negotiated readings, since the simple consensus of grief or moral outrage could no longer provide a common language for multiple viewpoints.

The evolving humanistic discourse did not, however, seek to dissolve identities. Demonstrations took place almost daily throughout late February and early March 2005, some drawing only thousands, others tens of thousands of participants. The numbers were not generally as important as the perceived need to inscribe messages on the landscape. Specific groups, including women, professional associations, and students, each held their own protest on given days. Others participated in vast human flag formations or massive candle arrangements that spelled "The Truth" in three languages when viewed from a great distance. Still others formed human chains or arranged mass bicycle and even scuba-diving demonstrations, each identity formation eager to produce an object-text to be read.

And all this while the busy bombers spent their spring on a road show of violence, blowing up one intellectual, leader, or statesman after another, apparently aiming at ratcheting fear into submission.

The rapidity and energy of the Uprising took by surprise the parties that had traditionally borne the mantle of popular progressive resistance, Hezbollah, the Lebanese Communist Party, and the Syrian Social Nationalist Party. These parties found themselves in the difficult position of facing a popular uprising against their Syrian patrons.[27] They responded by trying to reframe the anticolonial revolt from Syria to the United States. The smaller of these parties organized pro-Syrian counterdemonstrations against Western meddling in Lebanese affairs. Most of these demonstrations in Lebanon or in Syria itself were relatively small and consisted of male party members and supporters clapping and hopping rhythmically to the most common all-purpose chant in the Arab world: "With soul and with blood we sacrifice ourselves to _____ [fill in the blank]" (*bir rūḥ, bid damm nafdīk ya _____!*). This mode of political practice would seem to correspond to what Rancière associates with an oratorical discursive regime: a discrete meaning passing transparently from one will to another. Hyperbole, however, in the Arab world as elsewhere, can often signal a more complex performative. Lisa Wedeen's study of representation and power in Syria notes that most officially sanctioned "spontaneous" demonstrations are charades in which everyone is forced to participate without necessarily believing a word of what is affirmed.[28] Indeed "'real obedience' relies on *not believing.*"[29] While Lebanon is most assuredly not Syria, it is no stranger to fealty proven in the fires of absurdity as evidenced by the Syrian personality cult images and statuary throughout the country.[30] Thus assertions lacking evidential support such as that the Hariri slaying was a parricide served as an effective oath of loyalty to the Syrian regime more than as truth claims.

A far more cogent challenge to the Uprising came from the powerful and generally respected Hezbollah movement.[31] The Party of God's official position toward the Uprising was slow in coming, but after weeks of hedging, it pulled together a massive "Thank you, Syria" demonstration for 8 March. The vigor and rhetorical power of Hezbollah General-Secretary Sayyed Hassan Nasrallah bore nothing of the cowed and perfunctory obedience of the smaller pro-Syrian parties. Likewise, the Hezbollah pro-testors were no flunkies mouthing slogans, but a disciplined and committed host charged by their leader's every word. If the rally unfolded as a vertically organized, doctrine-centered affair, it also provided a stark vision of mobilized masses opposed to an Upris-ing that suddenly looked quaint by comparison. It was a remind-er that Hariri's assassination did not bridge all the gulfs within Lebanese society, that the Lebanese knack for assimilating other cultures is differentially directed, and that pro-Syrian movements could field some half million in support of the "special relation-ship" between the two countries.

By dwarfing all the opposition rallies since Hariri's funeral, the 8 March rally called the Uprising's popularity bluff, effectively demanding that it bring out its actual numbers. Syrian president Bashar al-Asad, clearly piqued by the popularity of the Uprising, claimed that it was an affair of few rabble-rousers and that this would be obvious if only the television cameras covering it would "zoom out." In response, and with no little desperation, Uprising organizers and grassroots activist networks launched televised appeals and text-message calls for a counter-rally on 14 March, the one-month anniversary of the explosion that killed the for-mer prime minister.[32] Well covered by the world's press, the event swamped all predictions, drawing more than a million partici-pants—between a quarter and a third of the entire in-country Lebanese population.

In this demonstration and the dozens that preceded and followed it, the movement dramatized its willingness to confront its more powerful adversaries firmly but without provocation, keeping the door open to the Lebanese Shiite Muslim parties and to normal bilateral relations with Syria.[33] The humanistic as opposed to identitarian priorities were manifest in the repeated injunctions in writing and around the podia to distinguish between the Syrian regime and the Syrian people. The openness to diverse opinion meant that even the Uprising's most ardent supporters criticized it from the beginning.[34] As a result, the movement succeeded in transforming the discourse of mourning into a humanistic discourse of resistance.

The humor, irony, and indirection that characterized this emerging discourse were also a practical necessity. In a fragmented, polarized nation, protesters of different sectarian, regional, and class affiliations needed to find common ground among themselves. The most common chant, "*Ayyy yal-la!... Sūriyya ʾṭalʿī barr-a!*" (roughly: Hey ho! . . . Syria's gotta go!), conveyed the biggest demand in an upbeat mode, in stark contrast to the usual chanted promise to sacrifice "soul and blood" for a leader. Chants based in common demands reinforced the sense of group resolve and eased fears, especially during the early demonstrations. Indeed, the Lebanese army, which had been called out against protesters in the past, was fully deployed before and during most of the demonstrations. Only on 28 February, two weeks after the Hariri assassination, did it become clear that the army would not intervene, although the risk that provocateurs would infiltrate the rallies remained throughout the Uprising. Other chants evoked common beliefs and experiences. Thus protestors chanted that they wanted no Syrian *kʿak* in Lebanon. *Kʿak*, a flat, sesame-seed-covered disk of bread, was often sold in the street by Syrians who were widely suspected of being informers. Thus the homely *kʿak* became a humorous metonymy for the serious threat of denunciation and arbitrary arrest. Such expressions of hitherto privately held beliefs revivified public discourse by offering an alternative to decades of cliché-ridden fealty to Damascus.

Since irony and indirection depend on reading and interpretation, the same signifiers can also be read against the grain. Perhaps, as some bloggers have intimated, the *k'ak* chant indexed the chanters' class hatred and xenophobia more than any real threat from the security apparatus. Alternative symptomatic readings cannot be excluded out of hand in a modern regime of meaning, but they can often be contextually corroborated or not. In the case of Lebanon, few would seriously claim that the working classes are empowered to the point of causing a "bourgeois backlash" against the Syrian working class. Moreover, the notion that middle-class participation in the Uprising indexed a primarily bourgeois movement ignores heavy working-class participation, and not only during the Uprising itself but throughout the years since, including the yearly anniversaries of Hariri's death. Nevertheless, while Hariri himself was something of a man of the people as evidenced by the homage paid him by Lebanese of all classes, the middle-class intelligentsia did play a leading role in the Uprising, which does not imply that it was a bourgeois uprising. More to the point, the new rhetoric of resistance described here requires a literate population capable of breaking out of customary practices—be they those of ritual mourning or of traditional street protests—to engage in practices variously described here as demystification, *bricolage*, indirection, cultural appropriation, recoding, and willful misreading. These techniques imply some capacity to manipulate symbol systems such as often provided by a humanistic education, which is increasingly available only to a minority who can afford it, and not just in Lebanon. This is not to deny that class exploitation is the most intractable and neglected long-term problem in Lebanon—and again not only in Lebanon—but to point out that its invocation at a time of military occupation and political assassination is opportunistic, akin to quibbling about the economic loss to the local economy as a result of the withdrawal of the Israeli Defense Forces in 2000.

In stressing Lebanese identity, the Uprising did indeed indulge in the "othering" of Syria, but it remained on the level of discourse. Businesses named after Syrian cities such as the Shami Bakeries or Halabi Restaurants hastily plastered images of Lebanese flags all over their walls and windows as if to stress the purely arbitrary nature of the Syrian signifier. Reports of violence against Syrian workers were also rife as long-simmering Lebanese working-class resentment at cheap Syrian labor broke out, although reports of serious injury or death were almost certainly exaggerated.[35] Indeed, nonviolence was not only an article of faith among Uprising participants; it was a necessity given that the only political party legally permitted to possess arms outside the Palestinian refugee camps is Syria's ally, Hezbollah. Any hint of violence on the part of the Uprising would have been a welcome excuse for the Syrian-backed Lebanese government to unleash a crushing response.

The Uprising's particular reader-oriented discursive regime also shunned the rhetorical escalation of tensions. Demonstrators brandished no grim-reaper personifications of villains, burned no Syrian flags or effigies, and chanted no "Death to Syria" slogans. Such hyperbolic expressions are characteristic of the oratorical discursive regime whose success is measured by the degree to which it can evoke and mobilize powerful feeling. Extreme claims are also part of the discursive regime characteristic of Syrian authoritarianism, except, as I have argued, its hyperbole is a loyalty performative independent of semantic content. The absence of righteous rage in the Uprising was noteworthy as it suggested dispassionate reflection about visceral issues and consciousness of other perspectives. Humor, irony, and indirection left space for disagreement and negotiation. The sharpest accusations, such as banners reading "Syrial Killers" or those that mocked former president Emile Lahoud, muted the agon in irony. Even pictures of the infamous heads of the Lebanese state security apparatus contained only the caption addressed to the Syrian regime: "Take them with you!"[36] In practical terms, by avoiding the rhetoric of rage, the movement conveyed a sense of purpose and confidence without animosity.

The Uprising's reader-oriented humor often depended on appropriating elements of pop and consumer cultures in order to insinuate messages of resistance. Superficially similar to the kind of *Adbusters*-style "culture jamming," these signs and banners did not engage the ethics of consumerism but strove to "rewire" its signifiers into ethical-political stances. In such a diverse country, a gamut of cultural icons lay at hand in Arabic, English, and French appealing to a wide range of citizenry and interests. Humor, nestled between the pop vehicle and the ethical tenor, ensured that any effort to prosecute for slander or incitement would be ridiculed. Thus, just as the movement recoded the structures of mourning, so it recoded pop and consumer cultures. A people at ease in their second-nature consumerism hitched Johnny Walker's "Keep Walking" slogan to a demand for military evacuation (see Plate 5); revised Bob Marley's "No Women No Cry" to "No Syria No Cry," and printed Madonna's "Papa Don't Preach, I'm in Trouble Deep" over an image of Syrian president Bashar al-Asad and his strong-arm father, former president Hafez al-Asad. Rather than an oratorical *J'accuse!* of Lebanese president Emile Lahoud for being a quisling, the Uprising pegged him as a good candidate for *Star Academy,* the Lebanese equivalent of *American Idol.* Among the Arabic puns on UN Resolution 1559 calling for Syrian withdrawal from Lebanon was a sign representing the "1559/ Persil" laundry-detergent box that punned on the rhyme between Bekaa, the Lebanese valley containing a great number of Syrian soldiers, and the word for "stain," *buqʻa,* implying that 1559 will remove the occupying army like the detergent removes stains. Troping moral and national interests with everyday products and experiences channeled a diverse nation's unease into good-natured conviction and away from provocation and polarization. As a result, the mass of protestors emerged as a pragmatic, horizontally constituted coalition of small groups and friend networks such as "Civil Society" animated by thirty-four-year-old Asma Andraos.[37] These groups shunned doctrinaire stances and displayed a refreshing antihierarchical spirit. Thus when one of the leaders of the Uprising, Progressive Socialist Party leader Walid Jumblatt, issued a directive on acceptable behavior to the tent-city inhabitants, they reminded him that they owed him no fealty. Their presence in the tent city was testimony to ethical and civic principles, the bywords being *truth, freedom, sovereignty,* and *independence.* Their commitment to a noncontingent notion of truth and to the nation may not seem very progressive to some, but they provided the ethical ground of the movement and suggest that perhaps the term "progressivism" itself needs redefining.

The movement's humor was often willfully campy, sometimes almost kitschy, but the conditions of production in spontaneous response to violent death and national humiliation placed these representations within serious political and ethical frames of reference. Moreover, if the primary function of kitsch is to obscure humanity and mortality—what Hal Foster bluntly calls "shit and death"—behind a feel-good veil of sentimentality, the art of the Uprising sought to transform but never obscure the tragedy of violent death.[38] Akin to a globalized version of subculture style, these songs, chants, and graphics are "more usefully regarded as mutations and extensions of existing codes rather than as the 'pure' expression of creative drives."[39] Thus demonstrators recoded the debased pop and consumer sign systems in order to dignify death and steel ethics-based resistance. To turn the empty language of commodity fetishism against the empty language of violence and political coercion was a deft move and about the closest thing to a postmodern literature of commitment this century has yet to offer.

This was all, of course, a bit much for a gang of culturally challenged murderers to bear. Whoever they were, they apparently resented the refusal of so many to cower in the debris of their explosions. Predictably, they communicated according to their wont with a string of more bombings, which continued into 2008, targeting opposition activists, journalists, intellectuals, military personnel, and politicians. Samir Kassir—a journalist, university professor, and implacable critic of Syrian occupation—died in a targeted explosion on 2 June 2005. George Hawi, the former head of the Lebanese Communist Party, died in another. Both were leading figures in the Leftist opposition to Syrian control over Lebanon. Other victims hailed from the Right, the only link among them all being their commitment to

Lebanese sovereignty. Lacking the wherewithal to even identify the perpetrators, let alone seek redress, the Uprising met each bomb with peaceful expressions of defiance and a deeper rejection of Syrian influence over national affairs.

The dialogue of bombs and words became something of a test to see just how far the post–civil war commitment to nonviolence would go. When the fifteenth bomb killed another trenchant critic of Syria, Gibran Tueni, on 12 December 2005, an ensuing crisis led to a walk-out by Hezbollah members of the government. The tensions subsided only when the aged father of the murdered man, Ghassan Tueni, a distinguished newspaper publisher and former ambassador to the U.N., called for calm and spoke directly with Hassan Nasrallah. Shortly thereafter, journalists found a speech that the assassinated parliamentarian had given at the 14 March rally in which the million-plus participants repeated after him a pledge of allegiance to the multifaith nation. Almost overlooked in the euphoria of that day, this pledge took on a new life after the death of its author, being widely rebroadcast and reprinted.

The Uprising proper is plausibly thought to have peaked with the gigantic 14 March demonstration and then continued for another six weeks before the run-up to the spring elections reactivated the feudal-sectarian political machines. By late April 2005, the traditional political formations were busy co-opting the movement's prestige for the elections while abandoning its principles.[40] Not surprisingly, the tent city folded, and the pithy graffiti, chants, and slogans that responded to unfolding events gave way to mass-produced symbols and a raft of middle-brow art. Commercial culture, having been thoroughly poached by the movement, in turn now fed off the Uprising with patriotic advertising (see Plate 7). It was often clever but bore the whiff of commodified sentiment and therefore the end of the Independence Uprising as a genuine mass movement.

ORATORICAL AND DEMOCRATIC DISCOURSES

The Syrian regime's discursive practice, as epitomized in the "soul and blood" chant, flattens the referential function of public discourse to the point of reducing it to endlessly repeated statements of fealty. Inspired by Brezhnev- and ultimately Stalinist-era Soviet practices, the verbal embrace of absurdity is itself the best indicator of the stakes in dissent. As Wedeen suggests, institutional terror forces citizens "to surrender their sense of self, to become obedient, defeated, and sycophantic."[41] In such a context, when the Syrian regime began appropriating the Uprising's signifiers—members of the Syrian Parliament took to donning scarves in the colors of the Syrian flag and demonstrations featured young people lounging about and speaking to journalists—it signified nothing more than a riff on the "soul and blood" charade. Had these gestures been accompanied by the loosening of restrictions on free speech or by the release of political prisoners, their meaning would doubtless have altered.

Hezbollah's discursive practices are distinct from those of Syrian authoritarianism. Like the Uprising albeit in a different manner, Hezbollah employs both oratorical and reader-oriented discourses. The oratory of Sayyed Hassan Nasrallah is a vital part of Hezbollah's appeal. To a certain extent, his speeches depend on the same discursive regime as that of the inchoate Uprising during the mourning period. In both cases, a clearly defined ethics-based message responds to a situation of gross injustice and evokes in listeners a sense of solidarity and unity. During the mourning period of the Uprising, protestors' indignation at brutal crime extended to decades of occupation. Likewise, during the late 1970s through Musa Sadr's Amal movement, Shiite Muslims began voicing their indignation at historical injustices they suffered. By the 1980s, through Hezbollah, they battled exploitation by feudal landlords, neglect by the Lebanese state, humiliation by Palestinian fedayeen, and occupation by the Israeli Defense Forces (IDF) and their Lebanese surrogates. These grievances found their most articulate spokesperson in Hassan Nasrallah, whose position as a cleric, descendant of the Prophet Muhammad, and especially his central role as general-secretary of Hezbollah since 1992 have conferred upon him great authority. Added to this, when he lost his eldest son in an armed skirmish with the IDF in 1997, Nasrallah took the personal tragedy with dignity and aplomb. By 2005, Nasrallah's prestige extended to Lebanese of all communities who admired the party's rigor, efficacy, and success in expelling the IDF from south Lebanon. Clearly, Nasrallah's authority springs from his actions as much as from his talent as an orator.

Without diminishing Nasrallah's many achievements, it is also necessary to note that his popularity owes something to his mastery of the same oratorical discursive regime that was characteristic of the mourning period for Hariri but which soon appeared orotund. Rancière notes that this discursive regime has traditionally generated a direct current of authority from speaker to listeners: "Speaking was viewed as the act of the orator who is persuading the popular assembly. . . . It was viewed as the act of the preacher uplifting souls or the general haranguing his troops. The representational power of doing art with words was bound up with the power of a social hierarchy based on the capacity of addressing appropriate kinds of speech-acts to appropriate kinds of audiences."[42] Modern orators often mitigate this hierarchical relationship by maintaining a conversational tone characteristic of a "fireside chat" or by avoiding authoritative intonations and gesticulation. Not Nasrallah, who furrows his brow in righteous wrath, wags his index finger, and sends waves of tonic accents over his audience. Such polemicism is necessary since only so long as he can arouse moral fervor will listeners submit and he maintain the orator's hierarchical relationship to his audience. His religious and political-military roles mean that he is both "the preacher uplifting souls" and "the general haranguing his troops." Thus his word can clear the streets of rioters in minutes as when, on 15 June 2006, a local television program specializing in political caricature dared depict Nasrallah as it does other political figures of all tendencies. Within minutes, bands of angry youths had set up barricades of burning tires throughout Beirut and its suburbs until Nasrallah brought them to heel and spooked the producer of the program into submission. The rioters had very astutely seized on the danger of democratizing the image of Nasrallah through caricature. Such irreverence, if allowed to continue, would have made his oratorical authority look implausible and old-fashioned, so the ostensibly unconstrained rioters acted immediately and in contradiction to the self-discipline for which Hezbollah activists are famous. The incompatibility of oratory with democratic reader-oriented discursive regimes such as caricature means that Nasrallah not only protects himself from irony and parody, he also refuses almost all public interviews and enters no public discussion or debate with political opponents. Thus by his earned prestige and the party's careful construction of a wall of reverence around him, Nasrallah's oratory enjoys sanctuary from the modern "collapse of a hierarchical system of address."[43]

To be sure, Hassan Nasrallah is not the only Hezbollah leader, and as important as his role is, it is also limited. The movement also employs highly educated cadres and communications firms to convey its messages through reader-oriented regimes of meaning. The party's intellectual elite, like that of any modern organization, frames its activities according to the ideological proclivities of its intended audiences. Thus the extensive veiling and anti-alcohol campaigns, launched and paid for by Iran in the 1980s and now self-perpetuating, are framed not as a return to tradition, but as a return to authenticity.[44] This framing is part of what Lara Deeb calls Hezbollah's "pious modernity," a discourse that aims to situate itself between "backward traditionalism" and "empty modernity" that is coded as Western.[45] As with any attempt to construct a new discourse, a good deal of equivocation has resulted: "Constructing the pious modern was also an ambivalent process. Perhaps the most fraught manifestation of this ambivalence lay in the contradictory deployments of multiple discourses about modern-ness simultaneously. While pious Shi'is made an effort to undermine western standards for defining modern-ness, at the same time, they used those same western standards to claim value as equally modern/civilized as the West."[46] In reframing the Sharia and Shiite Muslim social practices according to the discourses of modernity, Hezbollah has displayed at least as much ingenuity as the Uprising in rereading the signs of popular culture. Thus, the party is adept at appropriating popular iconography, such as when it presented its own brand of a "rainbow coalition" englobing the pro-Syrian opposition to the current government.

Hezbollah's deployment of democratic discursive regimes, however, has always been in the service of an antidemocratic, hierarchical impulse. Hezbollah deputy leader Shaykh Naim Qassem stresses the three long-standing pillars of the party: (1) belief in Islam, (2) *jihād* or "struggle," and (3) jurisdiction of the Jurist-Theologian (*al-walī al-faqīh*), a position currently held by the Iranian cleric Grand Ayatollah Sayyed Ali Husseini Khamenei.[47] Numerous Shiite Muslims have difficulty accepting this platform, and most of Lebanon's Sunni, Druze, and Christian communities find it alienating. It is therefore downplayed outside Hezbollah's Shiite Muslim constituency but cannot be jettisoned except at the risk of alienating its bases of support. As a result, the party squares its ideological circles as any modern political party does. Only more so. Even its famously polemical 1985 open letter stressed tolerance: "We don't want to impose Islam upon anybody, as much as we don't want others to impose upon us their convictions and their political systems. . . . We call for the implementation of an Islamic order on the basis of direct and free choice as exercised by the populace, and not on the basis of force, as others might entertain."[48] Yet as Augustus Norton notes, "Unfortunately, the organization's history of violence against its political and ideological rivals casts doubt on Hezbollah's commitment to voluntarism."[49] The party also pointedly rejects sectarian politics, Qassem equating it with "familial, tribal or regional fanaticism" and declaring that Hezbollah is "neither a sectarian party nor a party for a particular sect."[50] Yet Qassem also maintains: "It is a Muslim party founded on the system and order of the Prophet (pbuh) and his family of disciples, bearing a comprehensive vision, and grouping in its ranks all those who believe in its ideology and discipline irrespective of their sectarian affiliation at birth."[51] Since a comprehensive religion-based governing ideology is a serviceable definition of sectarianism, it is unclear how a hypothetical non-Shiite member of Hezbollah could be anything but an outsider in the organization. As one specialist has observed, notwithstanding their claims to the contrary, party leaders engage in "precisely the game of confessional Lebanese politics that they previously had denounced."[52] Indeed, Joseph Alagha suggests that Hezbollah has taken sectarianism further than the other Lebanese parties:

> Hezbollah is organized like a Leninist party so they have their own workers' solidarity foundations. . . . This is why when Hezbollah entered the government, they asked for the Ministry of Labor. They use the government to benefit themselves. That's why this is the only Hezbollah minister who is coming to work almost every day despite the walk-out [from the government between December 2006 and May 2008]. This is very important for their constituency. The grass roots are the basis of their following and without them they cannot mobilize, so they must attend to their needs. Why not exploit the apparatus of the state? . . .
>
> Working-class solidarity is prioritized through the Shiite working class, not the national working class, but . . . they have to package it so that it appeals to all even if you can see that everything is divided along sectarian lines. The national union, for example, has hardly any Hezbollah members. Hezbollah considers it corrupt, so they have their own unions based on their constituency's interests.[53]

Likewise, the party has stated its commitment to parliamentary democracy but insists on retaining an independent armed presence and a power of veto with its coalition partners over the majority in government decisions. It has stated its commitment to the Lebanese nation but executes policies of a national scope that run counter to the constitution, the most well-known example being Hezbollah's refusal to accept the election of the only Hezbollah-endorsed candidate for the Lebanese presidency, leaving the country without a head of state for some six months.[54] The party receives, moreover, aid estimated in the hundreds of millions annually from Iran, which is deposited directly into party coffers, and partly as a result, Hezbollah is the second-largest employer in the country, having erected water, electricity, education, and health-care infrastructures parallel to those of the government.[55]

The party's stated commitment to pluralism has not prevented it either from seeking to topple the elected government in extensive and intimidating street protests that culminated in an armed attack on Beirut and numerous regions throughout the country beginning on 7 May 2008, and ending only days later after it had obtained its political objective of exercising veto power in the government. Finally, Hezbollah's stated commitment to free choice of lifestyles sits uneasily beside the high priority it places on public displays of piety. Deeb writes: "The pious modern is an ethos, a way of being in the world, and a self-presentation. It is an ideal, hegemonic in a Gramscian sense, institutionalized for pious Shi'is as an infrastructure, a social norm, and a desired experience."[56] These contradictions are not without their effect on Hezbollah's prestige, yet at the same time its military exploits, its care for its constituency as well as the comparative weakness of the central government reinforce the party's appeal.

The hierarchical and authoritarian nature of Hezbollah comes through in a rhetoric of the "with us or against us" variety. Qassem writes that Lebanon must declare "either allegiance to Syria or an allegiance to Israel"; that the nation is "left with but two alternatives: surrender versus confrontation"; that the world is faced today with "two sets of logic: the first is that adopted by those materialist devotees to life who practically believe that the world is the end of all existence and who thus place in life all their efforts. . . . The second is the logic of the believers in God who go through life as a trail leading to the hereafter."[57] None of these binaries is radically different for being opposed to the binary thinking made famous by U.S. president George Bush and various other populist leaders. Moreover, the use of an exceedingly supple modern discourse combined with a gamut of coercive practices is not anomalous among modern institutions. Indeed, in its stress on the appearance of propriety over its reality, battlefield prowess over negotiation, and parochial over national interests, Hezbollah is not so much a pariah organization as an apotheosis of modern political practices. Even the argument that Hezbollah is structurally dependent on enmity and ongoing war is no more compelling than the same argument with respect to Israel.

Yet there remains for the moment a significant difference among institutions that are structurally committed to ongoing war and little else and those that can at the same time prosper and provide conditions for human fulfillment. Qassem extols Hezbollah's "culture of martyrdom" that "reinforces one's readiness for death for the sake of God."[58] In order to justify and maintain such a vision of perpetual conflict and readiness for martyrdom, Hezbollah supporters must be maintained under a state of constant mobilization, not unlike that of Israeli society, and indeed Hezbollah and the Israel often seem only too eager to provide each other justification for ever-readiness. Thus "mobilization" (al-ta'bi'a) campaigns are constantly whipping up enthusiasms and looking out for supporters and fellow travelers. As Joseph Alagha notes: "Nobody is bored" in Hezbollah-dominated neighborhoods and villages.[59]

SECTARIAN TO NATIONAL CONSCIOUSNESS

Since it did little to change the stranglehold of established Lebanese parties and feudal families on the political process, the Uprising has become the object of some fashionable scorn.[60] Its contribution to twenty-first-century political practice, however, goes beyond its political objectives and beyond Lebanon's borders. In Lebanon, the Uprising ratified a high degree of political maturity in a people once so famous for in-fighting that the rest of the world called it Lebanization whenever a state broke up into ethnic-sectarian chaos. The peaceful mass commitment to the idea of their nation in the face of continued brutal intimidation earned the world's respect for showing what imperfect human beings can do on a good day.

The more general contributions of the Uprising include the insight it provides into a discourse of national consciousness formation that is not necessarily jingoistic. The deeper sense of commitment to Lebanon as a nation, which emerged during the Uprising,

was a surprise, but maybe it should not have been since it corresponds to what Ashis Nandy writes regarding another colonial
struggle: "In retrospect, colonialism *did* have its triumphs after
all. It did make Western man definitionally non-Eastern."[61] Likewise, the Uprising showed that three decades of Syrian colonial
occupation managed only to make many Lebanese definitionally
non-Syrian. While a boon for Lebanese identity, one might imagine this as an undesirable outcome from the standpoint of the Syrian regime and wonder what happened to give many Lebanese today a clearer sense of their separateness from Syria, a country and
culture most recognize as closely related to their own. The 1976
entry of Syrian forces into Lebanon, billed as a "helping hand,"
was also clearly an assimilationist colonial venture.[62] After the
war ended in 1990, a paternalist rationale took over, not unlike
that of another colonial power, the British Raj, which regarded
the Indians as "crypto-barbarians who needed to further civilize
themselves," except that the Lebanese were viewed as crypto-an-
archists who needed to learn self-control under the tutelage of a
more level-headed power.[63]

The paternalist rationale for Syrian control over Lebanon came
closest to public articulation when the former Syrian security chief
in Lebanon, the late Ghazi Kanaan, remarked to Lebanese journalists shortly after the civil war ended in 1990: "You Lebanese,
you are shrewd, creative and successful merchants. Soon, you are
going to have 12 million [Syrian] neighbors coming toward you.
Create light industries. Engage in trade and commerce. Indulge
in light media, which does not affect security. Shine all over the
world by your inventiveness, and leave politics to us. Each has his
domain in Lebanon: yours is trade; ours, politics and security."[64]
It is uncontroversial to say that this political and economic divi-
sion of labor with its gross imbalance of power exploited the Lebanese economy. The paternalist rationale depended on numerous
ideological assumptions about difference that infect most colonial
ventures: Syria was the staunch guardian of Arabism, Lebanon
the bowerbird collector of foreign tinsel; Syria the chaste male,
Lebanon the salacious female; Syria obedient and quiet, Lebanon

unruly and outspoken; Syria noble Caliban, Lebanon effete Prospero; Syria authoritarian tradition, Lebanon babbling democratic modernity. Never mind that among other contradictions to this neat set of binaries, Israel has for decades enjoyed its most secure border with the staunch guardian of Arabism in exchange for not a square inch of territory. In Lebanon, however, the Syrian army and security services, their Lebanese intermediaries, the unmonitored Syrian work force, and Syrian border policy all enforced a sense of the country's dependence on Syria.

In the end, even many of those who had the most to gain from continued fealty to Damascus deemed the price exacted for domestic calm in Lebanon too great to bear. This is at first blush surprising and counterintuitive. After all, Lebanon can hardly avoid foreign interference in its internal affairs, and all of its leaders understood the high priority Syria placed on the "Lebanon file." Moreover, Syria may be a disciplinary society in which "people obey because they *fear* being punished," but nobody demanded genuine belief, only the outward signs of obedience.[65] Thus since nobody was really demanding (as the chant has it) a "soul and blood" commitment, it was imprudent from a pragmatic standpoint for the Lebanese to risk their blood and economic prosperity for the luxury of simply voicing publicly what nobody prevented them from thinking privately. Somewhere, Syria must have blundered in the management of its dependency.

Without discounting the usual reasons for imperial failure—hubris, overexploitation, or miscalculation of interests—it is also not implausible that many Lebanese could no longer see themselves functioning under a Syrian discursive regime. The paternalist rationale hides a contradiction that many Lebanese may well have found unbearable between freewheeling capitalism and authoritarianism. Many especially coastal Lebanese are, in Kanaan's words, "shrewd, creative and successful merchants" plugged into capitalist markets and intimately acquainted with capitalism's attendant democratic discursive regime. Many others are from the agricultural hinterlands and are more attuned to the oratorical tradition associated with feudal hierarchies and which,

I have tried to show, are also suited for conveying unambiguous moral stances (see Plate 6). Throughout twenty-nine years of occupation the Lebanese were essentially being asked to be both good capitalists adept at manipulating the codes of a democratic discursive regime and good vassals who interiorize a hierarchical discursive regime. This worked during the 1990s as the coastal population engaged in business and the southern Hezbollah-dominated population fought to liberate the country from Israeli occupation. When Israel evacuated in 2000, Hezbollah needed a new role and at the same time the Beirut-based pro-business interests began to chafe under the Syrian yoke. In response, the Syrian regime could imagine nothing more creative than to insist on the same old terms. When the Uprising erupted, the Beirut-based reader-oriented rhetoric of resistance fell on Syrian-Hezbollah ears more attuned to an oratorical rhetoric of authority. By the same token, Hezbollah's oratorical rhetoric of moral authority fell on ears more attuned to the reader-oriented rhetoric of democracy. Thus when the famous question burst out of the Uprising in Syrian dialect: "Faja'nākum! Mū?" (We Surprised You! Didn't We?), it obliquely referred—in its merry and dialogical way—to the rise of a new democratic rhetoric of resistance.

CONCLUSION: RUINS OF A HUMANISTIC RESISTANCE

I have tried to show how the rhetoric of resistance characteristic of the Uprising was essentially modern and distinguished from authoritarian and oratorical regimes of meaning. Yet it also split from contemporary political discourses as apotheosized by Hezbollah taking semantic contingency to the point of couching religious fundamentalism in the discourse of modernity. The Uprising stopped short of this extreme. The romp across discursive registers—a song blending Christian liturgical rhythms and a political speech, a banner blending silly consumerist imagery and a demand for military withdrawal—could have quickly led to the kind of semiotic fungibility whereby anything can be equated with anything else, which is another way of saying authoritarianism. The greatest contribution of the Uprising, therefore, was to center the "phantasmagoric fabric of poetic signs" characteristic of democratic discursive regimes around an elegiac consciousness of death and ruin that is sharply distinguished from Hezbollah's, Israel's, and the American populists' doctrine of Manichean armed struggle.[66] The discourse that emerged from and drew tens and ultimately hundreds of thousands was predicated on a humanistic consciousness of death and ruin as tragedy, not as martyrdom or collateral damage. From this consciousness sprang the demand for truth about the assassination and the demand for national sovereignty, but not a will to vanquish. When these ethical imperatives wilted under the sun of election expediencies in the spring of 2005, so did the Uprising, but not before leaving traces, "ruins" as it were, of a humanistic resistance that blends the elegiac and the modern. As nationhood struggles to grow in the rocky Middle East, these traces of successful unarmed resistance merit attention, and not just from the Lebanese.

"We're All Hezbollah Now"

Throughout this book, I have made the case for the existence of a minority aesthetic in wartime and postwar Lebanon, calling it "elegiac humanism" and arguing that it provides a cultural framework for an alternative to the long-term sectarian revanchism that has plagued this tiny nation. At various points throughout, I have contrasted this aesthetic with the dominant aesthetic of mythic utopianism that, in its Lebanese form, is essentially sectarian. This is not to set up a reified binary relationship between good elegiac humanism and bad mythic utopianism.[1] Nor is it to call for the replacement of one coercive dominant by another. The purpose has been to draw attention to the existence of a wider range of aesthetic practices than commonly thought exist in Lebanon in order to cast into relief the potential for the cultural realm to respond flexibly to changing social and political circumstances. Failing this, a dominant aesthetic practice such as sectarian utopianism is conceived of as a one-size-fits-all inevitability and a natural corollary to "endemic" sectarianism.

The first two chapters centered on how the standing-by-the-ruins topos evolved in the novel and feature film according to changing historical conditions from the Lebanese civil war in the late 1970s to 2005. By way of showing how quickly the aesthetic response to changing conditions can occur, I explored in chapter 3 the rapid rise to prominence of elegiac humanism in early 2005 Lebanon and its equally precipitous decline when the conditions of spring parliamentary elections enjoined a return to sectarian affiliations. A year later, conditions had again changed. The country was embroiled in the 2006 "July War" between Hezbollah and the Israeli Defense Forces (IDF), and immediately the cultural sphere responded. Again songs and iconography responded to violence. Again ruins imagery figured prominently in scenes of bombed-out homes, bridges, ambulances. Yet the conditions surrounding this violence were different than those of the civil war and the post–civil war. The massive air, land, and sea attack on the country, coupled with the world's support or acquiescence, evoked a response sharply at variance with the elegiac humanist aesthetic. Artists in all media and genres and from all points of the political compass, even among those with no sympathy for Hezbollah and who recognized the Party of God's role in initiating a border skirmish, embraced the logic of redemptive self-sacrifice and its mythic utopian aesthetic.

A song sung by Zayn al-ʿAmr is typical. The title, "Shumūkh," translates as "pride" and is used in the sense of haughty disdain directed against the attackers and those who endorse their actions. Its evocation of ruins does not evoke self-examination as a novel published in the midst of the civil war might have, or a longing for human community beyond sectarian identities as a song published during the 2005 Independence Uprising might have. Indeed, the July War of 2006 exposed the incapacity of elegiac humanism to deal with barbarous destruction.[2] An aesthetic directed at exploring the moral complexity of self-responsibility in civil war is inadequate to respond to massive attack from without. These, however, are perfect conditions for a revival of what had by then become an almost discredited mythic utopian aesthetic. Thus ruins in "Pride" set up a polarized self-other relationship and a will to self-sacrifice that appealed to a people who felt abandoned, and not for the first time, on the altar of geopolitical interests:

> Whenever they destroyed a house in my land,
> They built castles with my determination.
> They bargained for my land with my blood,
> So drink, my land, from my blood.[3]

The endorsement of a self-sacrificial ethos clearly departs from the elegiac humanist vision of a past that must be assumed in order to build a tolerable present. This song, one of many that proliferated during the July War, draws from the mythic well of blood and land in an effort to convert random war death into self-sacrifice for a cause. In addition to the new batch of songs produced for this war, others from past conflicts were dusted off and replayed for the familiar context of unequal war. Marcel Khalife's "Muntaṣib al-Qama 'Imshī" (I Walk Upright) is perhaps the best known, dating back to the 1980s during the first Israeli invasion:

> I walk upright, with my head held high
> I hold an olive branch in my hand
> And my coffin on my shoulders.[4]

Most of these songs transmute the struggle from the brutality of the here and now to a reference point in the hereafter.

Humiliation is the most prominent leitmotif. From abroad, the war might have looked like a gratuitous attack on the part of Hezbollah followed by an inordinate but more or less understandable response on the part of the IDF. From within Lebanon, it looked more like a serious but limited cross-border raid of which Israel took advantage to cripple the Lebanese economy, environment, and modern infrastructure.[5] From within this frame, the sense of humiliation trumped self-responsibility and served to rally the nation to a position very close to that of Hezbollah. Practically, the nation's unity in the face of adversity meant that communities throughout the country took in hundreds of thousands of refugees during the thirty-four-day war and erstwhile opponents voiced support for Hezbollah throughout the war. A song, "Lubnān, yā

Lubnān" (Lebanon, Oh Lebanon), sung by Joanna Mallah, voices precisely the polarized choice the war imposed:

Lebanon, Oh Lebanon,
The attacker is asking:
Death or humiliation?
Death is sweeter to us.[6]

The pathos of a humiliated population attempting to reclaim some measure of dignity by pretending to welcome death was lost in Western journalistic accounts that preferred to interpret this response as a manifestation of a "culture of death." The war thus vindicated Hezbollah's long-standing claim that the neighbors to the south sought peace by humiliation.

For a population made vulnerable to arbitrary attack by the IDF in the summer of 2006, the rhetorical embrace of death was the only dignified response. By the same token, the attack exposed the ideological pretensions of the world community that endorsed it. Thus the war also ratified Hezbollah's claim that liberal humanism is hypocritical and self-serving. Popular songs such as Pascale Machalany's "Waynak, yā Insān" (Where Are You, Human Being?) decry an absence of conscience in world opinion. Others, like Mikaella's "Nahnā Rāh Mindafaʿa" (We Will Resist) indict world opinion and morality:

We will resist.
We will not yield,
Neither to the sound of cannon,
Nor to the eyes of the world.
. . . .
You, people of civilization, you peacekeepers,
You visited us a thousand times, and sold us only words.[7]

Most of the songs or singers cited here were not affiliated with Hezbollah, nor were most listeners. Wartime conditions brought together otherwise divergent points of view. Thus events, in the form of an internationally sanctioned war on the nation, ratified

Figure 10. Mock graveyard: *Top of pyramid,* names of war dead; *large type,* "A Greeting of Loyalty"; *bottom,* "From the union of civil society associations for freedom and life to the martyrs killed intentionally by America and Israel." Photo by Ken Seigneurie.

Hezbollah's brand of militant martyrdom and discredited all alternatives, humanist or other.

Under normal conditions, a little mythic utopianism goes a long way. Self-sacrifice makes sense to most only under conditions of extreme duress such as those that prevailed during the thirty-four-day war. In the wake of the war, aesthetic visions of its violence branched into three styles. The first used political posters and installations to depict wartime deaths as atrocities, thereby legitimating future vengeance according to a mythic utopian aesthetic. A mock graveyard set up in the downtown area commemorated those who died in the war while driving home the message that their deaths were the responsibility of the United States and the state of Israel (see Figure 10). Another exhibit near the clock tower in the downtown included a lurid photo display of the war's toll on children juxtaposed to quotes from mostly U.S. leaders. In these cases, mourning was enlisted as part of a political rhetoric, as it often is elsewhere in cases of polarized opposition.

A second response to the war coded it as a victory. Well publicized in the world press, this response centered on billboards, especially in Hezbollah-dominated areas. It often featured images of militia fighters at work or Hezbollah leader Hassan Nasrallah smiling benevolently next to texts extolling "the divine victory" (see Plate 9). This aesthetic, too, corresponds to mythic utopianism by claiming to offer a glimpse of the pride and future peace that redemptive self-sacrifice can offer.

The incapacity of elegiac humanism to respond effectively to the conditions of this war probably put an end to it as a viable alternative to mythic utopianism for the foreseeable future. It may well continue as a minor key discourse attuned to exploring self-responsibility and bridging differences among interlocutors of good faith, but by definition it lacks the energizing potential of righteous hatred. The war's end, however, did open the door to a third response. Within days of the cease-fire, ruins imagery festooned Lebanon's billboards. These images did not evoke a pristine past as elegiac humanism often does, nor did they seek to steel a here-and-now militant resistance as mythic utopianism does. Instead, they were part of a massive commercial recuperation of the 2006 war that dwarfed that which was deployed in the wake of the 2005 Independence Uprising (see Plates 8 and 10). These ads ignored the moral resonances of the war and looked to the practical future, tapping into the Lebanese determination to get on with life after armed conflicts.

According to the logic implicit in this ad campaign, the war was a boring interlude that had to be erased by renewed and somewhat frenetic investment and construction. The campaign played neatly into the paradigm of capitalistic "creative destruction" that was already sketched out in several of the novels and films treated in this study.[8] Stripped of the moral hand-wringing of elegiac humanism and of the eye-for-eye moral pretexting of mythic utopianism, this capitalist aesthetic is exceptionally supple, capable of turning loss to gain and humiliation into pride provided one is not too fussy about memory.

The aesthetic of elegiac humanism may well have run its course over the thirty-year period culminating in the Independence Uprising. It may also be the case that mythic utopianism will become an anachronism, although this is much less likely given its obvious value during wartime and its utility in promoting sectarian interests. The third aesthetic briefly sketched in this conclusion—the marriage of pragmatic economic interests and postmodern iconography—might well become the dominant aesthetic, and not only in Lebanon. Even so, the generation of Lebanese novelists, filmmakers, and producers of popular culture from 1975 to 2005 has shown courage, artistic ingenuity, and indomitable will in defending human dignity under dire conditions. Today's artists positioned in the thin space between modern sectarian and capitalist aesthetics will find their example inspiring in the search for new ways to stand by the ruins and remember civil society.

APPENDIX

A Selected Bibliography
of Lebanese War Novels

Abu al-Faraj, Ghalib Hamza. *Wa-Ihtaraqat Bayrut* (And Beirut Burned). Beirut: Dar al-Afaq al-Jadida, 1983.

Al-Ashqar, Yusuf Habshi. *Al-Mizallah wa-l-Malik wa-Hajis al-Mawt* (The Umbrella, the King, and the Obsession with Death). Beirut: Dar al-Nahar, 1980.

——. *Al-Zill wa-l-Sada* (Shadows and Echoes). Beirut: Dar al-Nahar, 1989.

Barakat, Halim. *Al-Rahil bayna al-Sahm wa-l-Watar* (The Departure between the Arrow and the Bow). Beirut: al-Mu'assasat al-'Arabiyyh li-l-Dirasat, 1979.

Barakat, Hoda. *Hajar al-Dahik*. London: Riad al-Rayyes, 1990. Translated by Sophie Bennett as *The Stone of Laughter*. London: Garnet, 1994.

——. *Ahl al-Hawa*. Beirut: Dar al-Nahar, 1993. Translated by Marilyn Booth as *Disciples of Passion*. Syracuse, N.Y.: Syracuse University Press, 2005.

Barakat, Najwa. *Bas al-Awadim* (Bus of Decent People). Beirut: Dar al-Adab, 1996.

——. *Ya Salam*. Beirut: Dar al-Adab, 1999.

Al-Daif, Rashid. *Fusha Mustahdafa bayna al-Nu'as wa-l-Nawm*. Beirut: Mukhtarat, 1983. Translated by Nirvana Tanoukhi as *Passage to Dusk*. Austin: University of Texas Press, 2001.

———. *Ahl al-Zill* (People of Shadow). Beirut: Mukhtarat, 1987.

———. *Taqniyyat al-Bu's* (Techniques of Misery). Beirut: Mukhtarat, 1989.

———. *'Azizi al-Sayyid Kawabata*. Beirut: Mukhtarat, 1995. Translated by Paul Starkey as *Dear Mr Kawabata*. London: Quartet, 1999.

———. *Nahiyat al-Bara'a*. Beirut: al-Massar, 1997. Translated by Paula Haydar as *This Side of Innocence*. New York: Interlink, 2001.

Daoud, Hassan. *Binayat Mathilde*. Beirut: Dar al-Tanwir, 1983. Translated by Peter Theroux as *The House of Mathilde*. London: Granta, 1999.

———. *Makyaj Khafif li-Hadihi al-Laylah* (Light Makeup for Tonight). Beirut: Riad al-Rayyes, 2003.

Fattouh, Rafif. *Tafasil Saghirah* (Minor Details). Beirut: al-Mu'assasat al-'Arabiyya li-l-Dirassat, 1980.

Hamdan, Umaya. *Nuqtat al-Bikar* (The Compass Point). Beirut: Dar al-Ittihad, 1979.

———. *Al-Azraq al-Qadim m'a al-Rih* (The Blue That Comes with the Wind). Beirut: Dar al-Afaq al-Jadida, 1980.

Jaber, Rabi'. *Shay Aswad* (Black Tea). Beirut: Dar al-Adab, 1995.

———. *Ralf Rizq Allah* (Ralph Rizk-Allah). Beirut: Dar al-Adab, 1997.

Khoury, Elias. *Al-Jabal al-Saghir*. Beirut: Dar al-Adab, 1977. Translated by Maria Tabet as *The Little Mountain*. Manchester, U.K.: Carcanet Press, 1989.

———. *Abwab al-Madina*. Beirut: Dar Ibn Rushd, 1981. Translated by Paula Haydar as *Gates of the City*. Minneapolis: University of Minnesota Press, 1993.

———. *Al-Wujuh al-Bayda* (White Faces). Beirut: Dar Ibn Rushd, 1981.

———. *Mamlakat al-Ghuraba*. Beirut: Dar al-Adab, 1989. Translated by Paula Haydar as *The Kingdom of Strangers*. Fayetteville: University of Arkansas Press, 1996.

———. *Rihlat Ghandi al-Saghir*. Beirut: Dar al-Adab, 1989. Translated by Paula Haydar as *The Journey of Little Gandhi*. Minneapolis: University of Minnesota Press, 1994.

————. *Bab al-Shams*. Beirut: Dar al-Adab, 1998. Translated by Humphrey Davies as *Gate of the Sun*. London: Harvill Secker, 2005.

————. *Yalo*. Beirut: Dar al-Adab, 2002. Translated by Peter Theroux as *Yalo*. New York: Archipelago, 2008.

Nasrallah, Emily. *Tilka al-Dhikriyat* (Those Memories). Beirut: Mu'assasa Naufal, 1980.

————. *Al-Iqla' 'aks al-Zaman* (The Flight against Time). Beirut: Mu'assasa Naufal, 1981.

Samman, Ghada. *Bayrut 75*. Beirut: Dar al-Adab, 1975. Translated by Nancy N. Roberts as *Beirut 75*. Fayetteville: University of Arkansas Press, 1995.

————. *Kawabis Bayrut*. Beirut: Dar al-Adab, 1977. Translated by Nancy N. Roberts as *Beirut Nightmares*. London: Quartet Books, 1997.

Sawma, Adel. *Lubnaniyun fi al-Mansa*. Beirut: Dar al-Farabi, 1997.

Al-Shaykh, Hanan. *Hikaya Zahrah*. Beirut: privately published by author and Najah Tahir, 1980; Beirut: Dar al-Adab, 2004. Translated by Peter Ford as *The Story of Zahra*. London: Readers International, 1986.

————. *Barid Bayrut*. Cairo: Dar al-Hilal, 1992. Translated by Catherine Cobham as *Beirut Blues*. New York: Anchor Books, 1995.

Usayran, Layla. *Qalat al-Usta* (Usta's Citadel). Beirut: Dar al-Nahar, 1979.

————. *Jisr al-Hajar* (Stone Bridge). Beirut: Dar al-'Awda, 1982.

Yunis, Iman Humaydan. *Ba' Mithil Bayt . . . Mithil Bayrut*. Beirut: al-Massar, 1997. Translated by Max Weiss as *B as in Beirut*. London: Interlink, 2008.

NOTES

INTRODUCTION

1. Theodor Hanf stresses the vulnerability of a neutral Lebanon in the aftermath of the 1973 October War: "No foreign power was willing to defend the interests of the Lebanese state. They stood by and watched as Lebanon's barely armed neutrality was eroded, and some purposively contributed" (*Coexistence in Wartime Lebanon* [London: Centre of Lebanese Studies, 1993], 175).

2. Open war endured sporadically for fifteen years, dwarfing all other armed conflicts in modern Lebanese history. Richly funded from all points of the compass, it left 170,000 dead and injured out of a population of 3.5 million, and forced more than a million to flee their homes and often the country. It ruined the economy, infrastructure, and long-term confidence in the nation (see Fawwaz Traboulsi, *A History of Modern Lebanon* [London: Pluto Press, 2007], 238).

3. Stressing the secular nature of the conflict in the early 1970s, Hanf writes: "The remarkable feature was the absence of 'confessional' undertones. They were not conflicts between communities but between social and economic groups and interests" (*Coexistence in Wartime Lebanon*, 109).

4. Traboulsi, *A History of Modern Lebanon*, 231.

5. On the modernity of sectarianism, Eisenstadt writes that these groups appropriate space and time according to their respective utopian visions and that these are often "imbued with very strong eschatological components which place them at the end of history, with a message of messianic redemption often following an imminent catastrophe—an ontology which comes to full fruition in their specific 'enclave' culture"

(*Fundamentalism, Sectarianism, and Revolution* [Cambridge: Cambridge University Press, 1999], 90). See also Juan Cole, *Sacred Space and Holy War* (London: Tauris, 2002), 189–211; Lara Deeb, *An Enchanted Modern* (Princeton: Princeton University Press, 2006), 3–41; and Ussama Makdisi, *The Culture of Sectarianism* (Berkeley and Los Angeles: University of California Press, 2000), 1–14.

6. Hanf, *Coexistence in Wartime Lebanon*, 193.

7. Eisenstadt argues that the roots of modern fundamentalism may be traced to the nineteenth-century United States (*Fundamentalism, Sectarianism, and Revolution*, 82–83). Makdisi affirms that Lebanon's role as a hothouse of modern sectarianism goes back to the nineteenth century (*The Culture of Sectarianism*, 174). Sectarianism, as an element of modernity, is clearly as transnational and locally inflected as other elements of modernity.

8. Traboulsi, *A History of Modern Lebanon*, 233.

9. Hanf, *Coexistence in Wartime Lebanon*, 160.

10. Rashid al-Daif discusses the relationship between these three subgenres and Western antecedents in "al-Nitaj al-Riwa'i fi Lubnan: Tayyarat wa Ittijahat" (Novelistic Production in Lebanon: Currents and Trends), *Fusul* 16, no. 4 (Spring 1998): 167–72. See also Stefan G. Meyer's *The Experimental Arabic Novel* (Albany: State University of New York Press, 2001), 15–69. For the purposes of this introduction, the literary context may be extended to the realms of film and popular culture, which will receive fuller analyses in the relevant chapters.

11. For compendious introductions in English to commitment literature in Arabic, see Verena Klemm's "Different Notions of Commitment (*Iltizām*) and Committed Literature (*al-Adab al-Multazim*) in the Literary Circles of the Mashriq," *Arabic and Middle Eastern Literatures* 3 (2000): 51–62; and M. M. Badawi's "Commitment in Contemporary Arabic Literature," in *Critical Perspectives on Modern Arabic Literature*, ed. Issa J. Boullata (Boulder, Colo.: Three Continents Press, 1980), 23–44.

12. See especially Lewis 'Awwad's *al-Ishtirakiyya wa-l-Adab* (Socialism and Literature) (Beirut: Dar al-Adab, 1963), 8–10.

13. Klemm, "Different Notions," 57. See also Roger Allen's *The Arabic Novel* (Syracuse, N.Y.: Syracuse University Press, 1995), 57–60.

14. Ghassan Kanafani, *Fi-al-Adab al-Sihyuni* (On Zionist Literature) (Beirut: Munazzamat al-Tahrir al-Filistiniyya, Markaz al-Abhath, 1967), 146.

15. Ahmad Mohammad A'tiya, *al-Iltizam wa-l-Thawra fi-al-Adab al-*

'Arabiyya al-Haditha (Commitment and Revolution in Modern Arabic Literature) (Beirut: Dar al-'Awda, 1974), 9. For the role of literature in Zionist ideology, see Yael Zerubavel, *Recovered Roots* (Chicago: University of Chicago Press, 1995), 83. I offer a condensed history of Zionist commitment literature culled from English-language sources in "A Survival Aesthetic for Ongoing War," *Crisis and Memory*, ed. Ken Seigneurie (Wiesbaden: Reichert, 2003), 16–21.

16. A'tiya, *al-Iltizam wa-l-Thawra*, 7.

17. Elise Salem, *Constructing Lebanon: A Century of Literary Narratives* (Gainesville: University Press of Florida, 2003), 122.

18. Klemm, "Different Notions," 58.

19. Badawi, "Commitment in Contemporary Arabic Literature," 42; Barbara Harlow, *Resistance Literature* (New York: Methuen, 1987), 164.

20. Tawfiq Yusuf 'Awwad, *Tawahin Bayrut* (Beirut: Maktabat Lubnan, 1972), translated by Leslie McLoughlin as *Death in Beirut* (Boulder, Colo.: Three Continents Press, 1984); Ghada Samman. *Bayrut '75* (Beirut: Dar al-Adab, 1975), translated by Nancy N. Roberts as *Beirut '75* (Fayetteville: University of Arkansas Press, 1995).

21. I argue for the difference in paradigms between 1968 Paris and 1976 Beirut in "Ongoing War and Arab Humanism," *Geomodernisms*, ed. Laura Doyle and Laura Winkiel (Bloomington: Indiana University Press, 2005), 108–9.

22. Numerous studies of mythic or religious topoi in Arabic literature have appeared in recent years. See, in particular. *Myths, Historical Archetypes and Symbolic Figures in Arabic Literature*, ed. Angelika Neuwirth et al. (Beirut: Orient-Institut der DMG, 1999). See also Michelle Hartman's *Jesus, Joseph and Job: Reading Rescriptings of Religious Figures in Lebanese Women's Fiction* (Wiesbaden: Reichert, 2002); Maher Jarrar's "The Arabic Novel Carries Its Cross," in *Poetry's Voice-Society's Norms*, ed. Andreas Pflitsch and Barbara Winckler (Wiesbaden: Reichert, 2006), 61–92; Friedericke Pannewick's "Death and the Power of the Word," in Pflitsche and Winckler, 49–60; Pannewick's edited book *Martyrdom in Literature* (Wiesbaden: Reichert, 2004); and Sasson Somekh's "Biblical Echoes in Modern Arabic Literature," *Journal of Arabic Literature*, 26, no. 1–2 (1995): 186–200.

23. Neuwirth, *Myths, Historical Archetypes*, xv.

24. Zeina Maasri, *Off the Wall* (New York: Palgrave Macmillan, 2009). Prior to the publication of Maasri's book, she put together an exhibit entitled Signs of Conflict: Political Posters of Lebanon's Civil War

that displayed hundreds of war posters (Beirut, Ashkal Alwan, April 2008). See also Paula Schmitt's refreshing and insightful *Advertised to Death: Lebanese Poster Boys* (Beirut: Arab Printing Press, 2009). Noteworthy also is the exhibition entitled The "War" through Its Memorials: Photo Exhibition in Progress (Haret Hreik UMAM Documentation and Research Center, 12–29 June 2009).

25. Maasri, *Off the Wall*, 87

26. Ibid., 49.

27. Aziz al-Azmeh stresses the necessary disjunction between scriptural and real registers in *Islams and Modernities* (London: Verso, 1996): "The secret of fundamentalism resides in the absence of specification, in the very tokenism of the letter, in the parallelism but never in the identity of the scriptural and the real registers. The latter can therefore be the meaning of the former through the imputation of such meaning by the agency that has the power and authority to posit, consolidate, and enforce meaning. . . . Without the distinction between the registers which allows the powers that be to penetrate the script and infuse it with their power, fundamentalism becomes redundant, an idle chiliasm without a chance in this world" (156).

28. Maasri, *Off the Wall*, 61.

29. Neuwirth, *Myths, Historical Archetypes*, xiv.

30. Two fine books on the nexus among war, culture, and memory in Lebanon have appeared recently: Sune Haugbolle's *War and Memory in Lebanon* (Cambridge: Cambridge University Press, 2010); and Franck Mermier and Christophe Varin's edited volume, *Mémoires de Guerres au Liban (1975–1990)* (Paris: Sindbad, 2010).

31. Aaron Santesso, *A Careful Longing* (Newark: University of Delaware Press, 2006), 16.

32. David Kennedy, *Elegy* (London: Routledge, 2007), 20.

33. John J. Su, *Ethics and Nostalgia in the Contemporary Novel* (Cambridge: Cambridge University Press, 2005), 3.

34. See Christopher Woodward, *In Ruins* (New York: Vintage, 2001), respectively, 88, 51, 66, 89, 179.

35. Francesco Orlando, *Obsolete Objects in the Literary Imagination* (New Haven: Yale University Press, 2006), 7, emphasis in original.

36. Ibid., 15.

37. See "*nasīb*" in *The Encyclopaedia of Islam* (Leiden: Brill, 1993), 7: 978–83.

38. Jaroslav Stetkevych, *The Zephyrs of Najd: The Poetics of Nostal-*

gia in the Classical Arabic Nasīb (Chicago: University of Chicago Press, 1993), 26–27.

39. Ibid., 52.

40. Raymond Williams, *Marxism and Literature* (Oxford: Oxford University Press, 1977), 132. Williams distinguishes "structures of feeling" from "more formal concepts of 'world-view' or 'ideology'" by stressing that they are "meanings and values as they are actively lived and felt" and goes on to note that structures of feeling are "explicit and recognizable in specific kinds of art" (132, 135). These characteristics correspond closely to the ruins topos and the associated feelings of yearning discussed throughout this book.

41. Renate Jacobi, "Time and Reality in *Nasīb* and *Ghazal*," *Journal of Arabic Literature* 16 (1985): 15–16.

42. Several excellent studies have already explored the functionality of the ruins topos (see Stefan Sperl's *Mannerism in Arabic Poetry* [Cambridge: Cambridge University Press, 1989]; and Andras Hamori's *On the Art of Medieval Arabic Literature* [Princeton: Princeton University Press, 1974]).

43. ʿAza Hasan, *Shʿir al-Wuqūf ʿala al-Atlal min al-Jahiliya ila Nihayat al-Qarn al-Thalith* (Damascus: University of Damascus Press, 1968), 117–18.

44. Shukri Faysal, *Tatawwur al-Ghazal bayna al-Jahiliya wa-l-Islam*, 2nd ed. (Damascus: University of Damascus Press, 1964), 63.

45. It is important not to overstate or essentialize this difference. From Odysseus lashed to the mast to hear the Sirens' song but never to possess them to *Remembrance of Things Past*, longing and memory are not necessarily less, only differently, expressed in Western cultures. More fruitful Western correlates to the ruins topos than *ubi sunt* may include the ruins motif in Romantic poetry or the longing for earthly paradise described by Jean Delumeau in *Un histoire du paradis* (Paris: Arthème Fayard, 1992). Nevertheless, it is interesting to note that the few examples Woodward cites of longing in the "Arabic mode" are mostly from non-Western cultures such as the poem about the return of a Chinese soldier, in the first century B.C., to an abandoned home and his subsequent longing before the overgrown ruins (45). The exotic feel of Ezra Pound's loose translation from Li Po's Chinese in "The River Merchant's Wife: A Letter" arises from the deployment of a ruins topos relatively rare in modern Western literatures.

46. Stetkevych, *The Zephyrs of Najd*, 50. Hussein ʿAtwan's three-vol-

ume study tracing the fortunes of the ruins motif consistently notes its resilience despite criticism of it going back to the Abbasside period (750–1258) (*Muqaddimat al-Qasidat al-'Arabiyya*. 3 vols. [Cairo: Dar al-Ma'rifa bi-Misr, 1970]).

47. In trying to explain the longevity of the ruins topos and its associated structure of feeling, one might note that Islam also doubtless contributes to its appeal and longevity. The undisputed preeminence of the seventh-century Qur'an as the model of eloquence in Arabic means that history may be less apt to obscure archaic meanings in Arabic than in other languages. Moreover, 'Atwan and Stetkevych each note how the dispersal of Islam from central Arabia to Damascus and then to Baghdad and Andalusia established longing for Arabia as a topos in Arab-Muslim culture (see 'Atwan, *Muqaddimat al-Qasidat al-'Arabiyya fi-al-'Asr al-'Umawi*, 13–25; and Stetkevych, *The Zephyrs of Najd*, 50–102).

48. Enchantment, according to Sarah Cole, "refers to the tendency to see in violence some kind of transformative power," whereas the ruins topos evokes a contemplative regard for the past stopping well short of utopianism. Nor, however, does this topos correspond to Cole's notion of disenchantment, the idea that literature "must expose rather than elevate the violence of war" (Cole, "Enchantment, Disenchantment, War, Literature," *PMLA* 124, no. 5 [2009]: 1633, 1640).

49. Stetkevych's translation is slightly modified to eliminate reference to the Arabic dual form (*The Zephyrs of Najd*, 110).

50. Sinan Antoon, "Returning to the Wind: On Darwish's 'La Ta'tadhir 'amma Fa'alta,'" in *Mahmoud Darwish: Exile's Poet*, ed. Hala Khamis Nassar and Najat Rahman (Northampton, Mass.: Olive Branch Press, 2008), 216.

51. Hilary Kilpatrick, "Literary Creativity and the Cultural Heritage: The *Atlal* in Modern Arabic Fiction," in *Tradition, Modernity, and Postmodernity in Arabic Literature: Essays in Honor of Professor Issa F. Boullatta*, ed. Kamal Abdel-Malek and Wael Hallaq (Leiden: Brill, 2000), 42. To my knowledge, Kilpatrick was the first scholar to explore the ruins motif in the modern Arabic novel, although Elliot Colla did briefly note the relevance of the *nasib* to a film on the Lebanese civil war in "The Image of Loss: Jalal Toufic's Filmic Beirut," *Visual Anthropology* 10 (1998): 314. With respect to the broader question of the contemporary tendency to reassimilate traditional forms, Birget Embaló has identified *ghazal* motifs in the modern novel in "The City, Mythical Images and Their Deconstruction: The Image of Beirut in Contemporary Works of Arabic

Literature," in *Myths, Historical Archetypes and Symbolic Figures in Arabic Literature: Towards a New Hermeneutic Approach*, ed. Angelika Neuwirth, Birgit Embaló, Sebastian Günther, and Maher Jarrar (Stuttgart: Steiner, 1999), 583–603. Critics are thus beginning to see what Robin Ostle has aptly termed "the most important feature of Arabic literature of the past fifty years," the Arabic novel's "reassimilation of tradition"— a happy departure from the still-entrenched view that the Arabic novel is always and everywhere derivative of Western models ("Excellence in Modern Arabic Literature," paper presented at American University of Beirut, 23 March 2006).

52. Hanf writes: "The irresponsibility of the Lebanese political class prepared the ground for this disaster [of the civil war]." The Palestinian fedayeen themselves, according to Hanf, did little to make their presence less burdensome: "Lebanon was not the Palestinian organizations' country of choice—that was Jordan—but their bastion of last resort. They mercilessly exploited its weaknesses. For, in their view all Arab states were duty-bound to make every sacrifice for the Palestinian cause, a cause concerning all Arabs. The fact that Lebanon was the only country they could force to do so was no reason for them not to do so" (*Coexistence in Wartime Lebanon*, 177).

53. Svetlana Boym, *The Future of Nostalgia* (New York: Basic Books, 2001), xv.

54. Clifton R. Spargo, *The Ethics of Mourning* (Baltimore: John Hopkins University Press, 2004), 9.

55. Consider, for example, the problem of disciplinary definitions. The philosopher David E. Cooper equates humanism with the notion that the only world we can know is a human world, which makes humanists out of avowedly antihumanist poststructuralists who accept the human world hypothesis but who see humanism as a coercive ideology within that world (*The Measure of Things* [Oxford: Clarendon Press, 2002], 7). An anthropological perspective such as that of Tsvetan Todorov would stress that humans possess essential attributes such as the capacity for free action (*The Imperfect Garden* [Princeton: Princeton University Press, 2002], 30–31). Intellectual historians might respond that any essential definition of what humans are boils down to racism (see H. M. Bracken, "Essence, Accident, and Race," *Hermathena* 116 [Winter 1973]: 92–93). A trimmed-down humanism such as that of Frantz Fanon that avoids defining the human and simply asserts a moral priority on humanity as opposed to divine or parochial interests would be fine if

it did not beg the question of who defines what is moral (*The Wretched of the Earth* [London: Penguin Books, 1967], 198). Finally, a rigorously historical humanism defined as a "specific intellectual program" characteristic of the early European Renaissance downplays the troublesome sociological and moral accretions of the term, but by the same token sidesteps the question of human identity (Ernst Cassirer, Paul Oskar Kristeller, and John Herman Randall Jr., eds., *The Renaissance Philosophy of Man* [Chicago: Chicago University Press, 1948], 2–3).

56. In addition to Cooper, *The Measure of Things*, and Todorov, *The Imperfect Garden*, books that seek to clarify humanism include: Tony Davies, *Humanism* (London: Routledge, 1997), Jeff Noonan, *Critical Humanism and the Politics of Difference* (Montreal: McGill-Queen's University Press, 2003), Edward W. Said, *Humanism and Democratic Criticism* (New York: Columbia University Press, 2004), Paul Sheehan, *Modernism, Narrative and Humanism* (Cambridge: Cambridge University Press, 2002), Kate Soper, *Humanism and Anti-Humanism* (London: Hutchinson, 1986), and Stephane Toussaint, *Humanismes / Antihumanismes* (Paris: Belles Lettres, 2008).

57. Thus Michael Hardt and Antonio Negri chronicle a centuries-long struggle between an immanent human-centered modernity and a transcendent constituted power (*Empire* [Cambridge: Harvard University Press, 2000], 69–92); Stephen Toulmin identifies a problematic Cartesian program for philosophy that "swept aside the 'reasonable' uncertainties and hesitations of 16th-century skeptics, in favor of new, mathematical kinds of 'rational' certainty and proof. In this, it may . . . lead philosophy into a dead end" (*Cosmopolis* [Chicago: University of Chicago Press, 1992], 75); Max Horkheimer and Theodor Adorno's famous indictment of Enlightenment rationality sees it as a machine out of control such that "its own ideas of human rights then fare no better than the older universals" (*Dialectic of Enlightenment* [Stanford: Stanford University Press, 2002], 3); Cooper finds in Prometheus an apt symbol for a nineteenth-century philosophy "which seemingly denies the answerability of human thought and purpose to any independent measure which might prove to be their nemesis" (*The Measure of Things*, 52); Frantz Fanon underscores the paradox of simultaneously fetishizing and negating humanity: "When I search for Man in the technique and the style of Europe, I see only a succession of negations of man, and an avalanche of murders" (*The Wretched of the Earth*, 252).

58. Heidegger writes: "In defining the humanity of man humanism

not only does not ask about the relation of Being to the essence of man; because of its metaphysical origin humanism even impedes the question by neither recognizing nor understanding it" ("Letter on Humanism," in *Basic Writings* [New York: Harper-Collins, 1993], 226); Foucault claims: "For man did not exist . . . and the human sciences did not appear when, as a result of some pressing rationalism, some unresolved scientific problem, some practical concern, it was decided to include man . . . among the objects of science—among which it has perhaps not been proved even yet that it is absolutely possible to class him; they appeared when man constituted himself in Western culture as both that which must be conceived of and that which is to be known" (*The Order of Things* [London: Routledge, 2002], 76); Althusser writes: "The recourse to ethics so deeply inscribed in every humanist ideology may play the part of an imaginary treatment of real problems. Once known, these problems are posed in precise terms; they are organizational problems of the forms of economic life, political life and individual life" ("Marxism and Humanism," in *For Marx* [London: Verso, 1996], 247); Spivak identifies the object of French deconstructive criticism as: "the rationalist narratives of the knowing subject, full of a certain sort of benevolence towards others, wanting to welcome those others into his own—and I use the pronoun advisedly—into his own understanding of the word, so that they too can be liberated and begin to inhabit a world that is the best of all possible worlds" (*The Post-colonial Critic* [London: Routledge, 1990], 19).

59. This terminology is borrowed from William Spanos, who writes that "traditional humanism has been able to transcend the limitations of imperial power's overt use (its vulnerability to insurrection) by internalizing the systematics of coercion through knowledge production (the truth that is incumbent on ostensibly disinterested inquiry)" (*The Legacy of Edward W. Said* [Urbana: University of Illinois Press, 2009], 156).

60. See Said, *Humanism*; Todorov, *The Imperfect Garden*; Lorenzo Simpson, *The Unfinished Project* (London: Routledge, 2001); *Emmanuel Levinas, Humanism of the Other* (Urbana: University of Illinois Press, 2005); and Martin Halliwell and Andy Mousley, *Critical Humanisms* (Edinburgh: Edinburgh University Press, 2003).

61. Paul Sheehan, *Modernism, Narrative and Humanism* (Cambridge: Cambridge University Press, 2002), 6.

62. Toussaint points to the distinction between Renaissance *humanitas* and Enlightenment-era anthropological definitions of the human

with which most poststructuralists take issue: "La notion d'*humanitas* précède, et de loin, plus qu'elle ne l'anticipe, toute l'anthropologie occidentale. . . . L'histoire de l'*humanitas* humaniste d'une part, et l'histoire de l'humanité anthropologique d'autre part, ne coïncide jamais depuis la même origine." [The notion of *humanitas* precedes, and by far, more than it anticipates any Western anthropology. . . . From the beginning, the history of humanistic *humanitas* on the one hand and the history of anthropological humanity on the other never coincide] (*Humanismes / Antihumanismes*, 39–40).

63. Cooper, *The Measure of Things*, 28, emphasis in original.

64. Ibid., 38. The open-ended ontology of humanism appears most famously in Pico della Mirandola's fifteenth-century "Oration on the Dignity of Man," in which he presents a scene in which God says to Adam: "We have given you, O Adam, no visage proper to yourself, nor endowment properly your own, in order that whatever place, whatever form, whatever gifts you may, with premeditation, select, these same you may have and possess through your own judgement and decision. The nature of all other creatures is defined and restricted within laws which We have laid down; you, by contrast, impeded by no such restrictions, may, by your own free will, to whose custody We have assigned you, trace for yourself the lineaments of your own nature." See also Davies, *Humanism*, 93–104.

65. William J. Bouwsma, *The Waning of the Renaissance 1550–1640* (New Haven: Yale University Press, 2000), 22.

66. Louis Dupré, *Passage to Modernity* (New Haven: Yale University Press, 1993), 105. Nor does Dupré hesitate to declare the stakes in such a liberation, noting elsewhere that the "combustive mixture" of human creativity and nominalist theology sparked the "cultural explosion" of modernity itself (3). For the role of nominalism in humanist thought, see also Cooper, *The Measure of Things*, 24–32; and Toussaint, *Humanismes / Antihumanismes*, 155–57. To my knowledge, Hans Blumenberg was the first to trace the nominalist pedigree of modernity in *The Legitimacy of the Modern Age* (Cambridge: MIT Press, 1985), 145–79.

67. See, respectively, Cooper, *The Measure of Things*, 36–50; Anthony Grafton, "The New Science and the Traditions of Humanism," in *The Cambridge Companion to Renaissance Humanism*, ed. Jill Kraye (Cambridge: Cambridge University Press, 1996), 206; Bouwsma, *The Waning of the Renaissance*, 65; Charles Nauert, *Humanism and the Culture of Renaissance Europe* (Cambridge: Cambridge University Press, 2006),

17–20; J. R. Milton, "Delicate Learning: Erudition and the Enterprise of Philosophy," *Humanism and Early Modern Philosophy* (London: Routledge, 2000), 159–71; and James Hankins, "Humanism and the Origins of Modern Political Thought," in Kraye, *Cambridge Companion*, 129–31.

68. Most of the time, the non-European constituents of "Western" humanism are simply ignored even among otherwise trenchant critics who would not normally be prone to orientalist thinking. Thus William V. Spanos neglects a half century of scholarship in his approval of Heidegger's distinctively mid-twentieth-century identification of Western humanism with ancient Rome (*The Legacy of Edward W. Said*, 153–54).

69. Sylvain Gouguenheim, *Aristote au Mont Saint-Michel* (Paris: Seuil, 2008). See also the review by Roger Pol Droit, "Et si l'Europe ne devait pas ses savoirs à l'Islam ?" *Le Monde des Livres*, 3 April 2008, www.lemonde. fr/web/recherche_resultats/1,13–0,1–0,0.html. Thierry Leclère recounts the debate in "Polémique autour d'un essai sur les racines de l'Europe," 28 April 2008, www.telerama.fr/idees/polemique-autour-d-un-essai-sur-les-racines-de-l-europe,28265.php. See also Blaise Dufal, "Choc des civilisations et manipulations historique: Troubles dans la médiévistique," http://cvuh. free.fr/spip.php?article180; Max Lejbowicz, "Saint-Michel historiographe: Quelques aperçus sur le livre de Sylvain Gouguenheim"; and the text of a petition, "Prendre de vieilles lunes pour des étoiles nouvelles, ou comment refaire aujourd'hui l'histoire des savoirs," *La Revue internationale des livres et des idées* (4), http://revuedeslivres.net/index.php?idH=225.

70. Petrarch's denigration of an Arab role in the following letter to his physician in 1370 suggests a degree of willful denial: "I implore you to keep these Arabs from giving me advice about my personal condition. Let them stay in exile. I hate the whole lot. I know that the Greeks were once most ingenious and eloquent men. Many very excellent philosophers and poets; outstanding orators and mathematicians have come from Greece. That part of the world has brought forth princes of medicine. You know what kind of physicians the Arabs are. I know what kind of poets they are. Nobody has such winning ways; nobody, also, is more tender and more lacking in vigor, and, to use the right words, meaner and more perverted. The minds of men are inclined to act differently; but, as you used to say, every man radiates his own peculiar mental disposition. To sum up: I will not be persuaded than any good can come from Arabia" (qtd. in Ernst Cassirer, Paul Oskar Kristeller, and John Herman Randall Jr., eds., *The Renaissance Philosophy of Man* [Chicago: Chicago University Press, 1948], 142).

71. Michael G. Carter traces the links between the Arab and Western humanist traditions along five different axes, summarizing the scholarship in support of each ("Humanism and the Language Sciences in Medieval Islam," in *Humanism, Culture, and Language in the Near East*, ed. Asma Afsaruddin and A. H. Mathias Zahniser [Winona Lake, Ind.: Eisenbrauns, 1997]).

72. Joel L. Kraemer, *Humanism in the Renaissance of Islam: The Cultural Revival during the Buyid Age* (Leiden: Brill, 1986), 10.

73. See Fedwa Malti-Douglas's *Structures of Avarice* (Leiden: Brill, 1985) for a sense of the semantic range of the term *adab* (7–16), but see also Doris Behrens-Abouseif's account of *adab* as a virtual equivalent of "preciosity" in *Beauty in Arabic Culture* (Princeton: Markus Weiner, 1999), 85–87.

74. George Makdisi, "Inquiry into the Origins of Humanism," in *Humanism, Culture, and Language in the Near East*, ed. Afsaruddin and Zahniser, 25. Makdisi argues for the relationship between *adab* and *ars dictaminus* in *The Rise of Humanism in Classical Islam and the Christian West with Special Reference to Scholasticism* (Edinburgh: Edinburgh University Press, 1990), 294–331.

75. See Mohammad Arkoun, *Contribution à l'étude de l'humanisme arabe au IVe/Xe siècle* (Paris: Vrin, 1970), 355–65; Marc Bergé, *Pour un humanisme vécu* (Damascus: Institut français de Damas, 1979), 174; and Makdisi, "Inquiry," 19–21. For more on the remarkable Buyid dynasty, see John Donohue's *The Buwayhid Dynasty in Iraq 334 H./945 to 403 H./1012* (Leiden: Brill, 2003).

76. Kraemer, *Humanism in the Renaissance of Islam*, 115.

77. María Rosa Menocal, *The Arabic Role in Medieval Literary History* (Philadelphia: University of Pennsylvania Press, 1987). See also Abdulla al-Dabbagh, "Modern Universalism and the Myth of Westerness," *Comparatist* 27 (2003); Alain de Libéra, *La philosophie médiévale* (Paris: Presses Universitaires de France, 1993), 485–87; and Makdisi, *The Rise of Humanism*, 352–54.

78. Mohammed Arkoun, *Pour une critique de la raison islamique* (Paris: Maisonneuve et Larose, 1984).

79. Arkoun, *Contribution*, 14, emphasis in the original.

80. If it is the case that, for example, the tenth-century Buyids were a pivotal force in the development of humanist thought, it is noteworthy that this was a Persian dynasty and that many scholars were non-Arab or non-Muslim such as the Christian Ibn ʿAdi cited above. Considered

along with Menocal's compelling argument for the pan-Mediterranean hybridity of Andalusian Spain and late-medieval Sicily in *The Arabic Role*, it is not difficult to see how de Libéra can argue for a one-thousand-year medieval Mediterranean cultural symbiosis that breaks down precisely at the dawn of the European Renaissance when *humanisti* such as Petrarch attack various "barbarian" elements in the effort to achieve cultural homogeneity (*La philosophie médiévale*, 485–87).

81. In addition to the explicitly modern priorities mentioned here, Charles Taylor argues that the symbolic levels of ritual and art in modernity may be coded as traditional and that a third level, that of embodied understanding or habitus, may be considered feudal. Thus observers who fail to see the modernity of sectarianism may be regarding it primarily from the standpoint of its traditional symbolism and feudal habitus ("Two Theories of Modernity" *Alternative Modernities*, ed. Dilip Parameshwar Gaonkar [Durham: Duke University Press, 2001], 188).

82. "Letter on Humanism," in *Basic Writings* (New York: HarperCollins, 1993), 225–26.

83. For discussion of the key concepts of "standing reserve" (*Bestand*) and "enframing" (*Gestell*), see Heidegger's "The Question Concerning Technology." in *The Question Concerning Technology and Other Essays* (New York: Harper Torchbooks, 1977), 17–20.

84. Jacques Derrida, "The Ends of Man," *Margins of Philosophy* (Chicago: University of Chicago Press, 1982), 121, emphasis in the original.

85. Martin Heidegger, "Letter on Humanism," 220.

86. Ibid., 221.

87. Ibid., 223.

88. Rex Gilliland writes: "Derrida's view [is] that we are constantly pulled back into the closure of metaphysics of presence, even when we restrict ourselves to a language of the beyond as minimal and indirect as negative theology—a language of impossibility, alterity, and undecidability. The appropriate response to the tireless undertow of metaphysics is not an attempted escape but to vigilantly problematize these issues over and over again by reinscribing one's relationship to the impossibility of presence" ("What Becomes of the Human after Humanism?: Heidegger and Derrida," *Proceedings of the North American Heidegger Conference*, http://home.southernct.edu/~gillilandr1/jobs/WhatBecomesoftheHumanafterHumanism5.htm).

89. Derrida, "The Ends of Man," 127.

90. Ibid., 133.

91. Jacques Derrida, *Specters of Marx* (New York: Routledge, 1994), 29.

92. Nor is this aesthetic hostile toward religion in the manner of traditional "secular" humanism. Indeed, as an alternative to sectarianism, it corresponds more closely to a theology that refuses circumscriptions of God such as that of Jean-Luc Marion, who crosses out the "o" of the signifier "God" to indicate the unthinkable nature of the deity: "G⊗d is expressed neither as a being nor as Being, nor by an essence. We have learned again to be amazed that metaphysics should have been able, starting with Descartes, to think G⊗d on the basis of causality (efficient moreover) and to impose *causa sui* upon him as a first name. We are in the process of discovering . . . that it is not self-evident that an *ousia* or that concept should be able to determine in what way this might be G⊗d. It remains to be glimpsed, if not with Heidegger, at least in reading him, and, if really necessary, against him, that G⊗d does not depend on [*relève de*] Being/being, and even that Being/being depends on distance. *Relève.* Neither abolition, nor continuation, but a resumption that surpasses and maintains. In other words, among the divine names, none exhausts G⊗d or offers the grasp or hold of a comprehension of him" (*God without Being* [Chicago: University of Chicago Press, 1991], 106).

93. The Lebanese novel and feature film are minor constellations in a Lebanese cultural firmament dominated by music, television, grand spectacles, and religion-oriented arts.

CHAPTER 1: ABSENCE AT THE HEART OF YEARNING

1. The claim that the distinguishing feature of realism is its reliance on a single horizon of meaning comes from Elizabeth Deeds Ermarth: "Fictional realism is an aesthetic form of consensus, its touchstone being the agreement between the various viewpoints made available by a text. To the extent that all points of view summoned by the text agree, to the extent that they converge upon the 'same' world, that text maintains the consensus of realism" (*Realism and Consensus in the English Novel: Time, Space, and Narrative* [Princeton: Princeton University Press, 1998], ix).

2. The prominent Lebanese intellectual Elias Khoury goes so far as to claim that the Lebanese novel as such was "born during the war," emerging "in the void left by the decay of a central government, the destruction of the middle-class, and of the Lebanese democratic system"

("al-Riwaya wa-l-riwa'i wa-l-harb" [The Novel, the Novelist and the War], "Mulhaq al-Thaqafi li-l-Nahar," 22 January 2006, 14.

3. The arguments in this chapter cap a decade's work on a clutch of Lebanese war and postwar novels. See also: "Anointing with Rubble: Ruins in the Lebanese War Novel," *Comparative Studies of South Asia, Africa and the Middle East* 28, no. 1 (2008): 50–60; "Ongoing War and Arab Humanism," in *Geomodernisms: Race, Modernism , Modernity,* ed. Laura Doyle and Laura Winkiel (Bloomington: Indiana University Press, 2005), 96–113; and "A Survival Aesthetic for Ongoing War," in *Crisis and Memory: The Representation of Space in Modern Levantine Narrative,* ed. Ken Seigneurie (Wiesbaden: Reichert, 2003), 11–32.

4. Franco Moretti's method of "distant reading" pushes the practice of extrapolating insights from a cursory reading of a wide sample to its logical conclusion in "Conjectures on World Literature," *New Left Review,* January–February 2000, 54–68. Douglas McGray describes Moretti's project to use a mainframe computer to "read" and confirm claims of vast literary-historical implications ("Hyper Texts: How One Professor Applies Quantitative Analysis to Classic Literature," *Wired,* December 2009, 78).

5. Hassan Daoud's *Binayat Mathilde* (Beirut: Dar al-Tanwir, 1983), translated by Peter Theroux as *The House of Mathilde* (London: Granta, 1999); Hoda Barakat's *Hajar al-Dahik* (London: Riad al-Rayyes, 1990), translated by Sophie Bennett as *The Stone of Laughter* (London: Garnet, 1994); Rashid al-Daif's *'Azizi al-Sayyid Kawabata* (Beirut: Mukhtarat, 1995), translated by Paul Starkey as *Dear Mr Kawabata* (London: Quartet, 1999); Najwa Barakat's 1999 *Ya Salam* (Beirut: Dar al-Adab, 1999), untranslated (Good Heavens); and Rabi' Jaber's *Berytus: Madina taht al-Ard* (Beirut: Dar al-Markaz al-Thaqafi al-'Arabi and Dar al-Adab, 2005), untranslated (Berytus: City Underground).

6. I do not broach the question of what constitutes the fraught category of "Lebanese" literature. For my purposes, I am interested in the novels written by those who have been acculturated to contemporary Lebanese Arab society by education and long experience in the country. Elise Salem discusses the problem of defining "Lebanese" literature in *Constructing Lebanon: A Century of Literary Narratives* (Gainesville: University Press of Florida, 2003).

7. As this book seeks to make a sliver of Arabic literature more accessible to a wider audience, all citations are to the English translation when available unless otherwise noted. Translations of *Ya Salam* (Good

Heavens) and *Berytus: Madina taht al-Ard* (Berytus: City Underground) are my own. A selected bibliography of Lebanese Arabic novels about the war and postwar along with available English translations is contained in the appendix.

8. Hassan Daoud, interview by the author, Beirut, 13 July 2010. See also my "The Flickering Light of Literature: 8–18 February 2000," *Profession 2000* (New York: Modern Language Association, 2000): 46–53.

9. Daoud interview. See also John Donohue, S.J. and Leslie Tramontini, eds., *Crosshatching in Global Culture: A Dictionary of Modern Arab Writers: An Updated English Version of R.B. Campbell's "Contemporary Writers"* (Beirut: Orient Institute, 2004), 303; and "Muthaqafun Lubnaniyyun Yu'ayyidun Haydar Haydar: Isti'mal al-Din Mu'shshir Inhitat," *al-Nahar*, 17 May 2000.

10. In a previous study, I attempted to understand these layered, almost subjectless conflicts through the lens of represented social spaces (see "The Everyday World of War in Hassan Daoud's House of Mathilde," in *Crisis and Memory: The Representation of Space in Modern Levantine Narrative*, ed. Ken Seigneurie [Wiesbaden: Reichert, 2003], 101–14). For a structuralist analysis of space in the novels treated in this chapter as well as numerous others, see Wafa' Abdel-Nour, "al-Makan fi-al-Riwayat al-Lubnaniyya, 1980–2000" (Place in the Lebanese Novel, 1980–2000) (Ph.D. diss., Université Saint-Joseph, Beirut, 2010).

11. Hassan Daoud, *The House of Mathilde*, trans. Peter Theroux (London: Granta, 1999), 3–4; hereafter cited parenthetically.

12. The fact that observations are products of the narrator's interpretation is revealed more clearly in the last sentence of the Arabic, which translates literally (and less elegantly) as: "Not only the steps and railing, but I think [a'taqud] the small, front balconies . . ." (Daoud, *Mathilde*, 11 [Arabic]).

13. "*Qifa Nabki*" is also the title of a popular blog on Lebanese politics, underscoring the transformation of the topos to sociopolitical purposes—and ironically revealing the blogger's attitude toward Lebanese politics (http://qifanabki.com/).

14. Hoda Barakat, telephone interview by the author, 17 July 2010. See also Donohue and Tramontini, eds., *Crosshatching*, 218–19; and Youssef Rakha, "Hoda Barakat: Starting Over," *al-Ahram Weekly*, 457, 25 November–1 December 1999.

15. Numerous memorials, such as the statue in Martyrs' Square, are themselves damaged and essentially ruins in addition to being art. Architecture and monumental sculpture are privileged means of coding traumatic memory in Lebanon as elsewhere. On the erasure of architectural and monumental records, see Miriam Cooke, "Beirut Reborn: The Political Aesthetics of Auto-Destruction," *Yale Journal of Criticism* 15, no. 2 (2002): 393–424; and Saree Makdisi, "Laying Claim to Beirut: Urban Narrative and Spatial Identity in the Age of Solidère," *Critical Inquiry* 23, no. 3 (Spring 1997): 661–705. For a discussion of the broader problem of postwar memory, see Sune Haugbolle, "Public and Private Memory of the Lebanese Civil War," *Comparative Studies of South Asia, Africa and the Middle East* 25, no. 1 (2005): 191–203.

16. Hoda Barakat, *The Stone of Laughter,* trans. Sophie Bennett as *The Stone of Laughter* (London: Garnet, 1994), 16–21; hereafter cited parenthetically.

17. For a broader view of the representation of masculinity in Arabic fiction, see Samira Aghacy's *Masculine Identity in the Fiction of the Arab East since 1967* (Syracuse, N.Y.: Syracuse University Press, 2009).

18. The question of Khalil's homosexuality according to this reading is a red herring. The important question is whether he can forge a masculine gender identity, gay or straight, that is not complicit with atrocity. By this light, allusions to his feminization simply clue his failure to reach manhood and have little to do with the question of whether he is gay.

19. Rashid al-Daif, interview by the author, Beirut, 14 July 2010. See also Donohue and Tramontini , eds., *Crosshatching;* and Youssef Rakha, "Rashid al-Daif: Writing to Yasunari," *al-Ahram Weekly,* 770, 24–30 November 2005.

20. Portions of this section of the chapter are drawn from my article "The Importance of Being Kawabata: The Narratee in Today's Literature of Commitment," *JNT: Journal of Narrative Theory* 34, no. 1 (Winter 2004): 54–73.

21. Al-Daif, *Dear Mr Kawabata,* trans. Paul Starkey (London: Quartet, 1999), 81; hereafter cited parenthetically.

22. Italics in English translation. The Arabic original most often has the italicized passages in parentheses.

23. Najwa Barakat, interview by the author, Beirut, 5 July 2010. See also Hasan al-Zayn, "Hiwar Najwa Barakat ʿan Riwayatiha al-Jadid *Ya Salam,*" *al-Nahar,* 20 February 1999; and Marie al-Qusayfi, "*Ya Salam* li-

Najwa Barakat: Shukhus Ma baʿd al-Harb fi-al-Qatl wa al-Siyada" (Najwa Barakat's *Ya Salam*: Postwar Characters in Killing and Sovereignty), *al-Nahar* (Beirut), 21 April 1999. *al-Nahar* 24. Najwa Barakat, *Ya Salam* (Beirut: Dar al-Adab, 1999), 171; hereafter cited parenthetically.

24. These novels are part of what might profitably be conceived of as a subgenre of modern Promethean limit-texts.

25. On the significance of names in this novel, see Marie al-Qusayfi's "*Ya Salam* li-Najwa Barakat," *al-Nahar*. This article also deals with the notions of comeuppance and cleansing violence.

26. N. Barakat interview.

27. Ibid.

28. In discussing her work, Barakat clearly distinguishes Loris's murders from the crimes of other characters (ibid.). See also Hassan al-Zayn's "Hiwar Najwa Barakat ʿan Riwayatiha al-Jadid *Ya Salam*" (Discussion with Najwa Barakat on Her New Novel *Ya Salam*), *al-Nahar* (Beirut), 20 February 1999.

29. Rabiʿ Jaber, *Taqrir Milis* (The Mehlis Report) (Beirut: Dar al-Markaz al-Thaqafi al-ʿArabi, 2005).

30. Abdu Wazen, *Riwayat al-Harb al-Lubnaniyya: Madkhal wa Namadij* (The Novel of the Lebanese War: Introduction and Models) (Dubai: Dar al-Sada, 2009), 115.

31. General biographical information in this paragraph is drawn from a phone conversation with Rabiʿ Jaber, 14 July 2010, and information provided by Samuel Shimon, editor of *Beirut 39: New Writing from the Arab World* (London: Bloomsbury), 2010.

32. See, for example, Rachel Falconer, *Hell in Contemporary Literature: Western Descent Narratives since 1945* (Edinburgh: Edinburgh University Press, 2009).

33. The Arabic *ṣayyād* could mean "hunter" or "fisher." I choose to translate it as "hunter" since it is specifically mentioned that "nobody fishes" in Berytus (61), and, moreover, the term "hunter" resonates more accurately with the function of *ṣāda*, to "hunt" those who stray too close to any of the five gates of Berytus.

34. Rabiʿ Jaber, *Berytus: Madina taht al-Ard* (Beirut: Dar al-Markaz al-Thaqafi al-ʿArabi and Dar al-Adab, 2005), 12; hereafter cited parenthetically.

35. I am taking the liberty of translating *ḥamām* as "dove," although it could just as easily be "pigeon." For that matter, the biological difference between doves and pigeons is nugatory as both belong to the same family of Columbidae.

CHAPTER 2: "SPEAK, RUINS!"

1. The summary of pre-1975 Lebanese film is indebted to: Ibrahim al-ʿAris, *al-Sura al-Multabisa, al-Sinama fi Lubnan: Mubdiʿuha wa Aflamuha* (The Ambiguous Image: Cinema in Lebanon: Its Achievements and Its Films) (Beirut: Dar al-Nahda al-ʿArabiyya, 2010); Viola Shafik, *Arab Cinema* (Cairo: American University Press, 1998); Hady Zaccak, *Le cinéma libanais* (Beyrouth: Dar al-Mashriq, 1997); Lina Khatib, *Lebanese Cinema* (London: Tauris, 2008); and interviews with Aimée Boulos and Reine Mitry of the "Fondation Liban Cinéma" at Saint Joseph University (March 2007), and with Zhafer Henri ʿAzar of the "Centre National Ciné-Tévé" at the Lebanese Ministry of Culture (May 2007).

2. The question of what constitutes a national film is variously and inadequately addressed by citing the source of production, the language used in the film, the directors' nationality or that of the principal actors or crew members, the site of shooting, or the studio location. For my purposes, a Lebanese film is one at least coproduced in Lebanon. Additionally, I have tried to limit the object of my study to feature films directed by Lebanese citizens who have spent a good deal of time in Lebanon. I have not been concerned about the original language of the film although all except *Hors la vie* were originally made primarily in Arabic.

3. Fawwaz Traboulsi analyzes the political subtexts of the work of Fayrouz and ʿAssi and Mansour Rahbani in *Fayruz wa-l-Rahabina* (Beirut: Riad al-Rayyes, 2006).

4. Christopher Stone discusses how the Rahbani vision of *turāth* (heritage) was itself a construction designed to impose unity on Lebanon's cultural diversity ("Ziyad Rahbani's 'Novelization' of Lebanese Musical Theater or the Paradox of Parody," *Middle Eastern Literatures* 8, no. 2 (July 2005): 151–70).

5. Viola Shafik makes the case for the refracted images of social tensions in Arab melodrama, arguing: "Notwithstanding all the trivial commercialism that might have governed the genre, it was just like realism a vessel for social dissent, or in other words, it represented a different strategy for dealing with the same ideological tensions and, in turn reflected the very same ambiguities, last not least towards women" ("Women, National Liberation and Melodrama in Arab Cinema," *al-Raida* 16, no. 86–87 (1999): 13).

6. See Zaccak, *Le cinéma libanais*, 47–54.

7. Zaccak deems them "sans valeur, mettant en scène des histoires banales, des personnages préfabriqués et des situations artificielles, dont le but primordial est de réaliser des bénéfices" (of no value, highlighting banal stories, prefab characters, and artificial situations whose primary aim was to turn a profit) (*Le cinéma libanais*, 103).

8. Muhammad Swayd, *al-Sinama al-Mu'ajala: Aflam al-Harb al-Ahliyya al-Lubnaniyya* (Beirut: Mu'assasat al-Abhath al-'Arabiyya, 1986), 70.

9. Principal sources for this paragraph include interviews with Burhan 'Alawiyya (Beirut, 12 February 2007), Joana HadjiThomas (20 July 2010), Jean Chamoun (21 July 2010), and Assad Fouladkar (26 July 2010). See also Zhafer Henri 'Azar, *Nazra 'ala al-Sinama al-'Alamiyya al-Mu'asira* (Beirut: al-Mu'assasa li-l-Dirasat wa-l-Nashr, 1987); 'Adnan Madanat, *Tahawwulat al-Sinama al-'Arabiyya al-Mu'asira* (Damascus: Dar Kana'an, 2004); Swayd, *al-Sinama al-Mu'ajala*; and Zaccak, *Le cinéma libanais*.

10. The penury suffered by Lebanese filmmakers is well known. See Khatib's *Lebanese Cinema*, 36–44, for the problem of funding Lebanese films; and Nana Asfour's "The Politics of Arab Cinema" for a more general discussion of Arab cinema and its political and economic woes (*Cinéaste* 26 [2000]: 46).

11. Burhan 'Alawiyya, interview by the author, Beirut, 12 February 2007.

12. 'Azar, *Nazra 'ala al-Sinama al-'Alamiyya al-Mu'asira*, 47.

13. Khatib, *Lebanese Cinema*, 34–36; Zaccak, "Regard," 189–90.

14. Swayd provides the most thorough bibliography of Lebanese war films. Unfortunately, his book was published in 1982. For more recent titles, see Khatib's filmography in *Lebanese Cinema*, 207–8.

15. "Al-'Adas al-'Arabiyya" (The Arabic Lens), *al-Jazeera International*, 1 May 2006, http://www.aljazeera.net.NR/exeres/AB9C8751–98B8–4A75–8CF7–A861A4DE537A.HTM.

16. 'Alawiyya interview. See also Kamel Jaber, "Burhan 'Alawiyya: Kayfa Nashfa min Zaman al-Harb?" (Burhan 'Alawiyya: How to Heal from the War Era?), *al-Akhbar*, 29 July 2009; and Hovig Habshian, "Hayat al-Mukhrij Ahamm min al-Sinama" (The Director's Life Is More Important Than the Cinema), *al-Nahar*, 12 May 2007.

17. 'Azar, *Nazra 'ala al-Sinama*, 52.

18. This information is gleaned from: Ibrahim al-'Aris, *al-Hulm al-*

Mu'allaq: Sinama Marun Baghdadi (The Suspended Dream: The Cinema of Maroun Baghdadi) (Beirut: Dar al-Nahar, 1994); and Rima al-Mismar, "Marun Baghdadi fi Dikra Rahilihi al-Khamisat Ashra" (Maroun Baghdadi: In Commemoration of the Fifteenth Anniversary of his Death), *al-Mustaqbal*, 19 February 2008.

19. It is instructive, by comparison, to consider Rikke Schubart's analysis of the theme of acceleration in the Hollywood action film. One could do worse than to consider driving through the ruins and acceleration as analogous attempts to convey parallel sociopsychological contexts ("Passion and Acceleration: Genetic Change in the Action Film," in *Violence and American Cinema*, ed. David Slocum [New York: Routledge, 2001], 192–207).

20. Hippolyte Girardot's acting in this sequence is particularly convincing. Ibrahim al-'Aris notes that during production of the film, Baghdadi would ostracize Girardot on the set as a way of permitting the actor to better experience the role (*Al-Hulm al-Mu'allaq: Sinama Marun Baghdadi* [Beirut: Dar al-Nahar, 1994], 112–13).

21. 'Aris, *al-Hulm al-Mu'allaq*, 104.

22. Joana Hadji Thomas, telephone interview by the author, 20 July 2010. See also George Kaydi, "*al-Bayt al-Zahr* li-Khalil wa Juanna Jorayge Isti'ara li-l-Harb wa-l-Watan wa-l-Dakira" (*The Pink House* of Khalil and Joanna Joreige: A Metaphor for War, Nation and Memory), *al-Nahar*, 7 September 1998.

23. The debate is worth citing in some detail. Miriam Cooke's critique is directed at Solidère's Saifi Village project: "The Master Plan calls Saifi an 'urban village' and although construction is clearly new, the Plan vaunts the 'large number of existing buildings that have been retained.' The buildings in this formerly working class area resemble their antecedents. But not quite. And it is this 'not quite' that is so important because it serves to cloud the memory. The slick lines and surfaces of housing blocks targeting the wealthy middle classes cannot harbor the unpredictable collective memories that lurked in the thick green of the weed-choked downtown ruins." ("Beirut Reborn: The Political Aesthetics of Auto-Destruction," *Yale Journal of Criticism* 15, no. 2 [2002]: 409). Cooke argues that a Solidère-sponsored publication, *Beirut Reborn: The Restoration and Development of the Central District* by Gavin Angus and Ramez Maluf (London: Academy Editions, 1996), puffed the project at the expense of historical memory. One of the book's coauthors, Ramez Maluf, responded to this claim to me in a personal e-mail that

he has approved for publication: "There was a lot of romanticizing and nostalgia about the pre-war downtown, most of it uninformed. To those of us who lived in Beirut before the war and knew the area well, that part of the city had its appeal of course. But by the early 1970s it was also an area you wanted to avoid going through or visiting. . . . The view to the sea was totally blocked. One major culprit was the Rivoli building that was built illegally and against demonstrations by Beirut residents. Later, when Solidère demolished it, some criticized the demolition of a Beirut 'icon.' . . . A lot of people . . . bemoaned the loss of the traditional downtown with all of its quaint neighborhoods and accused Solidère of creating too beautiful a place beyond the reach of the average Lebanese. Well, maybe. But this is the problem of capitalism, not of urban planning. . . . A newly rebuilt area, with elegant sidewalks, parks, archaeological gardens, nice restaurants, etc. is bound to be expensive. The other option, advocated in all seriousness by some journalists who reviewed the book, was to make downtown Beirut look like the rest of the areas around it, I assume with narrow sidewalks, no green space, uneven streets. . . . I want a beautiful city as my capital. Let the other neighborhoods emulate the downtown, not the other way around" ("Re: Cooke on 'Beirut Reborn,'" e-mail to Ken Seigneurie, 4 May 2007).

24. Among the numerous publications devoted to the Lebanese postwar, the special issue of *Parachute*, edited by Chantal Pontbriand, 108 (2002); and *Tamass: Contemporary Arab Representations*, dir. Catherine David (Barcelona: Fundació Antoni Tàpies, 2002) are particularly insightful for their discussion of how the postwar intersects with artistic practice. On the topic of urbanism, consider also Peter G. Rowe and Hashim Sarkis's *Projecting Beirut: Episodes in the Construction and Reconstruction of a Modern City* (Munich: Prestel, 1998); and the special issue of *Autrement: Beyrouth, la brûlure des rêves*, ed. Jade Tabet, 127 (2001).

25. See Madanat, *Tahawwulat al-Sinama*, 201.

26. Joseph Schumpeter defines "creative destruction": "The opening up of new markets, foreign or domestic, and the organizational development from the craft shop and factory to such concerns as U.S. Steel illustrate the same process of industrial mutation—if I may use that biological term—that incessantly revolutionizes the economic structure *from within*, incessantly destroying the old one, incessantly creating a new one. This process of Creative Destruction is the essential fact about capitalism. It is what capitalism consists in and what every capitalist

concern has got to live in" (*Capitalism, Socialism and Democracy* [1942] [New York: Harper, 1975], 82). For planned demolition of sections of Beirut during the war, see Saree Makdisi's "Laying Claim to Beirut: Urban Narrative and Spatial Identity in the Age of Solidère," *Critical Inquiry* 23 (Spring 1997): 667–68.

27. Jean Chamoun, interview by the author, Beirut, 21 July 2010. See also "al-ʿAdas al-ʿArabiyya" (The Arabic Lens), al-Jazeera International, 21 April 2006, www.aljazeera.net.

28. For a discussion of the "standing reserve" (*Bestand*), see Heidegger's "The Question Concerning Technology," in *The Question Concerning Technology and Other Essays* (New York: Harper Torchbooks, 1977), 17–20.

29. Madanat, *Tahawwulat al-Sinama*, 207–8.

30. Five years after the release of this film, "The Truth" became the most powerful slogan of the Lebanese *Intifāḍat al-Istiqlāl* movement, with hundreds of thousands demanding to know the facts around the dozens of hushed-up political assassinations as well as the fates of the seventeen thousand still missing from the war.

31. Assad Fouladkar, telephone interview by the author, 30 July 2010. See also Rania al-Rafaʿi, "Asad Fuladkar ʿan Filmihi *Lamma Ḥikyit Maryam*" (Assad Fouladkar on His Film *When Maryam Spoke*), al-Nahar, 16 December 2002. Fouladkar notes that while filming *When Maryam Spoke*, he saw other films containing similar plot lines including Dariush Mehriui's 1998 Iranian feature film *Leila*.

32. Hamid Naficy, *An Accented Cinema* (Princeton: Princeton University Press, 2001), 103.

33. Ibid.,105.

34. For a feminist study that compares the film *Take Care of Zuzu* to the popular American film *Pretty Woman*, see Dima Dabbous-Sensenig, "Who Is the Prettiest One of All?: Hollywood Cinema, Egyptian Cinema, and the Recycling of Fairy Tales: A Structural Feminist Analysis," *al -Raida* 16, no. 86–87 (1999): 40–47.

CHAPTER 3: ELEGIAC HUMANISM AND POPULAR POLITICS

1. This chapter expands and reinflects the argument I made in "The Wrench and the Ratchet: Cultural Mediation in a Contemporary Liberation Struggle," *Public Culture*, 21, no. 2 (2009): 377–402. I depart from

IJMES norms in this chapter by fully transliterating the titles of Lebanese popular songs since otherwise the dialectical renderings might lead to confusion.

2. To frame the contemporary conflict between Lebanon and Syria as a "colonial struggle" may be counterintuitive to those who find the concept difficult to apply to neighboring Arab countries sharing deep cultural affinities. From this standpoint, an independent Lebanon implies a further fragmentation of an already splintered Arab world as well as the creation of a de facto outpost of Western influence in the Arab world, an antechamber to Israel where the Zionist entity could plunder water, dump its industrial wastes, and expel its surplus or troublesome Palestinian population. Such a view is no more sinister than the historical record supports. Yet the problem with this scenario is its thralldom to empirically discredited ideologies and its consequent blindness to facts. To complain about a "fragmented" Arab world is to accept one vision of Pan Arabism or Pan Islamism as normative. To think of a free Lebanon as a pawn of the West is to ignore the current reality and twentieth-century history of this feisty nation. On the other hand, whether one defines colonialism as the exercise of political, economic, and military control over a dependency, or as the implantation of settlers, or as the ideological homologies that buttress dominance of one country over another, the term plausibly describes the role Syria played in Lebanon from 1976 to 2005. Thus, in keeping with this preference for observation of phenomena that actually occur and in the conviction that the highest stakes in colonial struggles are usually local, this essay leaves to others the task of arguing that the Lebanese movement to throw off twenty-nine years of Syrian tutelage was a proxy struggle in a greater global game. A representative sample of this camp would include Charles Ayoub's writings in the Beirut daily *al-Diyar* since February 2005; Alain Gresh, "Offensive concertée contre le régime syrien," *Le Monde Diplomatique* (Paris), December 2005, 12; Charles Glass, "An Assassin's Land," *London Review of Books*, 4 August 2005, 15–18; the late Joseph Samaha's writings in the Beirut daily *al-Safir* and *al-Akhbar* since 2005; and Trish Schuh, "Faking the Case against Syria," *Counterpunch*, 18 November 2005.

3. The term "pious modern" is borrowed from Lara Deeb, *An Enchanted Modern: Gender and Public Piety in Shi'i Lebanon* (Princeton: Princeton University Press, 2006), 30.

4. Numerous recent books make note of exclusionary nativism in

the Middle East. Walter Armbrust shows how Egyptian films strive to construct a normative *ibn al-balad* (Egyptian salt-of-the-earth) figure in *Mass Culture and Modernism in Egypt* (Cambridge: Cambridge University Press, 1996), 204–20. Lila Abu-Lughod extends and develops the analysis of the *ibn al-balad* figure to television serials in *Dramas of Nationhood: The Politics of Television in Egypt* (Cairo: American University in Cairo Press, 2005), 135–61. Joseph A. Massad shows how Jordanian authorities mobilize culture to exalt "Bedouin life" over alternatives in *Colonial Effects: The Making of National Identity* (New York: Columbia University Press, 2001), 250–58. Lisa Wedeen shows how popular imagery ensconces Syrian identity in a patriarchal model with Hafez al-Asad at its head in *Ambiguities of Domination: Politics, Rhetoric, and Symbols in Contemporary Syria* (Chicago: University of Chicago Press, 1999), 32–66. Yael Zerubavel traces the discursive indigenization of the European Jewish settler in Palestine in *Recovered Roots: Collective Memory and the Making of Israeli National Tradition* (Chicago: University of Chicago Press, 1995).

5. Some of work on Hezbollah would include: Joseph Elie Alagha, *The Shifts in Hizbullah's Ideology: Religious Ideology, Political Ideology, and Political Program* (Leiden: Amsterdam University Press, 2006); Abdallah Balqaziz, *Hizbullah min al-Tahrir ila al-Rad': 1982–2006* (Hezbollah from liberation to deterrence: 1982–2006) (Beirut: Markaz Dirasat al-Wahda al-'Arabiyya, 2006); H. E. Chehabi, *Distant Relations: Iran and Lebanon in the Last 500 Years* (London: Center for Lebanese Studies/Tauris, 2006); Judith Palmer Harik, *Hezbollah: The Changing Face of Terrorism* (London: Tauris, 2005); Emile El-Hokayem "Hizballah and Syria: Outgrowing the Proxy Relationship," *Washington Quarterly* 30, no. 2 (Spring 2007): 35–52; Sabrina Mervin, ed., *Les Mondes chiites et l'Iran* (Paris: Karthala, 2007); Augustus Richard Norton, *Hezbollah: A Short History* (Princeton: Princeton University Press, 2007); Naim Qassem, *Hizbullah: The Story from Within*, trans. Dalia Khalil (London: Saqi, 2005); Amal Saad-Ghorayeb, *Hizbu'llah: Politics and Religion* (London: Pluto Press, 2002); Waddah Sharara, *Dawlat Hizbullah: Lubnan Mujtama'an Islamiyyan* (The Hezbollah State: Lebanon as an Islamic Society) (Beirut: Dar al-Nahar, 2006). For a study of Hezbollah's cultural policy, see especially Deeb, *An Enchanted Modern*.

6. I do not want to overstate the case for the scholarly split between culture and politics when it comes to the Arab world. Nu-

merous trenchant studies on the intersection of Arab culture and politics do exist. See, for example: Rebecca L. Stein and Ted Swedenburg, eds., *Palestine, Israel, and the Politics of Popular Culture* (Durham: Duke University Press, 2005); Armbrust, *Mass Culture and Modernism in Egypt;* and Walter Armbrust, ed., *Mass Mediations: New Approaches to Popular Culture in the Middle East and beyond Authenticity and Distinction in Urban Syria* (Bloomington: Indiana University Press, 2004). Even so, the role of cultural mediation in Lebanon has received scant attention, and little of a scholarly nature has been written about Lebanon's 2005 Independence Uprising other than Rita Chemaly's *Le printemps 2005 au Liban: Entre mythes et réalités* (Paris: L'Harmattan, 2009). Journalistic studies of the movement include: *The Beirut Spring* (Beirut: Dar al-Nahar and Quantum Communications, 2005); *Middle East Report,* 236 (Fall 2005); *Le printemps inachevé,* special issue, *L'Orient-Express* (Beirut), December 2005; *L'Orient-Le Jour: L'espoir en lettres de sang* (Beirut), 13 February 2006; and Nicholas Blanford, *Killing Mr Beirut: The Assassination of Rafik Hariri and Its Impact on the Middle East,* (London: Tauris, 2006). For an account of the events within a historical context, see Michael Young's *The Ghosts of Martyrs Square* (New York: Simon and Schuster, 2010).

7. See, for example, the collection of annual speeches from 1996 through 2003 by Sélim Abou, Rector of Saint Joseph University during this period, *Freedoms: Cultural Roots of the Cedar Revolution* (Beirut: Presses de l'Université Saint-Joseph, 2005).

8. Key moves in the immediate run-up to 2005 included UN Security Council Resolution 1559 calling for the withdrawal of foreign troops from Lebanon along with the disarmament of all militias, and the Syrian regime's decision to extend the unpopular Lebanese President Emile Lahoud's mandate. The documentary film *Kuluna li-l-Watan* (We Are All the Nation), dir. Jean Aoun (Beirut: LBC1, 2006), contains interviews with numerous key figures involved in the 2004 decisions.

9. See Nathalie Khankan, "Reperceiving the Pre-Islamic *Nasīb,*" *Journal of Arabic Literature,* 33, no. 1 (2002): 1–23.

10. The exception was Hariri's hometown of Sidon, where angry demonstrators burned tires and dared to voice anti-Syrian comments soon after the assassination.

11. Leila Hatoum and Jessy Chahine, "Beirut Bombing Draws Sor-

row, Fear and Anger from the People," *Daily Star* (Beirut), 15 February 2005.

12. Ziad Majid, *'An Rabi' Bayrut wa-l-Dawla al-Naqisa* (On the Beirut Spring and the Incomplete State) (Beirut: Dar al-Nahar, 2006), 74–75. For a critical view of Hariri's role in the downtown Beirut reconstruction project, see Saree Makdisi, "Laying Claim to Beirut: Urban Narrative and Spatial Identity in the Age of Solidère," *Critical Inquiry* 23, no. 3 (Spring 1997): 661–705. For a positive view, see Samir Khalaf, *Heart of Beirut: Reclaiming the Bourj* (London: Saqi, 2006).

13. Although no member of the Syrian regime has been indicted for the Hariri assassination or any of the others that plagued the country from late 2004 through 2008, paragraph 9 of the report of the International Independent Investigation Commission established pursuant to United Nations Security Council resolution 1595 (2005), (Mehlis I), 19 October 2005, states: "Building on the findings of the Commission and Lebanese investigations to date and on the basis of the material and documentary evidence collected, and the leads pursued until now, there is converging evidence pointing at both Lebanese and Syrian involvement in this terrorist act. It is a well-known fact that Syrian Military Intelligence had a pervasive presence in Lebanon at the least until the withdrawal of the Syrian forces pursuant to resolution 1559. The former senior security officials of Lebanon were their appointees. Given the infiltration of Lebanese institutions and society by the Syrian and Lebanese intelligence services working in tandem, it would be difficult to envisage a scenario whereby such a complex assassination plot could have been carried out without their knowledge." Paragraph 123 of the same document states: "Conclusion: There is probable cause to believe that the decision to assassinate former Prime Minister, Rafiq Hariri, could not have been taken without the approval of top-ranked Syrian security official [*sic*] and could not have been further organized without the collusion of their counterparts in the Lebanese security services" (cited in Chibli Mallat, *March 2221: Lebanon's Cedar Revolution: An Essay on Non-Violence and Justice* [Beirut: Gubernare, 2007], 104, 106).

Since 2006 until this writing in early 2011, suspicion for the assassination has focused increasingly on Hezbollah. In response, the Party of God affirms that it has evidence that Israel committed the crime. As the issue of the indictment ripens, the concerned parties seem to be scrambling to come to some kind of consensus to ensure the stability of Lebanon (see "Hariri: Sau-

di-Syrian Deal Finalized but Requires Steps from Other Camp,"*Naharnet,*
6 December 2010, www.naharnet.com/domino/tn/NewsDesk.nsf/0/232E4
E8F1A322C0EC22578100066F9E8?OpenDocument).

14. The Labor Ministry reported in 2008 that "dozens" of Syrians
were registered with the labor authorities (see Rima Abushakra, "Syrian
Laborers Face Tough Times amid Lebanon's Political Divide," *Daily Star*
[Beirut], 17 March 2008, 4).

15. Walid Choucair, "Lebanon Loses Its Protective Umbrella," *Daily
Star* (Beirut), 19 February 2005, 1.

16. Michel de Certeau defines *bricolage* as "artisan-like inventiveness" in *The Practice of Everyday Life,* trans. Steven Rendall (Berkeley
and Los Angeles: University of California Press, 1984), xviii.

17. Mark R. Beissinger cites six characteristics of these peaceful revolutions, none of which corresponds more than partially to the Independence Uprising ("Structure and Example in Modular Political Phenomena: The Diffusion of Bulldozer/Rose/Orange/Tulip Revolutions,"
Perspectives on Politics 5, no. 2 [June 2007]: 261).

18. See Graeme P. Herd, "Russia and the 'Orange Revolution': Response, Rhetoric, Reality?" *Quarterly Journal* 2 (June 2005): 15. For
Georgian activists' "paranoia" about becoming unwitting tools of U.S.
foreign policy, see Paul Manning, "Rose-Colored Glasses?: Color Revolutions and Cartoon Chaos in Postsocialist Georgia," *Cultural Anthropology* 22, no. 2 (May 2007): 171–213.

19. The well-known singer and songwriter Ahmad Qabur recalls
composing with his lyricist "Say Allah, Stand up Yalla" ("Qūlū Allah,
Qūmū Yalla") on the night of the Hariri assassination. From an unpub-
lished interview with Zoha Abdulsater, Beirut, 25 September 2007.

20. In noting the mourning songs' direct mode of address, I do not
imply that they are in any way "pure" products. The hybrid form of
Arab pop militates against such essentialist associations (see Joseph A.
Massad, "Liberating Songs: Palestine Put to Music," in *Palestine, Israel,
and the Politics of Popular Culture,* ed. Rebecca L. Stein and Ted Swedenburg [Durham: Duke University Press, 2005], 179).

21. *Maʿqūl ẓulm al-bashar yiqtul fīnā l-ḥilim / Maʿqūl yibkī l-ḥajar
min qaswat ha l-ẓulum.*

22. *Lā mā khulṣit al-ḥikāya / Lā, lā mish haydī al-nihāya / Lā māʾnsīnā
bʿadak fīnā / Wa-bʿadū al-waṭan huwwi l-ghāyeh.*

23. *Innī astawdiʿu Allāha hadhā al-balad al-ḥabīb, Lubnān wa-*

sh'abahu al-ṭayyib. / Lā titkhallah 'annā / 'aynak 'ā waṭanā bil-ayyām 's-ṣa'beh

24. Jacques Rancière, "The Politics of Literature" *SubStance* 33, no. 1 (2004): 14.

25. Ibid., 20. Judging by the large quantity and breadth of graffiti, songs, chants, and homemade signs, I take these reading practices to be widespread throughout the movement, and not the brainchild of an intellectual advertising elite. It is almost certainly the case that the Uprising unfolded as both a grassroots upheaval and as a catch-as-catch-can effort on the part of political elites to channel it. This is not to deny that movement leaders such as Samir Kassir worked with politicians and publicity experts such as representatives from Saatchi & Saatchi and Quantum, but to claim rather that the success of the Hariri family-funded "Independence '05" campaign depended on these people being in tune with the mass of citizens whose thoughts, feelings, and desires the organizers shared and channeled rather than manufactured or manipulated as Schuh in "Faking the Claim" alleges (see Scott Wilson and Daniel Williams, "A New Power Rises across Mideast," *Washington Post,* 17 April 2005).

26. Rancière, "Politics of Literature," 16.

27. El-Hokayem argues that since at least 2006, the terms "Syrian proxy" and "client" no longer apply to Hezbollah.

28. While poststructuralism teaches us that no initiative is ever entirely free and no authority absolute, it is crucial to distinguish between a will whose freedom is compromised and marching orders. Since there is little place for the public expression of personal values in the Syrian Baathist system, organized demonstrations are a part of what Wedeen calls the "strategy of domination based on compliance": "The regime produces compliance through enforced participation in rituals of obeisance that are transparently phony both to those who orchestrate them and to those who consume them. Asad's cult operates as a disciplinary device, generating a politics of public dissimulation in which citizens act *as if* they revere their leader. A politics of 'as if,' while it may appear irrational or even foolish at first glance, actually proves politically effective. It produces guidelines for acceptable speech and behavior; it defines and generalizes a specific type of national membership; it occasions the enforcement of obedience; it induces complicity by creating practices in which citizens are themselves 'accomplices,' upholding the norms constitutive of Asad's domination; it isolates Syrians from

one another; and it clutters public space with monotonous slogans and empty gestures, which tire the minds and bodies of producers and consumers alike" (*Ambiguities of Domination*, 6). The "Asad" Wedeen refers to is Hafez al-Asad, who ruled Syria from 1970 to the day of his death in 2000. Since 2000, his son Bashar al-Asad has ruled, although Wedeen's point remains as valid for the son as it was for the father.

29. Wedeen, *Ambiguities of Domination*, 74, italics in original.

30. Soon after the first protests following the Hariri assassination, pro-Syrian forces whisked away all statuary and images of Syrian authority throughout the country, underscoring the emotional investment in, and vulnerability of, political representation.

31. Hezbollah's prestige throughout all communities rested primarily on its successful campaign to push Israeli occupation forces from the south of Lebanon in 2000. For the history of how Hezbollah became the sole armed resistance force in south Lebanon, see Fawwaz Traboulsi, *A History of Modern Lebanon* (London: Pluto Press, 2007), 230.

32. A good deal of metonymic slippage results between, on the one hand, the events of 8 and 14 March 2005 and, on the other, the political movements that have come to be known by those dates. I focus here on the ten-week Independence Uprising that culminated on 14 March and, for all intents and purposes, ended by late April. Its claims do not necessarily extend to the political coalitions that have since come to be known as the "8 March" and "14 March" movements.

33. See, for example, Ziad Majid, 'An Rabi' Bayrut, 70–76.

34. See Kassir, "Intifada fi-al-Intifada" (Uprising within the Uprising), in *Intifadat al-Istiqlal kama Ruwaha* (The Independence Uprising as He Narrated It) (Beirut: Dar al-Nahar, 2005), 14–15. Lively debate was also evidenced in innumerable roundtables and debates among young people of all political and sectarian tendencies at Martyrs' Square and on televised prime-time talk shows such as Marcel Ghanem's *Kalam al-Nas* (People Talk).

35. Syrian laborers who cannot make a living in Syria come to Lebanon, where they earn about thirteen dollars for a twelve- to fourteen-hour workday on a typical construction site (see Abushakra, "Syrian Laborers Face Tough Times").

36. On 1 March 2009, the Special Tribunal for Lebanon (STL) ordered the release of senior security officials Raymond Azarm, Mustafa Hamdan, Ali Hajj, and Jamil Sayyed, who had been arrested in 2005 and held without trial since then.

37. See Rym Ghazal, "Asma Andraos Honored as 'Hero of Change,'" *Daily Star* (Beirut), 14 October 2005.

38. Hal Foster, "Yellow Ribbons," *London Review of Books* 29, no.13 (2005): 29–31.

39. Dick Hebdige, *Subculture: The Meaning of Style* (London: Routledge, 1979), 131.

40. Mai Masri's documentary film *Beirut Diaries: Truth, Lies and Videotape* (MTC, 2006), captures the sense of betrayal felt by protesters in the tent city as politicians began forming opportunistic election alliances.

41. Wedeen, *Ambiguities of Domination*, 82.

42. Rancière, "Politics of Literature," 14.

43. Ibid., 16.

44. Chehabi notes the importance of the alcohol and woman questions in *Distant Relations*, 218. Alagha notes the Iranian role in fostering these campaigns and Deeb notes the appeal to authenticity, *An Enchanted Modern*, 20.

45. Deeb, *An Enchanted Modern*, 30.

46. Ibid., 33.

47. Qassem, *Hizbullah: The Story from Within*, 21–58. *Jihād* does not necessarily imply armed struggle; it can also mean struggle against the demons of the self.

48. Translated by Joseph Elie Alagha in *The Shifts in Hizbullah's Ideology*, 228. Alagha's book contains numerous translations of key Hezbollah documents.

49. Norton, *Hezbollah: A Short History*, 40.

50. Qassem, *Hizbullah: The Story from Within*, 209, 210.

51. Ibid., 210.

52. Norton, *Hezbollah: A Short History*, 45.

53. Joseph Elie Alagha, interview by the author, Beirut, 7 March 2008.

54. The party has linked its acceptance of its own candidate to the formation of a national unity government as well as to changes to the electoral law.

55. Alagha interview. Robin Wright supports this point: "Hezbollah has become an enterprise in the dahiya [predominantly Shiite Muslim suburbs of Beirut], often outperforming the state. It runs a major hospital as well as schools, discount pharmacies, groceries and an orphanage. It runs a garbage service and a reconstruction program for homes damaged during Israel's invasion. It supports families of the young men it

sent off to their deaths. Altogether, it benefits an estimated 250,000 Lebanese and is the country's second-largest employer" ("Inside the Mind of Hezbollah," *Washington Post,* 16 July 2006).

56. Deeb, *An Enchanted Modern,* 228.

57. Qassem, *Hizbullah: The Story from Within,* 134, 263, 35–36.

58. Ibid., 47.

59. Alagha interview.

60. This misleadingly implies that the Uprising was aimed at the Lebanese political culture, which is patently not the case, even if frustration with Lebanese politics was among the unacknowledged reasons for the mass turnouts. The failure thesis also implies that toppling the pro-Syrian government, expelling the occupying army, calling for an international investigation to the Hariri assassination, and removing the compromised Lebanese security chiefs were all foregone conclusions or accomplished primarily by Western pressure. Besides remarking that international pressure should only be so efficacious elsewhere, the notion that weeks of massive public demonstrations could have no effect rests—like the argument that Israeli forces voluntarily evacuated the south of Lebanon in 2000—on the assumption that a small nation cannot possibly have a hand in its own history.

One of the Uprising's demands does remain unfulfilled, that of learning the fate of hundreds, if not thousands, of Lebanese citizens missing in Syria or under Syrian auspices. The humiliation of Hariri became a powerful synecdoche for these officially forgotten people.

61. Ashis Nandy, *The Intimate Enemy: Loss and Recovery of Self under Colonialism* (New Delhi: Oxford University Press, 1983), 71.

62. Traboulsi writes of Syrian President Hafez al-Asad in 1976 being "gripped by a strategic vision to unify under his leadership four peoples and three countries (Syria, Lebanon, Jordan and the Palestinians) as a counterweight to Sadat" (*A History of Modern Lebanon,* 194).

63. Nandy, *Intimate Enemy,* 7. The comparison with British India must not be pushed too far. Since present-day Lebanon was a part of Syria until the early twentieth century, Syrian colonialism is more akin to an irredentist campaign.

64. Cited in Traboulsi, *A History of Modern Lebanon,* 245–46.

65. Wedeen, *Ambiguities of Domination,* 146, italics in the original.

66. Rancière, "Politics of Literature," 19.

CONCLUSION

1. Militant sectarianism, along with its aesthetic corollary, is itself historically conditioned as Friederike Pannewick reminds us of late 1970s "red Shiʿism": "It was the mentors of the 'Islamic Revolution' who changed the 'Karbala paradigm' from an attempt to lend innocent suffering meaning to a call for rebellion and violent resistance against concrete social conditions. The most forceful figure was the influential Iranian sociologist Ali Shariati, who wanted to have the martyrdom of the Prophet's grandson understood as a call for struggle, and not, as had been the case since the Safavid dynasty, as a tragic incident that was to be mourned in passive suffering. He criticized the quietist 'Safavid Shia' and countered this with the active 'red Shia' of Ali and Husayn. The red Shia, so Shariati, is an Islam of fighters and martyrs, whereas the Safavid Shia is a religion for wailers. He categorically rejected the piety of those who solely proclaim their grief by crying, wailing and flagellating themselves in the course of the processions and assemblies held on religious feast days. Thinkers like Shariati politicized the 'Karbala paradigm' and prepared the way for a combative interpretation of martyrdom in the Shia (Pannewick, "Passion and Rebellion: Shiite Visions of Redemptive Martyrdom," in *Martyrdom in Literature: Visions of Death and Meaningful Suffering in Europe and the Middle East from Antiquity to Modernity*, ed. Nasrin Rahimieh [Wiesbaden: Reichert, 2004], 58).

2. I use the term "barbarous" in the sense of "savage cruelty" inasmuch as the IDF attack exceeded the theater of war in south Lebanon to include power stations, civilian factories, bridges, and infrastructure which could in no way be conceived of as supporting Hezbollah's war effort. Given that the state of Lebanon is forbidden by the United States from acquiring even a military radar much less the rest of an anti-aircraft defense system, the IDF air attack that terrorized the entire country, causing billions in infrastructure and ecological damage, was, for all intents and purposes, a turkey shoot.

3. "Pride":

Kullumā dammarū fī arḍī baytan shayyadū min ʿazmī quṣūran
Sāwamū ʿala arḍī min dammī fa ishrabī yā arḍī buḥūran

4. "I Walk Upright":

muntaṣib al-qāma imshī marfūʿ al-hāma imshī
fī kiffī qaṣbat zaytūn wa ʿala kitfī naʿshī

5. An Amnesty International Report states: "During more than four weeks of ground and aerial bombardment of Lebanon by the Israeli armed forces, the country's infrastructure suffered destruction on a catastrophic scale. Israeli forces pounded buildings into the ground, reducing entire neighborhoods to rubble and turning villages and towns into ghost towns, as their inhabitants fled the bombardments. Main roads, bridges and petrol stations were blown to bits. Entire families were killed in air strikes on their homes or in their vehicles while fleeing the aerial assaults on their villages. Scores lay buried beneath the rubble of their houses for weeks, as the Red Cross and other rescue workers were prevented from accessing the areas by continuing Israeli strikes. The hundreds of thousands of Lebanese who fled the bombardment now face the danger of unexploded munitions as they head home (*Lebanon: Deliberate Destruction or "Collateral Damage"?: Israeli Attacks on Civilian Infrastructure*, Amnesty International News Service No: 219, 23 August 2006, www.amnesty.org/en/library/info/MDE18/007/2006).

6. "Lebanon, Oh Lebanon":

Lubnān yā lubnān 'am yas'al al-'adwān
Minmūt aw ninhān? ilnā al-mawt aḥlā

7. "Where Are You, Human Being?"

naḥnā raḥ mindāfi' mush raḥ ninḥanā
'aṣawt al-madāfi' wa'a'ayn al-dunyā
Yā ahlu-l-ḥaḍāra yā rā'ī al-salām
'amaltū alf ziyāra wa ba'tūnā al-kalām

8. See, in particular, the discussion of Rabi' Jaber's 2005 novel *Berytus: Madina taht al-Ard* (Berytus: City Underground), Joana Hadjithomas and Khalil Joreige's 1999 film *al-Bayt al-Zahr* (The Pink House); and Jean Chamoun's 2000 film, *Tayf al-Madina* (In the Shadows of the City).

Abdel-Nour, Wafa'. "Al-Makan fi-al-Riwayat al-Lubnaniyya, 1980–2000" (Place in the Lebanese Novel, 1980–2000). Ph.D. diss., Université Saint-Joseph, Beirut, 2010.

Abou, Sélim. *Freedoms: Cultural Roots of the Cedar Revolution*. Beirut: Presses de l'Université Saint-Joseph, 2005.

Abu-Lughod, Lila. *Dramas of Nationhood: The Politics of Television in Egypt*. Cairo: American University in Cairo Press, 2005.

Abushakra, Rima. "Syrian Laborers Face Tough Times amid Lebanon's Political Divide." *Daily Star* (Beirut), 17 March 2008, 4.

Aghacy, Samira. *Masculine Identity in the Fiction of the Arab East since 1967*. Syracuse, N.Y.: Syracuse University Press, 2009.

Alagha, Joseph Elie. Interview by the author. Beirut. 7 March 2008.

———. *The Shifts in Hizbullah's Ideology: Religious Ideology, Political Ideology, and Political Program*. Leiden: Amsterdam University Press, 2006.

'Alawiyya, Burhan. Interview by the author. Beirut. 12 February 2007.

———. Interview by al-Jazeera International. "al-'Adas al-'Arabiyya" (The Arabic Lens). www.aljazeera.net.

Allen, Roger. *The Arabic Novel: An Historical and Critical Introduction*. Syracuse, N.Y.: Syracuse University Press, 1995.

Althusser, Louis. "Marxism and Humanism." In *For Marx*, translated by Ben Brewster, 221–47. London: Verso, 1996.

An al-Awan (The Time Has Come). Directed by Jean-Claude Codsi. 1993.

Angus, Gavin, and Ramez Maluf. *Beirut Reborn: The Restoration and Development of the Central District.* London: Academy Editions, 1996.

Antoon, Sinan. "Returning to the Wind: On Darwish's 'La Taʿtadhir ʿamma Faʿalta.'" In *Mahmoud Darwish: Exile's Poet,* edited by Hala Khamis Nassar and Najat Rahman. Northampton, Mass: Olive Branch Press, 2008.

Aoun, Jean, dir. *Kuluna li-l-Watan* (We Are All the Nation). 365 min. Beirut: LBC1, 2006.

Al-ʿAris, Ibrahim. *Al-Hulm al-Muʿallaq: Sinama Marun Baghdadi* (The Suspended Dream: The Cinema of Maroun Baghdadi). Beirut: Dar al-Nahar, 1994.

———. *Al-Sura al-Multabisa, al-Sinama fi Lubnan: Mubdiʿuha wa Aflamuha* (The Ambiguous Image: Cinema in Lebanon: Its Achievements and Its Films). Beirut: Dar al-Nahda al-ʿArabiyya, 2010.

Arkoun, Mohammad. *Contribution à l'étude de l'humanisme arabe au IVe/Xe siècle: Miskawayh, philosophe et historien.* Paris: Librairie Philosophique J. Vrin, 1970.

———. *Pour une critique de la raison islamique.* Paris: Maisonneuve et Larose, 1984.

Armbrust, Walter. *Mass Culture and Modernism in Egypt.* Cambridge: Cambridge University Press, 1996.

———. *Mass Mediations: New Approaches to Popular Culture in the Middle East and Beyond Authenticity and Distinction in Urban Syria.* Bloomington: Indiana University Press, 2004.

Asfour, Nana. "The Politics of Arab Cinema: Middle Eastern Filmmakers Face up to Their Reality." *Cineaste* 26 (2000): 46.

Aʿtiya, Ahmad Mohammad. *Al-Iltizam wa-l-Thawra fi-al-Adab al-ʿArabiyya al-Haditha* (Commitment and Revolution in Modern Arabic Literature). Beirut: Dar al-ʿAwda, 1974.

Atlal (The Last Man). Directed by Ghassan Salhab. Agat Film and Cie, 2006.

ʿAtwan, Hussein. *Muqaddimat al-Qasida al-ʿArabiyya* (Introduction to the Arabic Ode). 3 vols. Cairo: Dar al- Maʿrifa bi-Misr, 1970.

ʿAwwad, Lewis. *Al-Ishtirakiyya wa-l-Adab* (Socialism and Literature). Beirut: Dar al-Adab, 1963.

ʿAwwad, Tawfiq Yusuf. *Tawahin Bayrut.* Beirut: Maktabat Lubnan,

1972. Translated by Leslie Mcloughlin as *Death in Beirut*. Boulder: Three Continents Press, 1984.

Ayoub, Charles. *Al-Diyar* (Beirut), February 2005–February 2006.

ʿAzar, Zhafer Henri. Interview by the author. Beirut. May 2007.

———. *Nazra ʿala al-Sinama al-ʿAlamiyya al-Muʿasira: Asiya wa Ifriqi-yya wa-l-Buldan al-ʿArabiyya* (A Study of the Cinema of the Contemporary World: Asia, Africa, and the Arab Countries). Beirut: al-Muʾassasa li-l-Dirasat wa-l-Nashr, 1987.

Badawi, M. M. "Commitment in Contemporary Arabic Literature." In *Critical Perspectives on Modern Arabic Literature*, edited by Issa J. Boullata, 23–44. Boulder, Colo.: Three Continents Press, 1980.

Balqaziz, Abdallah. *Hizbullah min al-Tahrir ila al-Radʿ: 1982–2006* (Hezbollah from Liberation to Deterrence: 1982–2006). Beirut: Markaz Dirasat al-Wahda al-ʿArabiyya, 2006.

Barakat, Hoda. *Hajar al-Dahik*. London: Riad al-Rayyes, 1990. Translated by Sophie Bennett as *The Stone of Laughter*. London: Garnet, 1994.

———. Telephone interview by the author. 17 July 2010.

Barakat, Najwa. Interview by the author. Beirut. 5 July 2010.

———. *Ya Salam* (Good Heavens). Beirut: Dar al-Adab, 1999.

Bayrut, al-Liqaʾ (Beirut: The Meeting). Directed by Burhan ʿAlawiyya. France Media, 1981.

Al-Bayt al-Zahr (The Pink House). Directed by Joana HadjiThomas and Khalil Joreige. Djinn House Production, 1999.

Behrens-Abouseif, Doris. *Beauty in Arabic Culture*. Princeton, N.J.: Markus Weiner, 1999.

Beirut Diaries: Truth, Lies and Videotape. DVD. Directed by Mai Masri. 79 min. MTC Production, 2006.

The Beirut Spring. Beirut: Dar al-Nahar and Quantum Communications, 2005.

Beissinger, Mark R. "Structure and Example in Modular Political Phenomena: The Diffusion of Bulldozer/Rose/Orange/Tulip Revolutions." *Perspectives on Politics* 5, no. 2 (June 2007): 259–76.

Bergé, Marc. *Pour un humanisme vécu: Abū Hayyān al-Tawhīdī*. Damascus: Institut français de Damas, 1979.

Blanford, Nicholas. *Killing Mr Beirut: The Assassination of Rafik Hariri and Its Impact on the Middle East*. London: Tauris, 2006.

Blumenberg, Hans. *The Legitimacy of the Modern Age.* Translated by Robert M. Wallace. Cambridge: MIT Press, 1985.

Boulos, Aimée, and Reine Mitry. Interview by the author. Beirut. March 2007.

Bouwsma, William J. *The Waning of the Renaissance 1550–1640.* New Haven: Yale University Press, 2000.

Boym, Svetlana. *The Future of Nostalgia.* New York: Basic Books, 2001.

Bracken, H. M. "Essence, Accident, and Race." *Hermathena* 116 (Winter 1973): 81–96.

Carter, Michael G. "Humanism and the Language Sciences in Medieval Islam." In *Humanism, Culture, and Language in the Near East: Studies in Honor of Georg Krotkoff,* edited by Asma Afsaruddin and A. H. Mathias Zahniser, 27–38. Winona Lake, Ind.: Eisenbrauns, 1997.

Cassirer, Ernst., Paul Oskar Kristeller, John Herman Randall Jr., eds. *The Renaissance Philosophy of Man.* Chicago: Chicago University Press, 1948.

Certeau, Michel de. *The Practice of Everyday Life.* Translated by Steven Rendall. Berkeley and Los Angeles: University of California Press, 1984.

Chamoun, Jean. Interview by the author. Beirut. 21 July 2010.

Chehabi, H. E. *Distant Relations: Iran and Lebanon in the Last 500 Years.* London: Center for Lebanese Studies/Tauris, 2006.

Chemaly, Rita. *Le printemps 2005 au Liban: Entre, mythes, et réalités.* Paris: L'Harmattan, 2009.

Choucair, Walid. "Lebanon Loses Its Protective Umbrella." *Daily Star* (Beirut), 19 February 2005, 1.

A Civilized People. Directed by Randa Chahal. 1999.

Cole, Juan. *Sacred Space and Holy War: The Politics, Culture and History of Shiite Islam.* London: Tauris, 2002.

Cole, Sarah. "Enchantment, Disenchantment, War, Literature." *PMLA* 124, no. 5 (2009): 1632–47.

Colla, Elliot. "The Image of Loss: Jalal Toufic's Filmic Beirut." *Visual Anthropology* 10 (1998): 305–17.

Cooke, Miriam. "Beirut Reborn: The Political Aesthetics of Auto-Destruction." *Yale Journal of Criticism* 15, no. 2 (2002): 393–424.

Cooper, David E. *The Measure of Things: Humanism, Humility, and Mystery.* Oxford: Clarendon Press, 2002.

Al-Dabbagh, Abdulla. "Modern Universalism and the Myth of Westerness." *Comparatist* 27 (2003): 5–20.

Dabbous-Sensenig, Dima. "Who is the Prettiest One of All?: Hollywood Cinema, Egyptian Cinema, and the Recycling of Fairy Tales: A Structural Feminist Analysis." *Al-Raida* 16, no. 86–87 (1999): 40–47.

Al-Daif, Rashid. "Al-Nitaj al-Riwa'i fi Lubnan: Tayyarat wa Ittijahat" (Novelistic Production in Lebanon: Currents and Trends). *Fusul* 16, no. 4 (Spring 1998): 167–72.

———. *'Azizi al-Sayyid Kawabata.* Beirut: Mukhtarat, 1995. Translated by Paul Starkey as *Dear Mr Kawabata.* London: Quartet, 1999.

———. Interview by the author. Beirut. 14 July 2010.

Daoud, Hassan. *Binayat Mathilde.* Beirut: Dar al-Tanwir, 1983. Translated by Peter Theroux as *The House of Mathilde.* London: Granta, 1999.

———. Interview by the author. Beirut. 13 July 2010.

David, Catherine, dir. *Tamass: Contemporary Arab Representations Beirut/Lebanon 1.* Proceedings of the Contemporary Arab Representations Beirut/Lebanon Project, 3 May–14 July 2002, Barcelona. www.leftmatrix.com/tamass.html.

Davies, Tony. *Humanism.* London: Routledge, 1997.

Deeb, Lara. *An Enchanted Modern: Gender and Public Piety in Shi'i Lebanon.* Princeton: Princeton University Press, 2006.

Delumeau, Jean. *Un histoire du paradis: Le jardin des délices.* Paris: Arthème Fayard, 1992.

Derrida, Jacques. *Specters of Marx: The State of the Debt, the Work of Mourning, and the New International.* Translated by Peggy Kamuf. New York: Routledge, 1994.

———. "The Ends of Man." In *Margins of Philosophy*, translated by Alan Bass. Chicago: University of Chicago Press, 1982.

Donohue, John J., S.J. *The Buwayhid Dynasty in Iraq 334 H./945 to 403 H./1012: Shaping Institutions for the Future.* Leiden: Brill, 2003.

Donohue, John J., S.J., and Leslie Tramontini, eds. *Crosshatching in Global Culture: A Dictionary of Modern Arab Writers: An Updated English Version of R. B. Campbell's "Contemporary Writers."* Beirut: Orient Institute, 2004.

Dufal, Blaise. "Choc des civilisations et manipulations historique:

Troubles dans la médiévistique." Comité de vigilance face aux usages publics de l'histoire: http://cvuh.free.fr/spip.php?article180.

Dupré, Louis. *Passage to Modernity: An Essay in the Hermeneutics of Nature and Culture.* New Haven: Yale University Press, 1993.

Eisenstadt, S. N. *Fundamentalism, Sectarianism, and Revolution: The Jacobin Dimension of Modernity.* Cambridge: Cambridge University Press, 1999.

El-Hokayem, Emile. "Hizballah and Syria: Outgrowing the Proxy Relationship." *Washington Quarterly* 30, no. 2 (Spring 2007): 35–52.

Embaló, Birget. "The City, Mythical Images and Their Deconstruction: The Image of Beirut in Contemporary Works of Arabic Literature." In *Myths, Historical Archetypes and Symbolic Figures in Arabic Literature: Towards a New Hermeneutic Approach,* edited by Angelika Neuwirth, Birgit Embaló, Sebastian Günther, and Maher Jarrar, 583–603. Stuttgart: Steiner, 1999.

Ermarth, Elizabeth D. *Realism and Consensus in the English Novel: Time, Space, and Narrative.* Princeton: Princeton University Press, 1998.

Fanon, Frantz. *The Wretched of the Earth.* Translated by Constance Farrington. London: Penguin Books, 1967.

Faysal, Shukri. *Tatawwur al-Ghazal bayna al-Jahiliya wa-l-Islam* (Development of the Ghazal from the Jahiliya to Islam). 2nd ed. Damascus: University of Damascus Press, 1964.

Foster, Hal. "Yellow Ribbons." *London Review of Books* 29, no. 13 (2005): 29–31.

Foucault. Michel. *The Order of Things: An Archeology of the Human Sciences.* London: Routledge, 2002.

Fouladkar, Assad. Telephone interview by the author. 30 July 2010.

Ghazal, Rym. "Asma Andraos Honored as 'Hero of Change.'" *Daily Star* (Beirut), 14 October 2005.

Gilliland, Rex. "What Becomes of the Human after Humanism?: Heidegger and Derrida." *Proceedings of the North American Heidegger Conference,* May 2002. http://home.southernct.edu/~gillilandr1/jobs/WhatBecomesoftheHumanafterHumanism5.htm.

Glass, Charles. "An Assassin's Land." *London Review of Books,* 4 August 2005, 15–18.

Gouguenheim, Sylvain. *Aristote au Mont Saint-Michel: Les racines grecques de l'Europe chrétienne.* Paris: Seuil, 2008.

Grafton, Anthony. "The New Science and the Traditions of Humanism." In *The Cambridge Companion to Renaissance Humanism,* edited by Jill Kraye, 203–23. Cambridge: Cambridge University Press, 1996.

Gresh, Alain. "Offensive concertée contre le régime syrien." *Le Monde Diplomatique* (Paris), December 2005, 12.

Habshian, Hovig. "Hayat al-Mukhrij Ahamm min al-Sinama" (The Director's Life Is More Important Than the Cinema). *Al-Nahar,* 12 May 2007.

HadjiThomas, Joana. Telephone interview by the author. 20 July 2010.

Halliwell, Martin, and Andy Mousley. *Critical Humanisms: Humanist/ Anti-Humanist Dialogues.* Edinburgh: Edinburgh University Press, 2003.

Hamori, Andras. *On the Art of Medieval Arabic Literature.* Princeton: Princeton University Press, 1974.

Hanf, Theodor. *Coexistence in Wartime Lebanon: Decline of a State and Rise of a Nation.* Translated by John Richardson. London: Centre of Lebanese Studies, 1993.

Hankins, James. "Humanism and the Origins of Modern Political Thought." In *The Cambridge Companion to Renaissance Humanism,* edited by Jill Kraye, 118–41. Cambridge: Cambridge University Press, 1996.

Hardt, Michael, and Antonio Negri. *Empire.* Cambridge: Harvard University Press, 2000.

Harik, Judith Palmer. *Hezbollah: The Changing Face of Terrorism.* London: Tauris, 2005.

"Hariri: Saudi-Syrian Deal Finalized but Requires Steps from Other Camp," *Naharnet,* 6 December 2010. www.naharnet.com/domino/tn/NewsDesk.nsf/0/232E4E8F1A322C0EC22578100066F9E8?Open Document

Harlow, Barbara. *Resistance Literature.* New York: Methuen, 1987.

Hartman, Michelle. *Jesus, Joseph and Job: Reading Rescriptings of Religious Figures in Lebanese Women's Fiction.* Wiesbaden: Reichert, 2002.

Hasan, ʿAza. *Shʿir al-Wuquf ʿala al-Atlal min al-Jahiliya ila Nihayat al-Qarn al-Thalith* (Standing by the Ruins Poetry from the Jahiliya to the End of the Third Century [hegira]). Damascus: University of Damascus Press, 1968.

Hatoum, Leila, and Jessy Chahine. "Beirut Bombing Draws Sorrow, Fear and Anger from the People." *Daily Star* (Beirut), 15 February 2005, 1.

Haugbolle, Sune. "Public and Private Memory of the Lebanese Civil War." *Comparative Studies of South Asia, Africa and the Middle East* 25, no. 1 (2005): 191–203.

———. *War and Memory in Lebanon.* Cambridge: Cambridge University Press, 2010.

Hebdige, Dick. *Subculture: The Meaning of Style.* London: Routledge, 1979.

Heidegger, Martin. "Letter on Humanism." In *Basic Writings,* 217–65. New York: Harper-Collins, 1993.

———. "The Question Concerning Technology." In *The Question Concerning Technology and Other Essays,* translated by William Lovitt, 3–35. New York: Harper Torchbooks, 1977.

Herd, Graeme P. "Russia and the 'Orange Revolution': Response, Rhetoric, Reality?" *Quarterly Journal* 2 (June 2005): 15–28.

Horkheimer, Max, and Theodor W. Adorno. *Dialectic of Enlightenment: Philosophical Fragments.* Translated by Edmund Jephcott. Stanford: Stanford University Press, 2002.

Hors la vie (Beyond Life). Directed by Maroun Baghdadi. Video Collection International, 1991.

"Inside Syria and Lebanon." *Middle East Report* 236 (Fall 2005).

Al-I'sar (The Tornado). Dir. Samir Habshi. 1993.

Jaber, Kamel. "Burhan 'Alawiyya: Kayfa Nashfa min Zaman al-Harb?" (Burhan 'Alawiyya: How to Heal from the War Era?). *Al-Akhbar,* 29 July 2009.

Jaber, Rabi'. *Berytus: Madina taht al-Ard* (Berytus: City Underground). Beirut: Dar al-Markaz al-Thaqafi al-'Arabi and Dar al-Adab, 2005.

———. *Taqrir Milis* (The Mehlis Report). Beirut: Dar al-Markaz al-Thaqafi al-'Arabi, 2005.

Jacobi, Renate. "Time and Reality in *Nasib* and *Ghazal.*" *Journal of Arabic Literature* 16 (1985): 1–17.

Jarrar, Maher. "The Arabic Novel Carries Its Cross and Asks the Son of Man: Iconography of Jesus in Some Modern Arabic Novels." In *Po-*

etry's Voice—Society's Norms: Forms of Interaction between Middle Eastern Writers and Their Societies, edited by Andreas Pflitsch and Barbara Winckler, 61–92. Wiesbaden: Reichert, 2006.

Kanafani, Ghassan. *Fi-al-Adab al-Sihyuni* (On Zionist Literature). Beirut: Munazzamat al-Tahrir al-Filistiniyya, Markaz al-Abhath, 1967.

Kassir, Samir. "Intifada fi-al-Intifada" (Uprising within the Uprising). In *Intifadat al-Istiqlal kama Ruwaha* (The Independence Uprising as He Narrated It). Beirut: Dar al-Nahar, 2005.

Kaydi, George. "*Al-Bayt al-Zahr* li-Khalil wa Juanna Jorayge Istiʿara li-l-Harb wa-l-Watan wa-l-Dakira" (The Pink House of Khalil and Joanna Joreige: A Metaphor for War, Nation and Memory). *Al-Nahar*, 7 September 1998.

Kennedy, David. *Elegy*. London: Routledge, 2007.

Khalaf, Samir. *Heart of Beirut: Reclaiming the Bourj*. London: Saqi, 2006.

Khankan, Nathalie. "Reperceiving the Pre-Islamic *Nasīb*." *Journal of Arabic Literature* 33, no. 1 (2002): 1–23.

Khatib, Lina. *Lebanese Cinema: Imagining the Civil War and Beyond*. London: Tauris, 2008.

Khoury, Elias. "Al-Riwaya wa-l-Riwaʾi wa-l-Harb" (The Novel, the Novelist and the War). *Al-Mulhaq al-Thaqafi li-l-Nahar* (Beirut), 22 January 2006), 14.

Kilpatrick, Hilary. "Literary Creativity and the Cultural Heritage: The *Atlal* in Modern Arabic Fiction." In *Tradition, Modernity, and Postmodernity in Arabic Literature: Essays in Honor of Professor Issa F. Boullatta*, edited by Kamal Abdel-Malek and Wael Hallaq, 28–44. Leiden: Brill, 2000.

Klemm, Verena. "Different Notions of Commitment (*Iltizam*) and Committed Literature (*al-Adab al-Multazim*) in the Literary Circles of the Mashriq." *Arabic and Middle Eastern Literatures* 3 (2000): 51–62.

Kraemer, Joel L. *Humanism in the Renaissance of Islam: The Cultural Revival during the Buyid Age*. Leiden: Brill, 1986.

L'Orient-Le Jour: L'Espoir en lettres de sang (Beirut). 13 February 2006.

Lamma Ḥikyit Maryam (When Maryam Spoke). Directed by Assad Fouladkar. Lebanese American University, 2002.

"Lebanon: Deliberate Destruction or 'Collateral Damage'? Israeli Attacks on Civilian Infrastructure." Amnesty International News Ser-

vice No. 219, 23 August 2006. www.amnesty.org/en/library/info/
MDE18/007/2006.

Leclère, Thierry. "Polémique autour d'un essai sur les racines de l'Europe." *Télérama*, 28 April 2008. www.telerama.fr/idees/polemique-autour-d-un-essai-sur-les-racines-de-l-europe,28265.php.

Lejbowicz, Max. "Saint-Michel historiographe: Quelques aperçus sur le livre de Sylvain Gouguenheim." *La revue internationale des livres et des idées*, no. 4. http://revuedeslivres.net/index.php?idH=225.

Levinas, Emmanuel. *Humanism of the Other.* Urbana: University of Illinois Press, 2005.

Libéra, Alain de. *La philosophie médiévale.* Paris: Presses Universitaires de France, 1993.

Maasri, Zeina. *Off the Wall: Political Posters of the Lebanese Civil War.* New York: Palgrave Macmillan, 2009.

———. Signs of Conflict: Political Posters of Lebanon's Civil War. Exhibition. Beirut, Ashkal Alwan, April 2008.

Madanat, ʿAdnan. *Tahawwulat al-Sinama al-ʿArabiyya al-Muʿasira: Qadaya wa Aflam* (Changes in Contemporary Arabic Cinema: Issues and Films). Damascus: Dar Kanaʿan, 2004.

Majid, Ziad. *ʿAn Rabiʿ Bayrut wa-l-Dawla al-Naqisa* (On the Beirut Spring and the Incomplete State). Beirut: Dar al-Nahar, 2006.

Makdisi, George. "Inquiry into the Origins of Humanism." In *Humanism, Culture, and Language in the Near East: Studies in Honor of Georg Krotkoff*, edited by Asma Afsaruddin and A. H. Mathias Zahniser, 15–26. Winona Lake, Ind.: Eisenbrauns, 1997.

———. *The Rise of Humanism in Classical Islam and the Christian West with Special Reference to Scholasticism.* Edinburgh: Edinburgh University Press, 1990.

Makdisi, Saree. "Laying Claim to Beirut: Urban Narrative and Spatial Identity in the Age of Solidère." *Critical Inquiry* 23, no. 3 (Spring 1997): 661–705.

Makdisi, Ussama. *The Culture of Sectarianism: Community, History, and Violence in Nineteenth-Century Ottoman Lebanon.* Berkeley and Los Angeles: University of California Press, 2000.

Mallat, Chibli. *March 2221: Lebanon's Cedar Revolution: An Essay on Non-Violence and Justice.* Beirut: Gubernare, 2007.

Malti-Douglas, Fedwa. *Structures of Avarice: The Bukhalā' in Medieval Arabic Literature*. Leiden: Brill, 1985.

Maluf, Ramez. "Re: Cooke on 'Beirut Reborn.'" E-mail to Ken Seigneurie. 4 May 2007.

Manning, Paul. "Rose-Colored Glasses?: Color Revolutions and Cartoon Chaos in Postsocialist Georgia." *Cultural Anthropology* 22, no. 2 (May 2007): 171–213.

Marion, Jean-Luc. *God without Being: Hors-Texte*. 1982. Translated by Thomas A. Carlson. Chicago: University of Chicago Press, 1991.

Masri, Mai. *Beirut Diaries: Truth, Lies and Videotape*. N.p.: MTC, 2006.

Massad, Joseph A. *Colonial Effects: The Making of National Identity*. New York: Columbia University Press, 2001.

———. "Liberating Songs: Palestine Put to Music." In *Palestine, Israel, and the Politics of Popular Culture*, edited by Rebecca L. Stein and Ted Swedenburg, 175–201. Durham: Duke University Press, 2005.

McGray, Douglas. "Hyper Texts: How One Professor Applies Quantitative Analysis to Classic Literature." *Wired*, December 2009, 78.

Menocal, María Rosa. *The Arabic Role in Medieval Literary History: A Forgotten Heritage*. Philadelphia: University of Pennsylvania Press, 1987.

Mermier, Franck, and Christophe Varin, eds. *Mémoires de Guerres au Liban (1975–1990)*. Paris: Sindbad, 2010.

Mervin, Sabrina, ed. *Les mondes chiites et l'Iran*. Paris: Karthala, 2007.

Meyer, Stefan G. *The Experimental Arabic Novel: Post Colonial Literary Modernism in the Levant*. Albany: State University of New York Press, 2001.

Milton, J. R. "Delicate Learning: Erudition and the Enterprise of Philosophy." *Humanism and Early Modern Philosophy*, edited by Jill Kraye and M. W. F. Stone, 159–71. London: Routledge, 2000.

Al-Mismar, Rima. "Marun Baghdadi fi Dikra Rahilihi al-Khamisat Ashra" (Maroun Baghdadi: In Commemoration of the Fifteenth Anniversary of His Death). *Al-Mustaqbal*, 19 February 2008.

Moretti, Franco. "Conjectures on World Literature." *New Left Review* (2000): 54–68.

"Muthaqafun Lubnaniyyun Yu'ayyidun Haydar Haydar: Isti'mal al-Din Mu'shshir Inhitat" (Lebanese Intellectuals Support Haydar Haydar:

The [Political] Use of Religion Is an Indicator of Decay). *Al-Nahar*, 17 May 2000, 22.

Naficy, Hamid. *An Accented Cinema: Exilic and Diasporic Filmmaking.* Princeton: Princeton University Press, 2001.

Nandy, Ashis. *The Intimate Enemy: Loss and Recovery of Self under Colonialism.* New Delhi: Oxford University Press, 1983.

"Nasīb." *The Encyclopaedia of Islam.* Leiden: Brill, 1993.

Nauert, Charles G. *Humanism and the Culture of Renaissance Europe.* 2nd ed. Cambridge: Cambridge University Press, 2006.

Neuwirth, Angelika, Birgit Embaló, Sebastian Günther, and Maher Jarrar, eds. *Myths, Historical Archetypes and Symbolic Figures in Arabic Literature.* Beirut: Orient-Institut der DMG, 1999.

Noonan, Jeff. *Critical Humanism and the Politics of Difference.* Montreal: McGill–Queen's University Press, 2003.

Norton, Augustus Richard. *Hezbollah: A Short History.* Princeton: Princeton University Press, 2007.

Orlando, Francesco. *Obsolete Objects in the Literary Imagination: Ruins, Relics, Rarities, Rubbish, Uninhabited Places, and Hidden Treasures.* Translated by Gabriel Pihas, Daniel Seidel, and Alessandra Grego. New Haven: Yale University Press, 2006.

Ostle, Robin. "Excellence in Modern Arabic Literature." Paper presented at American University of Beirut, 23 March 2006.

Pannewick, Friederike. "Death and the Power of the Word." In *Poetry's Voice-Society's Norms: Forms of Interaction between Middle Eastern Writers and Their Societies*, edited by Andreas Pflitsch and Barbara Winckler, 49–60. Wiesbaden: Reichert, 2006.

———. "Passion and Rebellion: Shiite Visions of Redemptive Martyrdom." In *Martyrdom in Literature: Visions of Death and Meaningful Suffering in Europe and the Middle East from Antiquity to Modernity*, edited by Nasrin Rahimieh. Wiesbaden: Reichert, 2004.

Petrarca, Francesco. *Invectives.* Translated by David Marsh. Cambridge: Harvard University Press, 2008.

Pol Droit, Roger. "Et si l'Europe ne devait pas ses savoirs à l'islam?" *Le Monde des Livres*, 3 April 2008. www.lemonde.fr/web/recherche_resultats/1,13–0,1–0,0.html.

Pontbriand, Chantal, ed. "'Beirut': A Pivotal City between Contemporary Art and the Arab World." *Parachute* 108 (2002). www.parachute. ca/parachute.html.

Le printemps inachevé (Beirut). Special issue, *L'Orient-Express*, December 2005.

Qabur, Ahmad. Interview by Zoha. Beirut. 25 September 2007.

Qassem, Naim. *Hizbullah: The Story from Within*. Translated by Dalia Khalil. London: Saqi, 2005.

Al-Qusayfi, Marie. "*Ya Salam* li-Najwa Barakat: Shukhus Ma baʿd al-Harb fi-al-Qatl wa al-Siyada" (Najwa Barakat's *Ya Salam*: Postwar Characters in Killing and Sovereignty). *Al-Nahar* (Beirut), 21 April 1999.

Al-Rafaʿi, Rania. "Asad Fuladkar ʿan Filmihi *lamma Ḥikyit Maryam*" (Assad Fouladkar on His Film *When Maryam Spoke*). *Al-Nahar*, 16 December 2002.

Rakha, Youssef. "Hoda Barakat: Starting Over." *Al-Ahram Weekly*, 457, 25 November–1 December 1999.

———. "Rashid al-Daif: Writing to Yasunari." *Al-Ahram Weekly*, 770, 24–30 November 2005.

Rancière, Jacques. "The Politics of Literature." *SubStance* 33, no. 1 (2004): 10–24.

Rowe, Peter G., and Hashim Sarkis. *Projecting Beirut: Episodes in the Construction and Reconstruction of a Modern City*. Munich: Prestel, 1998.

Saad-Ghorayeb, Amal. *Hizbu'llah: Politics and Religion*. London: Pluto Press, 2002.

Said, Edward W. *Humanism and Democratic Criticism*. New York: Columbia University Press, 2004.

Salem, Elise. *Constructing Lebanon: A Century of Literary Narratives*. Gainesville: University Press of Florida, 2003.

Samaha, Joseph. *Al-Safir* (Beirut), February 2005–February 2006.

Samman, Ghada. *Bayrut '75*. Beirut: Dar al-Adab, 1975. Translated by Nancy N. Roberts as *Beirut '75*. Fayetteville: University of Arkansas Press, 1995.

Santesso, Aaron. *A Careful Longing: The Poetics and Problems of Nostalgia*. Newark: University of Delaware Press, 2006.

Schmitt, Paula. *Advertised to Death: Lebanese Poster Boys*. Beirut: Arab Printing Press, 2009.

Schubart, Rikke. "Passion and Acceleration: Genetic Change in the Action Film." *Violence and American Cinema*, edited by J. David Slocum, 192–207. New York: Routledge, 2001.

Schuh, Trish. "Faking the Case against Syria." *Counterpunch*, 18 November 2005.

Schumpeter, Joseph. *Capitalism, Socialism and Democracy.* 1942. New York: Harper, 1975.

Seigneurie, Ken. "Anointing with Rubble: Ruins in the Lebanese War Novel." *Comparative Studies of South Asia, Africa and the Middle East* 28, no. 1 (2008): 50–60.

——. "The Everyday World of War in Hassan Daoud's *House of Mathilde*." In *Crisis and Memory: The Representation of Space in Modern Levantine Narrative*, edited by Seigneurie, 101–14. Wiesbaden: Reichert, 2003.

——. "The Flickering Light of Literature: 8–18 February 2000." In *Profession 2000*, 46–53. New York: Modern Language Association, 2000.

——. "The Importance of Being Kawabata: The Narratee in Today's Literature of Commitment." *JNT: Journal of Narrative Theory* 34, no. 1 (Winter 2004): 54–73.

——. "Ongoing War and Arab Humanism." In *Geomodernisms: "Race," Modernism, Modernity*, edited by Laura Doyle and Laura Winkiel, 96–113. Bloomington: Indiana University Press, 2005.

——. "A Survival Aesthetic for Ongoing War." In *Crisis and Memory: The Representation of Space in Modern Levantine Narrative*, edited by Seigneurie, 11–32. Wiesbaden: Reichert, 2003.

——. "The Wrench and the Ratchet: Cultural Mediation in a Contemporary Liberation Struggle." *Public Culture* 21, no. 2 (2009): 377–402.

Shafik, Viola. *Arab Cinema: History and Cultural Identity.* Cairo: American University Press, 1998.

——. "Women, National Liberation and Melodrama in Arab Cinema. Some Considerations." *Al-Raida* 16, no. 86–87 (1999): 12–18.

Sharara, Waddah. *Dawlat Hizbullah: Lubnan Mujtam'an Islamiyyan* (The Hezbollah State: Lebanon as an Islamic Society). Beirut: Dar al-Nahar, 2006.

Al-Shaykha. Directed by Layla Assaf. 1993.

Sheehan, Paul, ed. *Becoming Human: New Perspectives on the Inhuman Condition.* Westport: Praeger, 2003.

————, ed. *Modernism, Narrative and Humanism*. Cambridge: Cambridge University Press, 2002.

Shimon, Samuel, ed. *Beirut 39: New Writing from the Arab World*. London: Bloomsbury, 2010.

Simpson, Lorenzo. *The Unfinished Project: Toward a Postmetaphysical Humanism*. London: Routledge, 2001.

Somekh, Sasson. "Biblical Echoes in Modern Arabic Literature." *Journal of Arabic Literature* 26, no. 1–2 (1995): 186–200.

Soper, Kate. *Humanism and Anti-Humanism*. London: Hutchinson, 1986.

Spanos, William V. *The Legacy of Edward W. Said*. Urbana: University of Illinois Press, 2009.

Spargo, Clifton R. *The Ethics of Mourning: Grief and Responsibility in Elegiac Literature*. Baltimore: John Hopkins University Press, 2004.

Sperl, Stefan. *Mannerism in Arabic Poetry: A Structural Analysis of Selected Texts*. Cambridge: Cambridge University Press, 1989.

Spivak, Gayatri Chakravorty. *The Post-Colonial Critic: Interviews, Strategies, Dialogues*. Edited by Sarah Harasym. London: Routledge, 1990.

Stein, Rebecca L., and Ted Swedenburg, eds. *Palestine, Israel, and the Politics of Popular Culture*. Durham: Duke University Press, 2005.

Stetkevych, Jaroslav. *The Zephyrs of Najd: The Poetics of Nostalgia in the Classical Arabic Nasīb*. Chicago: University of Chicago Press, 1993.

Stone, Christopher. "Ziyad Rahbani's 'Novelization' of Lebanese Musical Theater or the Paradox of Parody." *Middle Eastern Literatures* 8, no. 2 (July 2005): 151–70.

Su, John J. *Ethics and Nostalgia in the Contemporary Novel*. Cambridge: Cambridge University Press, 2005.

Swayd, Muhammad. *Al-Sinama al-Muʿajjala: Aflam al-Harb al-Ahliyya al-Lubnaniyya* (Urgent Cinema: Films of the Lebanese Civil War). Beirut: Muʾassasat al-Abhath al-ʿArabiyya, 1986; Syracuse, N.Y.: Syracuse University Press, 2009.

Tabet, Jade, dir. *Autrement: Beyrouth, la brûlure des rêves*. Paris, 2001.

Tayf al-Madina (In the Shadows of the City). Directed by Jean Chamoun. Arab Film Distribution. 2000.

Taylor, Charles. "Two Theories of Modernity." In *Alternative Moderni-*

ties, edited by Dilip Parameshwar Gaonkar, 172–96. Durham: Duke University Press, 2001.

Todorov, Tzvetan. *Imperfect Garden: The Legacy of Humanism.* Translated by Carol Cosman. Princeton: Princeton University Press, 2002.

Toulmin, Stephan. *Cosmopolis: The Hidden Agenda of Modernity.* Chicago: University of Chicago Press, 1992.

Toussaint, Stephane. *Humanismes/Antihumanismes: de Ficin à Heidegger.* Paris: Belles Lettres, 2008.

Traboulsi, Fawwaz. *Fayruz wa-l-Rahabina: Masrah al-Gharib wa-l-Kanz wa-l-Ujuba* (Fayruz and the Rahbanis: The Theater of the Stranger, the Treasure and the Wonder). Beirut: Riad al-Rayyes, 2006.

———. *A History of Modern Lebanon.* London: Pluto Press, 2007.

The "War" through Its Memorials: Photo Exhibition in Progress. Haret Hreik, Lebanon, UMAM Documentation and Research Center, 12–29 June 2009.

Wazen, Abdu. *Riwayat al-Harb al-Lubnaniyya: Madkhal wa Namadij* (The Novel of the Lebanese War: Introduction and Models). Dubai: Dar al-Sada, 2009.

Wedeen, Lisa. *Ambiguities of Domination: Politics, Rhetoric, and Symbols in Contemporary Syria.* Chicago: University of Chicago Press, 1999.

Williams, Raymond. *Marxism and Literature.* Oxford: Oxford University Press, 1977.

Wilson, Scott, and Daniel Williams. "A New Power Rises across Mideast." *Washington Post,* 17 April 2005, 1.

Woodward, Christopher. *In Ruins: A Journey through History, Art and Literature.* New York: Vintage Books, 2001.

Wright, Robin. "Inside the Mind of Hezbollah." *Washington Post,* 16 July 2006.

Young, Michael. *The Ghosts of Martyrs Square.* New York: Simon and Schuster, 2010.

Zaccak, Hady. *Le cinéma libanais: Itinéraire d'un cinéma vers l'inconnu (1929–1996).* Beirut: Dar al-Mashriq, 1997.

Al-Zayn, Hasan. "Hiwar Najwa Barakat 'an Riwayatiha al-Jadid *Ya Salam*" (Discussion with Najwa Barakat on Her New Novel *Ya Salam*). *Al-Nahar,* 20 February 1999.

Zerubavel, Yael. *Recovered Roots: Collective Memory and the Making of Israeli National Tradition.* Chicago: University of Chicago Press, 1995.